Colloquial
Urdu

The Colloquial Series

The following languages are available in the Colloquial series:

Afrikaans
Albanian
Amharic
Arabic (Levantine)
Arabic of Egypt
Arabic of the Gulf and
    Saudi Arabia
Basque
Bulgarian
* Cambodian
* Cantonese
* Chinese
Croatian and Serbian
Czech
Danish
Dutch
Estonian
Finnish
French
German
Greek
Gujarati
Hindi
Hungarian
Indonesian
Italian

Japanese
Korean
Latvian
Lithuanian
Malay
Mongolian
Norwegian
Panjabi
Persian
Polish
Portuguese
Portuguese of Brazil
Romanian
* Russian
Slovak
Slovene
Somali
* Spanish
Spanish of Latin America
Swedish
* Thai
Turkish
Ukrainian
* Vietnamese
Welsh

Accompanying cassette(s) (*and CDs) are available for the above titles. They can be ordered separately through your bookseller or send payment with order to Taylor & Francis/Routledge Ltd, ITPS, Cheriton House, North Way, Andover, Hants SP10 5BE, or to Routledge Inc., 29 West 35th Street, New York, NY 10001, USA.

COLLOQUIAL CD-ROMs: Multimedia Language Courses
Available in: Chinese, French, Portuguese and Spanish

Colloquial
Urdu

The Complete Course
for Beginners

Tej K. Bhatia and Ashok Koul

London and New York

To Shobha and Malini

First published 2000
by Routledge
11 New Fetter Lane, London EC4P 4EE

Simultaneously published in the USA and Canada
by Routledge
29 West 35th Street, New York, NY 10001

Routledge is an imprint of the Taylor and Francis Group

© 2000 Tej K. Bhatia and Ashok Koul

Typeset in Times Ten by Florence Production Ltd, Stoodleigh, Devon
and Accent on Type
Printed and bound in Great Britain by Clay Ltd, St Ives plc

British Library Cataloguing in Publication Data
A catalogue record for this book is available from the British Library

Library of Congress Cataloguing in Publication Data
Bhatia, Tej K.
Colloquial Urdu : a complete language course / Tej K. Bhatia and
Ashok Koul
Includes index.
1. Urdu language–Conversation and phrase books–English.
I. Koul, Ashok. II. Title
PK1975.B47 1997
491'.43983421–dc20   96–3689

ISBN 0–415–13540–0 (book)
ISBN 0–415–13541–9 (cassette)
ISBN 0–415–13542–7 (book and cassettes course)

Contents

Acknowledgements

We have contracted many debts in the process of writing this book. At the outset we are grateful to Simon Bell, for his commendable patience and encouragement. Our gratitude is also due to Drs Frank Ryan (Brown), William C. Ritchie (Syracuse) and Gopi Chand Narang (Delhi) for their comments and insightful suggestions. We owe special thanks to Adil Khan, Nuzhat Khan, Ali Abbas Rizwi, Tahsin Siddiqui, Ashish Tagore and Mangat R. Bhardwaj for their valuable comments, criticism and suggestions. Our heartfelt thanks are also due to Jennifer L. Smith, who provided editorial assistance for this work.

We are also indebted to our teachers, friends and colleagues Yamuna and Braj Kachru, Hans Hock, Rajeshwari Pandharipande, Meena and S.N. Sridhar, Sheela and M.K. Verma for their valuable discussions on matters of Hindi/Urdu teaching and linguistics. Finally, we also owe our debts to Dr P.R. Mehandiratta (Director, American Institute of Indian Studies, New Delhi) for his support and encouragement.

We are also grateful to Ankit and Kanika, who kept us going with their encouragement and support which enabled us to complete this work. Finally, no words can express our deepest appreciation to our brothers and families in India for their constant support during our entire careers.

There is no doubt in our minds that this work is not free from limitations. Therefore, we will be grateful for any comments, criticisms or suggestions that perceptive scholars might have on this book. Please send them to the first author at the following address: Linguistic Studies Program, 312 HBC, Syracuse University, Syracuse, New York-13244-1160.

Foreword

Urdu is one of the principal modern languages of South Asia. It is spoken by millions of people throughout North India and Pakistan and it is also widely understood in the rest of the Indian subcontinent.

Colloquial Urdu is a beginner's course in this important and fascinating language, offering a comprehensive introduction to both its written and spoken forms. Its structure makes learning both enjoyable and accessible, and on completion of the study programme it aims to enable the learner to communicate confidently with native speakers on a variety of topics. As the title suggests, the emphasis remains on Urdu as spoken everyday by educated native speakers. This has the added advantage of ensuring learners can communicate on a conversational level not only with Urdu speakers but also with Hindi speakers (the latter is the other principal language spoken in North India).[1] The advanced chapters towards the end of the book also introduce some of the more elegant, Persianized vocabulary, as a taste of the formal and literary registers encountered in Urdu.

The overall intention is that the course will not only develop your command of the language as it is spoken every day, but will perhaps also instil in you the same enthusiasm for Urdu that native speakers feel for it. For Urdu speakers are nothing if not passionate about their mother tongue. They will tell you of its romanticism, its rich literary heritage, and its role as a vehicle of *adab*, those complex rules of etiquette which have shaped Muslim South Asia's social mores for generations. They will explain how speakers of other Indian languages (e.g. Gujarati, Punjabi) will learn Urdu as a second language. This is due to its capacity to act as a *lingua franca*

---

[1] See note on the relationship between Urdu and Hindi

and its status as the idiom of decorum in the Indian subcontinent. And they will tell you with pride how their language has crossed national boundaries, and is spoken every day by overseas communities of South Asian origin all over the world (Urdu, for example, is one of the principal community languages spoken in the United Kingdom).

Such effusive praise may initially seem overwhelming – but don't let it surprise you! After all, Urdu represents to its speakers not only a means of communication, but also an expression of their identity and values. So learning the language will not only allow you to effectively negotiate your way around India, Pakistan and, indeed, wherever Urdu is spoken; it will also act as a gateway to the famously vast and varied cultural landscape of the Indian subcontinent – a landscape which has impressed both Mughal kings and British colonizers in the past and one which continues to captivate the interest of countless admirers today.

Note on the relationship between Urdu and Hindi

Due to their parallel historical development, the relationship between Urdu and Hindi is intimate and complex and is often a source of confusion for those meeting either language for the first time. It is therefore worth explaining in broad terms what the languages have in common and what differentiates them. Hindi is not spoken in Pakistan but is the national language of India. However, like Urdu, it is only spoken as a first language in the North Indian states.

In their spoken forms, it is sometimes difficult to establish where Urdu ends and Hindi begins. The languages share a virtually identical grammar and also possess a very large body of common vocabulary which consists mainly of words used in everyday, normal conversation. Although these words belong to the colloquial register of both languages, many come from Persian and Arabic, two languages which have exerted far greater influence on Urdu than on Hindi. Unsurprisingly, the use of common structures and words enables near-perfect mutual comprehension in day-to-day social situations between Urdu and Hindi speakers. They therefore converse with each other freely in much the same way as American and British speakers of English. In fact so similar are the spoken varieties of both languages that some refer to them as a single language, Hindustani (essentially 'simplified Urdu', due to the preponderance of Perso-Arabic words). Nevertheless, for cultural reasons, Muslims tend to term their colloquial speech Urdu and Hindus will refer to it as Hindi.

This extensive interface between the two languages coupled with the wide area over which either or both are spoken results in colloquial Urdu/Hindi being generally considered as the *lingua franca* of the Indian subcontinent. Yet there are important differences between the two and the most obvious manifests itself in the writing system – Urdu is written in a modified form of the Arabic script and Hindi in the Devanagari script which is also used for Sanskrit. In addition, although Urdu and Hindi share a large number of colloquial words, *formal* and *literary* Hindi and Urdu can differ markedly in terms of vocabulary. For higher registers, Urdu still continues to draw on Perso-Arabic resources, but Hindi turns to Sanskrit. It is in these contexts that Urdu and Hindi do become clearly distinct languages although it is worth noting that in certain areas, such as legal vocabulary, Hindi continues to make extensive use of Perso-Arabic words.

Adil Khan

Introduction

About the language

Urdu is a modern Indo-Aryan language spoken in South Asian countries (India and Pakistan) and also in other countries outside Asia (Mauritius, Trinidad, Fiji, Surinam, Guyana, and South Africa among others). Approximately 600 million people speak Urdu as either a first or a second language and it is ranked amongst the five most widely spoken languages of the world. Urdu is the national language of Pakistan and is spoken widely in cities such as Islamabad and Karachi. It is one of the sixteen regional languages recognized by the constitution of India and is the state language of Jammu and Kashmir. It is widely spoken in the Indian states of Delhi, Uttar Pradesh, Himachal Pradesh, Madhya Pradesh, Haryana, Rajasthan and Bihar. Besides, there are millions of Urdu speakers who live in Maharashtra, Andhra Pradesh and Karnataka.

Urdu is a Turkish loan word meaning 'army' or 'camp'. It was nursed in the camps and capitals of the Muslim rulers in India. Since Delhi was its first major centre of development, it is also called *Zabān-e-Dehlvi* 'The Language of Delhi'. Another term for this language is *Urdu-e-mu'alla* 'The Exalted Camp'. Historically, it was synonymous with Hindui, Hindawi, Rexta and KhaRi Boli. The terms *Hindi* and *Hindustani* are also employed to refer to a variety of this language. All these labels denote a mixed speech spoken around the area of Delhi, North India, which gained currency during the twelfth and thirteenth centuries as a contact language between native residents and the Arabs, Afghans, Persians and Turks.

Urdu is written in a modified form of the Arabic script. Like Arabic, Persian and Hebrew it is written and read from right to left. It is written in a cursive style. For more details see the section on the Urdu Writing System and Pronunciation.

The literary history of Urdu goes back to approximately the thirteenth century. Its first poet was Amir Khusro (1253–1325), who termed the language 'Zabān-e-Dehlvi' or 'Hindi' (see Beg 1988). The Deccan played an important role in the early stages of its development (see Haq n.d.; Shackle and Snell 1990). Later it found its impetus in North India (Delhi and Lucknow) when British rulers declared it as a court language and also as the medium of instruction in certain parts of the country. Urdu is particularly well known for its romantic literature. The two most famous genres of Urdu are the **masnawī** and **Gazal**, which are the gift of the mixing of the two great cultures – Hindu and Persian-Muslim. Some notable literary figures of Urdu literature are Inshah Alla Khan, Malik Muhammad Jaysi, Kabir, Mir, Mir Hasan, Daya Shankar Nasim, Bahadur Shah Zafar, Faiz Ahmad Faiz, Sirdar Jafari, Sadat Hasan Manto, Muhammad Iqbal and Mirza Ghalib. For more details see Dimock *et al.* (1978).

The two notable linguistic features of the language are as follows: (1) Urdu still retains the original Indo-European distinction between aspirated and unaspirated consonants which results in a two-way contrast as shown by the following example: kāl 'time', k^hāl 'skin' (2) It has the feature of retroflexion in its consonant inventory, cf. **Tāl** 'to put off' and **tāl** 'pond'. The retroflex consonant is transcribed as the capital *T*. For more details see the section on the Urdu Writing System and Pronunciation.

Urdu has an approximately three-centuries old, well-attested and rich grammatical tradition of its own. It is a by-product of the colonial era and was born shortly after the arrival of Europeans in India. For a detailed treatment of this topic in general and of the grammatical tradition in particular, see Bhatia (1987).

Because of their common Indo-European origin, you will find some striking similarities between Urdu and English. For example, the Urdu word for English 'name' is **nām**. The list goes on and on. The important thing to know is that Urdu belongs to the Indo-European language family and is similar to English in a number of ways. Learning to observe these similarities will make the process of learning this language full of pleasant surprises.

The book is grounded in current theories of language acquisition, learnability and language use. Unlike other books (even some of the latest ones), it never loses sight of the social–psychological aspects of language use. In this book, we have not attempted to act like a protector or saviour of a language by engaging in linguistically puritan tendencies. What you will find here is the way Urdu speakers use Urdu to communicate with each other in meaningful ways. No attempt is made to translate artificially an English word into Urdu if Urdu speakers treat the English word like any other Urdu word. We noticed in a widely circulated course on Urdu/Hindi in which the waiter asks his customers for their order, that the word 'order' was translated with the same verb as the English 'obey my order!' For more details see the section entitled 'English Prohibition?' in Unit 2.

How this book is organized

We have attempted to accommodate two types of learners: (1) those who want to learn the language through the Urdu (Perso-Arabic) script; and (2) those who wish to learn the spoken language in a relatively short period of time without the aid of the Urdu script. Such pragmatic considerations are an important feature of this book.

The book begins with the Urdu script and Urdu pronunciation. The main body of the book comprises ten conversational units which consist of the following parts: (1) vocabulary; (2) dialogues with English translation; (3) notes detailing pronunciation, grammar and usage involving the unit; and (4) exercises. The 'Tell me why?' and 'humour' texts together with notes explicitly deal with those aspects of Indian and Pakistani culture about which the present authors have frequently been asked. There are vocabulary lists for the new words used in the dialogues; the glossaries at the end of the book also provide the Urdu script for these words. You may wish to consult the vocabulary sections while doing exercises.

The Reference Grammar gives an overview of Urdu grammar with complete paradigms. This section complements the notes and grammar sections given in each conversation unit. The Urdu–English Glossary gives all the words used in the dialogues. The words are listed alphabetically in both Urdu and English. The English–Urdu Glossary classifies Urdu words into different semantic groups.

How to use this book

This book offers two courses to follow: (1) for those learners who want to adopt the English script path; and (2) for those who want to learn the Urdu script. Although the learning of the Urdu script is highly recommended, if you decide to choose the first track, you can bypass the units on the writing system. For every learner, whether on the first or the second track, the section on pronunciation is a must and familiarity with the salient phonetic features of Urdu together with the notes on transcription is imperative. Examples dealing with pronunciation are also recorded. The exercises with the cassette icon are recorded, so they require you to listen to the recording.

If you want to follow the Urdu script track, you will find all the dialogues in the conversation units in the Perso-Arabic transcription unit. There is an added incentive to consult the script units: their exercise sections supplement some of the very frequent expressions which any visitor will need in India and Pakistan.

Naturally, the vocabulary lists will involve memorization. The notes sections give you details of pronunciation, grammar and usage.

The Reference Grammar goes hand in hand with grammatical notes given at the end of each dialogue. Answers to the exercises can be found in the Keys.

Where to go from here

Obviously, we do not pretend to offer you everything that needs to be known about Urdu. Language learning can be a life-long venture. Your next step is to look for books offering intermediate and advanced Urdu courses. The reason we are stating this fact is to remove the misconception, which is quite widespread in the West, that there is a lack of language courses at intermediate and advanced levels in Asian and African languages. There is no shortage of material at the levels in question (e.g. Barker et al. 1975; Naim 1965; Narang 1968). The only difficulty you might face is that this material will invariably be in Perso-Arabic script. If that poses a problem for you, there are still many ways to continue to sharpen your linguistic skills, the most important of which are Hindi/Urdu films and Indo-Pakistani Urdu plays. India is the world's largest producer of films. Hindi/Urdu film videos are widely accessible in the East and the West. A taste for Hindi/Urdu films is also crucial for taking yourself to the advanced stages of Urdu language learning.

Tej Bhatia and Ashok Koul
Syracuse, New York

References

Barker, Muhammad, Abd-al-Rahman, Hasan Jahangir Hamdani, Khwaja Muhammad Shafi Dihlavi and Shafiqur Rahman. 1975. *A Course in Urdu*. Vols II–III. Ithaca, New York: Spoken Language Services.

Beg, M.K.A. 1988. *Urdu Grammar: History and Structure*. New Delhi: Bahri.

Bhatia, Tej K. 1987. *A History of the Hindi–Hindustani Grammatical Tradition*. Leiden: E.J. Brill.

Dimock, Edward C., Edwin Gerow, C.M. Naim, A.K. Ramanujan, Gordon Roadarmel and J.A.B. van Buitenen. 1978. *The Literatures of India: an Introduction*. Chicago: University of Chicago Press.

Haq, Abul (Maulavi). n.d. *Quaid-e-Urdu*. New Delhi: Naz.

Naim, C.M. 1965. *Readings in Urdu: Prose and Poetry*. Honolulu: East West Press.

Narang, Gopi Chand. 1968. *Readings in Literary Urdu Prose*. Madison, WI: University of Wisconsin, South Asia Centre.

Shackle, Christopher and Rupert Snell. 1990. *Hindi and Urdu since 1800: a Common Reader*. New Delhi: Heritage.

Urdu writing system and pronunciation

Introduction

This chapter briefly outlines the salient properties of the Urdu (Perso-Arabic) script and Urdu pronunciation. Even if you are not learning the script, this chapter is indispensable, because you need to know the pronunciation value of the Roman/English letters used in the conversation units. Furthermore, one or two unfamiliar symbols are drawn from the International Phonetic Alphabets (IPA). The transcription scheme followed here is used widely in the teaching of Urdu and in works on Urdu language and linguistics. We would strongly recommend you learn the Urdu script; however, if it is not possible due to constraints of time, you will still need to refer to the charts on pages 10 and 12 until you have mastered the letters and their pronunciation.

Listen to and repeat the pronunciation of Urdu vowels and consonants, together with their minimal pairs, on the recording accompanying this book.

The Urdu script

Like Urdu, a number of other languages are written in the Perso-Arabic script. Kashmiri, Punjabi and Sindhi are also written in a modified form of this script.

Urdu is written and read from right to left, unlike the Roman script; however, Urdu numerals are written from left to right. It is written in a cursive style, that is, most of the letters are joined together in a word. There are two common styles of calligraphy; (1) **nasx** and (2) **nasta'liq.** The first style is employed for the Quran and all Arabic publications are printed in this style. This style is also produced by Urdu typewriters. The second style is beautifully handwritten by professional scribes and then lithographed. It is most commonly used in Urdu publications. Besides some differences in shapes, the two styles are quite similar.

Many of the letters in the Urdu script have differing forms depending, broadly, on whether or not they are joined to another letter. The letters which are joined to a following letter in the same word are referred to as connectors, and those which are not connected to a following letter and may be joined only to a preceding letter, are called non-connectors.

It is important to note that the shape of a letter may differ according to its position in the word and also depends upon the letter which precedes or follows it. A connector may have four possible variants. These shapes are:

1   *detached (independent) shape,* which is not connected to another letter on either side.
2   *initial shape,* which is connected to the following letter only.
3   *medial shape,* which is connected on both sides.
4   *final shape,* which is connected on the right but not on the left.

These shapes will be detailed in the script units.

Below you will find the Urdu vowel and consonant charts.

The guiding principle of Arabic-origin scripts such as Urdu, is that the alphabet proper comprises consonants only. This means that the letters of the alphabet are all consonants; vowels are indicated either by special vowel signs, or by certain of the consonants which have secondary function as vowel indicators; or a combination of the two.

Readers should note that, in this book, the final choti is sometimes represented as **ah** in transcriptions. Words ending in **ah** are pronounced as **ā** (except for **vajah**).

Urdu vowels

There are ten vowels in Urdu. These vowels are indicated by four consonant letters:

alif ا
vāo و
cʰoT ī ye ی
baRī ye ے

These letters are further supplemented, where necessary, by the following vowel signs.

Short vowel signs

1 ´ , called **zabar**

It is pronounced **a** when written above the letter **alif**. Above a consonant it indicates a following **a**.

2 ˏ , called **zer**

It is pronounced **i** when written below the letter **alif**. Below a consonant it indicates a following **i**.

3 ´ , called **pesh**

It is pronounced **u** when written above the letter **alif**. Above a consonant it indicates a following **u**.

Long vowel signs

4 ´ , called **madd**

This sign is only written above the letter **alif** in the initial position and gives the sound of the long vowel **ā**.

5　ᶜ , called **ulTā pesh**

This sign is written over the letter **vāo** to indicate a long **ū**.

Vowel chart

Base forms:　**alif** ا　**vāo** و　**choTī ye** ی　and **baRī ye** ے

Vowels:　a ā i ī u ū e ɛ o au

Positional variants

vowel	initial	medial	final	vowel	initial	medial	final
a	اَ	◌َ		ā	آ	ا	ا
i	اِ	◌ِ	◌ٗ	ī	اِی	◌ی	ی
u	اُ	◌ُ		ū	اُو	◌و	و
e	اے	◌ے	ے	ɛ	اَی	◌َی	◌ے
o	او	و	و	au	اَو	◌َو	◌َو

Notes on the Urdu vowels

alif is always written when a word starts with a vowel, combined with some vowel signs or letters to indicate various vowels. In other words, if an Urdu word begins with a vowel, the consonant **alif** is used at the start of the word in Urdu script to 'carry' the vowel sign. Urdu vowels do not distinguish between the capital and non-capital form. However, it is important to note that the two vowel letters

ی c^hoT ī ye ے baRī ye

are *connectors* and may vary in appearance in a word. For more details please see the section in Script Unit 3.

Nasalization

In the production of a nasal vowel, the vowel is pronounced through the mouth and the nose at the same time. To indicate nasalization at initial and/or medial position, the symbol ⌣ called **ulTā jazm** may be written above the variants of the letter:

nūn ں

However, in final position **nūn-i-Gunah** ں (the letter **nūn** without a dot) is used to indicate nasalization. Usually long vowels are nasalized in Urdu. In our transcription, the symbol tilde ~ is used to indicate vowel nasalization, as in

kahã کہاں   **jāū̃** جاؤں   **cū̃c** چونچ   **cãd** چاند   **ãkh** آنکھ

Diphthongs

ɛ and **au** are pronounced as **a+i** and **a+u** in the eastern variety of Urdu, but are pronounced as single vowels in the Standard Urdu-speaking area (e.g. **pɛsā** 'money', **kauvā** 'crow')

Urdu consonants

The following grid classifies the sounds of Urdu according to where in the mouth and how they are pronounced. Consonants in a horizontal group share the same *place* of articulation. Consonants in the same column share the same *manner* of articulation. For example, all the sounds in the first horizontal line are pronounced with the tongue touching the soft palate (like k, g, ng in English), while all the consonants in the first column share the characteristic of being unvoiced and unaspirated. See below for a more detailed explanation.

	voiceless unaspirated	voiceless aspirated	voiced unaspirated	voiced aspirated	nasal
k-group	ک	کھ	گ	گھ	ن
	k	k^h	g	g^h	ŋ
c-group	چ	چھ	ج	جھ	ن
	c	c^h	j	j^h	ñ
T-group	ٹ	ٹھ	ڈ	ڈھ	ن
	T	T^h	D	D^h	N
t-group	ت/ط	تھ	د	دھ	ن
	t	t^h	d	d^h	n
p-group	پ	پھ	ب	بھ	م
	p	p^h	b	b^h	m
q-group	ق				
	q				

Others	ی	ر	ل	و	
	y	r	l	w/v	
	س/ص/ث	ش	ہ/ح	ذ/ز/ض/ظ	ف	غ	ژ
	s	sh	h	z	f	G	ž
	ڑ	ڑھ					
	R	R^h					
	ع						

' **ɛn** (see Script Unit 5)

Notes on Urdu consonants

Place of articulation

All consonants arranged within each of the six groups share the same place of articulation, as described below.

k-group

These consonants are also called 'velar' because the back of the tongue touches the rear of the soft palate, called the velum. They are similar to the English *k* and *ng*.

ﮎ   ﮐﮭ   ﮒ   ﮘ   ﮞ

k   **kʰ**   **g**   **gʰ**   **ŋ**

c-group

The body of the tongue touches the hard palate in the articulation of these sounds. **C** and **cʰ** are similar to English 'ch'. **Cʰ** is similar to the first sound of English 'church', while the unaspirated counterpart **c** is more the second 'ch' of the same English word. **J** is like English j, while **jʰ** has a noticeable aspirate. **Ñ** is like Spanish ñ or 'ni' in English 'o<u>ni</u>on'.

چ   چھ   ج   جھ   ن

c   **cʰ**   **j**   **jʰ**   **ñ**

T-group (the 'Capital T group')

ٹ   ٹھ   ڈ   ڈھ   ن

T   **Tʰ**   **D**   **Dʰ**   **N**

These consonants represent the distinctive features of the languages of the Indian subcontinent. They are also called 'retroflex' consonants. These sounds do not occur in Standard English, but are a noteworthy feature of English spoken by people from the subcontinent. In the articulation of these sounds, the tip of the tongue is curled back and the *underside* of the tongue touches the hard palate. The following diagram can be of further assistance in the production of these sounds.

Also, note that **R** and **Rʰ** are also pronounced with the same point of articulation.

t-group

The tip of the tongue touches the back of the teeth, and not the gum ridge behind the teeth as is the case in the pronunciation of the English *t* or *d*.

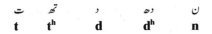

ت	تھ	د	دھ	ن
t	**tʰ**	**d**	**dʰ**	**n**

Study the following diagrams carefully in order to distinguish the Urdu t-group of sounds from the English t-group of sounds.

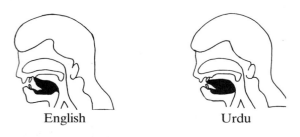

English   Urdu

p-group

These sounds are similar to English *p* ⌣ *b* and *m* sounds. They are pronounced by means of the closure or near closure of the lips.

پ	پھ	ب	بھ	م
p	**pʰ**	**b**	**bʰ**	**m**

q-group

This sound is called the uvular stop and is pronounced further back in the throat than velar **k**. In pronouncing this sound, the back of the tongue is raised to make firm contact with the uvula. This sound has been borrowed from Arabic.

ق

q

Manner of articulation

All columns in the six groups involve the same *manner of articulation*.

Voiceless unaspirated

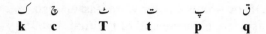

| k | c | T | t | p | q |

These sounds are like English *k* (as in 'skin' but not as in 'kin'), *p* (as in 'spin' but not as in 'pin'). In 'kin' and 'pin', the English sounds *k* and *p* are slightly aspirated, i.e. they are followed by a slight 'puff of air'. But in 'skin' and 'spin' the puff of air is much less - you can try this for yourself. So, for example, the distinction between the *p*'s in 'pin' and 'spin' is broadly the same as that between Urdu **p^h** and **p**. In order to pronounce the corresponding Urdu *k* and *p*, you need to reduce the stream of breath.

Voiceless aspirated

| k^h | c^h | T^h | t^h | p^h |

The superscript ^{h} means that these sounds are pronounced with the strong 'puff of air.' All you have to do is slightly increase the air stream in the pronunciation of the English *k* and *p* sounds.

Voiced unaspirated

| g | j | D | d | b |

In the production of these sounds the vocal cords vibrate. You should not encounter any difficulty in the production of these sounds as they are like English *g, j, d* and *b*.

Voiced aspirated (or breathy voiced)

If you pronounce the voiced unaspirated consonants with a 'puff of air', you will produce voiced aspirated sounds. The superscript ʰ indicates the presence of the 'puff of air.' If you have difficulties with these sounds, try pronouncing the voiced unaspirated consonants with an **h** (as in 'dog-house'). If you pronounce the words fast enough, you will obtain the voiced aspirate **gʰ** at the end of the first boundary between the two words.

گھ	جھ	ڈھ	دھ	بھ
gʰ	**jʰ**	**Dʰ**	**dʰ**	**bʰ**

Nasals

These sounds are called nasals because the air is released through the nose during the stopping phase in the mouth. In the Urdu script, there are two nasal consonants: ن and م. While م simply represents 'm', ن stands not only for **n**, but also for **ŋ**, **ñ**, and **N**.

ن	ن	ن	ن	م
ŋ	**ñ**	**N**	**n**	**m**

These sounds are similar to English nasal consonants, such as English *n* and *m*. **ŋ** and **ñ** are similar to the nasal consonants in the English words 'king' and 'bunch', respectively.

Others (miscellaneous)

The following consonants listed under the group 'others' are very similar to the English sounds, so they do not call for detailed phonetic description. The English transcription is sufficient to give you information about their pronunciation.

ی	ر	ل	و	ش	س	ہ
y	**r**	**l**	**w/v**	**sh**	**s**	**h**

The following two consonants are retroflex and so pronounced with the curled tongue, as explained earlier. However, the underside of the tongue is flapped quickly forward, thus touching the hard palate slightly instead of making the stop articulation with the hard palate, R^h is the aspirated counterpart of R.

ڑ   ڑھ

R R^h

Borrowed Perso-Arabic fricatives

The following five consonants are from Persian and Arabic. They exist in a number of words borrowed from these languages.

ژ	ف	ز،ذ	خ	غ
ž	f	z	x	G

Out of the above five, the last four are used quite frequently in Urdu. ž (IPAž) is a voiced palato-alveolar fricative. This sound is very rare in Urdu, and is found only in Persian loan words. It is similar to *s* in 'measure'. The next two sounds are similar to the English sounds *f* and *z*. The last two consonants are not found in English and call for detailed phonetic description. x is the final sound of the Scottish English 'lo<u>ch</u>' or the composer Ba<u>ch</u> and G is the same sound but voiced. In pronouncing these sounds the back of the tongue is raised towards the soft palate and the air escapes with friction.

ع This consonant has various pronunciations in Urdu. See Script Unit 5 for details.

Certain letters represent the same sound

As you must have noticed in the chart of Urdu consonants, some letters represent the same sound in Urdu, although in their original languages they have different sounds. These letters are:

       ت ط   represent *t*

     س ص ث all represent *s*

ز ذ ظ ض all represent *z*

ه ح represent *h*

It should be noted that the English alveolar sounds *t* and *d* are
perceived and written as *T* and *D* respectively. So the *t* and *d* in the
proper name 'Todd' will be written with the following letters: ٹ/ڈ

Pronunciation practice ◖◗

Vowels

Oral vowels

vowel	pronunciation cue (English near-equivalent)	Urdu words	
اَ a	*a*bout (i.e. unstressed [ə])	**mal**	rub
اَ ā	f*a*ther	**māl**	goods, wealth
اِ i	s*i*t	**din**	day
ای ī	s*ea*t	**dīn**	religion
اُ u	b*oo*k	**jul**	deception
او ū	b*oo*t, l*oo*t	**jūl**	line
ے e	l*a*te, d*a*te (without a *y*-glide)	**he**	hey
اَ ے ɛ	b*e*t	**hɛ**	is
او o	b*oa*t (without a *w*-glide)	**kʰolnā**	to open
اَ و au	b*ou*ght	**kʰaulnā**	to boil

Nasalized vowels

You need to practise the long nasalized vowels only.

nasalized vowels (long)	Urdu words	
ã	**mã**	mother
ĩ	**kahĩ**	somewhere

ũ̃	hũ̃	am
ẽ	mẽ	in
ɛ̃	mɛ̃	I
õ	gõd	gum
ãũ	cãũk	be alarmed, be startled

Minimal pair practice: words with oral and nasalized vowels

oral vowels			*nasalized vowels*		
ā	kahā	said (m. sg.)	ā̃	kahā̃	where
ī	kahī	said (f. sg.)	ī̃	kahī̃	somewhere
ū	pūcʰ	ask	ū̃	pū̃cʰ	a tail
e	me	the month of May	ẽ	mẽ	in
ɛ	hɛ	is	ɛ̃	hɛ̃	are
o	god	the lap	õ	gõd	gum
au	cauk	a crossing	ãũ	cãũk	be alarmed, be startled

Consonants

Listen to the recording and repeat the words.

Remember, the contrasts shown in the first four charts below are very critical in Urdu. Try and make the distinctions, because, as these examples show, sometimes they represent the only difference between two unrelated words. If you want to request food, **kʰānā** the failure to produce aspiration will result in **kānā** and you will end up asking for a one–eyed person. Similarly, if you do not distinguish the T–group from the t–group of consonants, rather than asking for **roTī** 'bread' you will end up reporting that a girl is crying (i.e. **rotī**).

Minimal pair practice: words with unvoiced unaspirated stops and unvoiced aspirated stops

	unvoiced unaspirated				*unvoiced aspirated*		
ک	**k**	کلی	**kalī**	bud	کھ	**kʰ**	کھلی	**kʰalī**	oil cake
چ	**c**	چنا	**cūnā**	lime	چھ	**cʰ**	چھونا	**cʰūnā**	to touch
ٹ	**T**	ٹاٹ	**TāT**	sackcloth	ٹھ	**Tʰ**	ٹھاٹھ	**TʰāTʰ**	splendour
ت	**t**	تان	**tān**	tune	تھ	**tʰ**	تھان	**tʰān**	roll of cloth
پ	**p**	پل	**pal**	moment	پھ	**pʰ**	پھل	**pʰal**	fruit

Minimal pair practice: words with voiced unaspirated stops and voiced aspirated stops

	voiced unaspirated				*voiced aspirated*		
گ	**g**	گرنا	**girnā**	to fall	گھ	**gʰ**	گھرنا	**gʰirnā**	to be surrounded
ج	**j**	جال	**jāl**	net	جھ	**jʰ**	جھال	**jʰāl**	soldering of metals
ڈ	**D**	ڈال	**Dāl**	a branch	ڈھ	**Dʰ**	ڈھال	**Dʰāl**	a shield
د	**d**	دار	**dār**	a piece of wood	دھ	**dʰ**	دھار	**dʰār**	sharpness
ب	**b**	بال	**bāl**	hair	بھ	**bʰ**	بھال	**bʰāl**	point of an arrow

Minimal pair practice: words with unvoiced aspirated stops and voiced aspirated stops

	unvoiced aspirated				*voiced aspirated*		
کھ	**kʰ**	کھانا	**kʰānā**	food	گھ	**gʰ**	گھانا	**gʰānā**	Ghana, the name of a country
چھ	**cʰ**	چھل	**cʰal**	cheat	جھ	**jʰ**	جھل	**jʰal**	to fan
ٹھ	**Tʰ**	ٹھک	**Tʰak**	tapping sound	ڈھ	**Dʰ**	ڈھک	**Dʰak**	to cover
تھ	**tʰ**	تھان	**tʰān**	roll of cloth	دھ	**dʰ**	دھان	**dʰān**	paddy
پھ	**pʰ**	پھوٗل	**pʰūl**	flower	بھ	**bʰ**	بھوٗل	**bʰūl**	mistake

Minimal pair practice: words with the T-group (retroflex) stops and the t-group (dental) stops

T-group				*t-group*			
ٹ	**T**	ٹال **Tāl**	postpone	ت	**t**	تال **tāl**	pond
ٹھ	**Tʰ**	ٹھک **Tʰak**	tapping sound	تھ	**tʰ**	تھک **tʰak**	be tired
ڈ	**D**	ڈال **Dāl**	branch	د	**d**	دال **dāl**	lentil
ڈھ	**Dʰ**	ڈھک **Dʰak**	cover	دھ	**dʰ**	ڈھک **dʰak**	palpitation, excitement

Minimal pair practice: words with the q-group (uvular) and the k-group (velar) stops

q-group				*k-group*			
ق	**q**	قاش **qāsh**	a piece of fruit	ک	**k**	کاش **kāsh**	may it happen

Nasal consonants

Listen to the following nasal consonants:

Nasal consonants		*Urdu words*		
ن	**ŋ**	گنگا	**gaŋgā**	Ganges
ن	**ñ**	رنج	**rañj**	sorrow
ن	**N**	انڈا	**aNDā**	egg
ن	**n**	نان	**nān**	bread
م	**m**	ماضی	**māzī**	past

Other consonants

Listen to the following words:

Consonants			Urdu words		
ے	y	یار	yār	pal	
ر	r	راز	rāz	secret	
ل	l	لال	lāl	red	
و	w/v	والد	vālid	father	
ش	sh	شال	shāl	shawl	
س	s	سال	sāl	year	
ہ، ح	h	حال	hāl	condition, state	

Minimal pair practice: fricatives vs. stops

fricatives					stops				
خ	x	خام	xām	raw	ک	k	کام	kām	work
خ	x	خطاب	xitāb	title	ک	k	کتاب	kitāb	book
غ	G	غُل	Gul	noise	گ	g	گُل	gul	flower
غ	G	غریب	Garīb	poor	ق	q	قریب	qarīb	near
ف	f	فانی	fānī	mortal	پ	p	پانی	pānī	water
ف	f	فن	fan	art	پھ	pʰ	پھن	pʰan	the hood of a snake
ز	z	زنگ	zaŋg	rust	ج	j	جنگ	jaŋg	war

Minimal pair practice: words with r, R and R^h

consonants			Urdu words		
ر	r		پَر	par	on, at
ڑ	R		پَڑ	paR	lie down, fall
ڑھ	Rʰ		پَڑھ	paRʰ	read, study

Punctuation marks

۔	=	full stop
،	=	comma
؛	=	semi colon
؟	=	question mark

Other punctuation marks are the same as those used in English. See Unit 10 for a set of special abbreviations and other symbols used in Urdu.

Syllables, stress and intonation

See unit beginning on page 231.

Dictionary order ▮▮

The dictionary order of the Urdu script is given below, working vertically down the columns. Each letter is given in its independent/detached shape. The name of the letter is given in the second column and in the third column its transliteration. It is very important, that you learn the names of these letters, as the name of the letter will be used when its variants are discussed.

letter	name	transliteration
ا	**alif**	a
ب	**be**	b
پ	**pe**	p
ت	**te**	t
ٹ	**Te**	T
ث	**se**	s
ج	**jīm**	j
چ	**ce**	c
ح	**he**	h
خ	**xe**	x
د	**dāl**	d
ڈ	**Dāl**	D

ذ	zāl	z
ر	re	r
ڑ	Re	R
ز	ze	z
ژ	že	ž
س	sīn	s
ش	shīn	sh
ص	svād	s
ض	zvād	z
ط	toe	t
ظ	zoe	z
ع	εn	' (see Script Unit 5)
غ	Gεn	G
ف	fe	f
ق	qāf	q
ک	kāf	k
گ	gāf	g
ل	lām	l
م	mīm	m
ن	nūn	n
و	vāo	v/w, o, ū, au
ہ	choTī he	h
ھ	do cashmī he	(aspiration)
ی	cʰoTī ye	y, ī
ے	baRī ye	e, ε

Listening exercises 🔘🔘

If you do not have the recording, either skip this section or seek the
assistance of a native speaker.

1 Listen to a list of three words and circle the word that is different.

Example:
you hear:

A	B	C
kar	kʰar	kar

answer: 1 B

1	A	B	C
2	A	B	C
3	A	B	C
4	A	B	C
5	A	B	C
6	A	B	C
7	A	B	C
8	A	B	C

2 Listen to a list of four words and circle the aspirated words.

Example:
you hear:

A	B	C	D
kar	kʰar	gar	gʰar

answer: B, D

1	A	B	C	D
2	A	B	C	D
3	A	B	C	D
4	A	B	C	D
5	A	B	C	D
6	A	B	C	D
7	A	B	C	D
8	A	B	C	D

3 Listen to the pair of words dealing with the contrast between the T-group (the retroflex) of consonants and the t-group (dental) of consonants.

A   B
Tik   tik

After the pair is pronounced, you will hear either (A) or (B). Underline the word that you hear the *third* time.

Example: you hear : **Tik**, then underline **Tik**:

A	B
1	tāk	**Tāk**
2	thak	**T^{h}ak**
3	dāg	**Dāg**
4	dhak	**D^{h}ak**
5	par	**paR**
6	sar	**saR**
7	karī	**kaR^{h}ī**
8	thīk	**T^{h}īk**

4 Listen to the pairs of words which contrast in terms of vowel.

A	B
din	**dīn**

After each pair is pronounced, you will hear either (A) or (B). Underline the word that you hear the third time.
Example: you hear: **dīn**, then underline **dīn**

A	B
1	**kām**	**kam**
2	**din**	**dīn**
3	**mil**	**mīl**
4	**cuk**	**cūk**
5	**mel**	**mɛl**
6	**ser**	**sɛr**
7	**bic**	**bīc**
8	**bāl**	**bal**

1 باب ایک: آداب

Greetings and social etiquette

By the end of this unit you should be able to:

- use simple greetings
- learn expressions of social etiquette
- use expressions for leave-taking
- ask simple questions
- make simple requests
- use personal pronouns (e.g. 'I', 'we', 'you', etc.)
- use some nouns and adjectives

Dialogue 1 🔲

Muslim greetings and social etiquette

Urdu greetings vary according to the religion of the speaker, but not according to the time of the day. In some cases, the speaker may choose to greet according to the religion of his/her listener.

Tahsin Siddiqui and Razia Arif run into each other in Hyde Park in London

TAHSIN:	as-salām 'alɛkum, raziā.
RAZIA:	va-'alɛkum as-salām. sab xɛriyat hɛ?
TAHSIN:	meharbānī hɛ, aur āp ke mizāj kɛse hɛ̃?
RAZIA:	allāh kā shukr hɛ.

(The conversation continues for some time.)

TAHSIN:	accʰā, xudā hāfiz.
RAZIA:	xudā hāfiz.

TAHSIN:	*Greetings Razia.*
RAZIA:	*Greetings. How are you?*
TAHSIN:	*Fine. And, how are you?*
RAZIA:	*I am fine.*
TAHSIN:	*Okay. Goodbye.*
RAZIA:	*Goodbye.*

Vocabulary

Note: It is a standard convention to transliterate Urdu words in lower case. This convention is used here. Therefore, the first letter of the first word in a sentence is not capitalized. The only exceptions are upper case T, D, N and R, which represent the retroflex sounds, and G, which represents the velar fricative sound.

as-salām 'alɛkum	hello (Muslim greeting)
va-'alɛkum as-salām	hello (replies to the greeting)
sab	all
xɛriyat (f.)	safety, welfare
meharbānī (f.)	kindness

āp ke	your
mizāj (m.)	temperament, nature
kɛse	how
hɛ̃	are
allāh kā shukr	fine
xudā hāfiz	goodbye

Notes

Muslim greetings and leave taking

as-salām 'alɛkum, (Hello) an Arabic greeting which literally means 'may peace be upon you' is a common greeting among Muslims. The proper reply to the greeting would be **va-'alɛkum as-salām**, which literally means 'may peace also be on you'. **salām** (an abbreviated form of **as-salām 'alɛkum**) is also used for 'hello' mostly in informal settings.

It is expressed by raising the right hand to the forehead. The expression for 'goodbye' is **xudā hāfiz** 'God, the protector'.

'How are you?'

The preferred way of saying 'How are you?' is 'Is everything fine?' or 'Is all well (with you)?' The expression for this is

> **sab   xɛriyat   hɛ?**
> all   welfare   is
> 'How are you?' (lit. Is everything fine with you?)

which is followed by the answer:

> **meharbānī   hɛ**
> kindness   is
> '(It is your) kindness', i.e. because of your kindness, every-
> thing is fine with me.

Yet another way of asking 'How are you?' is something like 'How are your habits?', as in the following sentence:

> **āp   ke   mizāj   kɛse   hɛ̃?**
> you   of   habits   how   are

This question is followed by the answer, 'With God's grace, everything is fine'. The Urdu expression for this is:

allāh kā shukr hε.
God   of   thank   is

The above exchange is used in formal situations.

What to do when speakers of different religions meet

When speakers of different religions greet each other, it is considered polite for the person who speaks first to greet the listener in the listener's religion. Respecting others' religious feelings is the rule of politeness. Nowadays the English word 'hello' can be used to stress neutrality and modernity at the same time.

Dialogue 2 ▣

Other forms of greeting

Mohan goes to see Shahid in his office in Southall, London. They know each other but are not close friends

MOHAN: ādāb arz janāb.
SHAHID: ādāb. kyā hāl hε mohan sāhab?
MOHAN: Tʰīk hε, aur āp?
SHAHID: mε̃ bʰī Tʰīk hū̃. hukam kījie.
MOHAN: hukam nahī̃, guzārish hε.
(The conversation continues for some time.)
MOHAN: accʰā, xudā hāfiz.
SHAHID: xudā hāfiz.

MOHAN: *Hello, sir.*
SHAHID: *Hello. How are you Mr Mohan?* (lit. What is (your) condition Mr Mohan?)
MOHAN: *Fine. And you?*
SHAHID: *I am fine too. What can I do for you?* (lit. please order).
MOHAN: *(It is) not an order, (but) a request.*

MOHAN: *Okay. Goodbye.*
SHAHID: *Goodbye.*

Vocabulary

ādāb arz	Muslim greeting, may be used by other religions too
janāb	sir
sāhab	sir, gentleman
kyā	what
hāl (m.)	condition
hɛ	is
Tʰīk	fine; OK
aur	and
āp	you (hon.)
mɛ̃	I
bʰī	also
hū̃	am
hukam (m.)	order
kījie	please do
nahī̃	not
guzārish (f.)	request

Pronunciation

In the eastern and southern regions of the Urdu-speaking area of India (e.g. in Hyderabad, India), the vowel ɛ in the words **mɛ̃** and **hɛ**, is pronounced as a diphthong, a combination of two vowels, i.e. [ai = a+i]. However, in the western Urdu-speaking area (e.g. in Delhi), it is pronounced as a vowel [ɛ], as in English words such as 'bet'. Since the vowel pronunciation is considered standard, it is given on the recording.

The verb form [kījie] can also be pronounced as [kījiye]. The semivowel [y] can intervene between the last two vowels. This word can be written with the semivowel too.

Notes

Other forms of greetings

namaste (literal meaning, 'I bow in your respect') is the most common greeting used by Hindus. It is expressed with the hands folded in front of the chest. It may be optionally followed by **jī** to show respect and politeness. A more formal alternative to **namaste** is **namaskār**. In rural areas many other variants such as **rām-rām** and **jɛ rām jī kī** are found. Sikhs prefer **sat srī akāl** instead of **namaste**. The gesture of folding hands, however, remains the same. The Hindu greetings do not vary at different times of the day.

   namaste (**sat srī akāl** by Sikhs) and its variants are used both for 'hello' and 'goodbye'.

   ādāb arz is used both for 'hello' and 'goodbye'. This polite form of greeting is commonly used mainly in areas influenced by Muslim culture, e.g. Kashmir, Lucknow, Hyderabad, etc.

   janāb 'sir' is used as a term of address.

   sāhab 'sir': the original meaning of Urdu **sāhab** is 'master' or 'lord'. This word is more formal than English 'sir'. It can be used in several ways:

1   after proper names, e.g. **mohan sāhab** 'Mr Mohan', **khan sāhab** 'Mr Khan'.
2   as a term of address, e.g. **āiye sāhab** 'Please come, sir'.
3   after titles, e.g. **DākTar sāhab** 'Doctor'.

   begam sāhab 'Madam' **mem sāhab** 'Mrs' (the former term is commonly used for upper-class Indian and Pakistani Muslim women and the latter term is usually used for Western women only).

   sāhab is also used as a word for 'boss', e.g. **vo mere sāhab hɛ̃** 'He is my boss'.

Other ways of saying 'How are you?'

Where an Urdu expression differs literally from its English translational equivalent, we will show this difference in notes by giving a word-for-word translation to show this difference. Observe the word-for-word translation of the Urdu equivalent of English, 'How are you?'

kyā   hāl   hɛ?
what   condition   is

and its reply.

Tʰīk   hɛ.
fine   is

Honorific pronoun

The honorific pronoun **āp** 'you' is grammatically plural, even if it refers to one person.

Politeness

If the speaker is being very polite in his/her speech, the listener is obliged to either match or outperform the speaker. The expression

hukam   kījie.
order   please do
'Please (give me) an order.'

is a very formal and cultured way of asking 'What can I do for you?' The listener appropriately uses an equally polite expression

hukam   nahī̃   guzārish   hɛ.
order   not   request   is
'It is not an order (but) a request.'

The polite expression **farmāiye**, 'to speak', 'to order' is also used in place of **hukam kījiye** (see Unit 10).

Word order

Note the difference between the word order of Urdu and English. In Urdu, the verb (e.g. 'is', 'am', 'are', etc.) usually appears at the end of the sentence. The object (e.g. 'order') appears before the verb.

Grammar

A vast majority of learners of Urdu as a foreign language find its grammar very simple. You will soon find out on your own the reasons for this perception. In this section we outline some salient features of Urdu grammar.

Word order in Urdu

The order of words in an Urdu sentence is not as rigidly fixed as it is thought to be by traditional grammarians. Although *usually* (but not invariably) an Urdu sentence begins with a subject and ends with a verb, if the sentence has an object, it is sandwiched between the subject and the verb. That is why Urdu is often called an SOV language (i.e. Subject-Object-Verb language). However, Urdu speakers or writers enjoy considerable freedom in placing words in an utterance to achieve stylistic effects. In dialogue 2 Shahid asks:

kyā   hāl   hɛ?
what   condition   is
'How are you?'

Usually the question word **kyā** 'what' does not appear in sentence-initial position. The usual form of the sentence is as follows:

hāl   kyā   hɛ?
condition   what   is
'How are you?'

The question word **kyā** 'what' is placed at the beginning of the sentence to give special emphasis to it. Also, you may have noticed the deletion of the possessive adjective 'your' in the conversation. Such deletions also affect Urdu word order. For example, in the same dialogue, Mohan responds to Shahid's question in the following way:

Tʰīk   hɛ.
fine   is
'I am fine.'

The reply by Mohan has no subject because the subject phrase is implied. The full version of the sentence is as follows:

merā	**hāl**	**Tʰīk**	**hɛ.**
my	condition	fine	is

'I am fine.' (lit. 'My condition is fine.')

The implied subject (i.e. **merā hāl**) is rarely spelled out in the reply.

Yes-no questions

Yes-no questions expect either an affirmative or a negative answer. In spoken Urdu, yes-no questions are much simpler than in English. They are usually formed by changing *intonation*, i.e. with a rising tone of voice at the end of the sentence. You do not need to place any form of the verb before the subject as you do in English. In dialogue 1 Razia asks

sab	**xɛriyat**	**hɛ?**
all	welfare	is

'Is all well?' or 'Is everything fine?'

simply by 'yes-no question intonation', i.e. raising the pitch of voice at the end of the sentence. The same sentence with a 'statement intonation' (pitch falling at the end), as in English, would mean 'All is well' = 'I am fine'.

Personal and demonstrative pronouns

The Urdu personal pronouns are

mɛ̃	I
ham	we
tū	you (sg.)
tum	you (pl.)
āp	you (hon.)
vo	she, he, it; that, they
ye	this, these

There is no gender distinction in Urdu pronouns.

tū is either intimate or very rude. We advise you not to use **tū** unless you are absolutely sure about your intimate relationship with the listener and your listener has already been using this pronoun in his/her exchanges with you. In short, you will not get much of a chance to hear and use **tū**. In the case of an emerging familiar relationship the only pronoun you will need is **tum**.

tum can be used with one or more than one person. However, like the English 'you', it never takes a singular verb form.

āp is used to show respect and politeness. Most often you will use this pronoun in exchanges with friends and strangers. South Asian society is changing quickly and you should avoid stereotyping. You may have heard about the distinction between lower- and higher-caste Indians. Our advice is, use **āp** for everybody regardless of his/her caste and status. This approach is the safest form of address in the final analysis. **āp** always takes a plural verb regardless of the number of speakers addressed.

vo is written as **vah**, but is pronounced as **vo** *most widely.* **vo** 'that, those' is also used to refer to person(s) or object(s) far from the speaker.

ye is written as **yah**, but is pronounced as **ye**. **ye** 'this, these' can be used to refer to both singular and plural person(s) or object(s) close to the speaker.

Number and gender (plural formation of unmarked nouns)

Urdu nouns (like Spanish, Italian and French) are marked for both number and gender. There are two numbers (singular and plural) and two genders (masculine and feminine). Adjectives and verbs *agree* with nouns in number and gender.

	singular	*plural*	
masculine	-ā	-e	
feminine	-ī	-iã̄	(nouns)
		-ī	(adjectives; verbs)

Here are some examples of nouns and adjectives. Verbs will be exemplified in the next unit. You will find slight changes in the feminine plural forms of verbs, which are discussed in Unit 6.

	masculine		
singular		*plural*	
beTā	son	**beTe**	sons
baccā	child (male)	**bacce**	children
burā	bad	**bure**	bad

	feminine		
singular		*plural*	
beTī	daughter	**beTiā̃**	daughters
baccī	child (female)	**bacciyā̃**	children
burī	bad	**burī**	bad

Nouns have gender too. Male human beings receive masculine gender, whereas females receive feminine gender. However, inanimate and abstract nouns can be either masculine or feminine. **foj** 'army', which (in India and Pakistan) does not admit women, is feminine; in addition, **dāRī** 'beard' is also feminine. Some animate nouns (species of animals, birds, insects, etc.) are either masculine or feminine. For example, **macchar** 'mosquito', **khaTmal** 'bug', **cītā** 'leopard' and **ullū** 'owl' are masculine in gender, and nouns such as **makkhī** 'fly', **macchlī** 'fish' are feminine. However, do not worry about gender in the case of inanimate and abstract nouns. The following are some guidelines for you.

Look at the following representative list of Urdu nouns and see if you can guess the gender rules:

masculine		*feminine*	
laRkā	boy	**laRkī**	girl
ghoRā	horse	**ghoRī**	mare
kamrā	room	**kursī**	chair
darvāzā	door	**khiRkī**	window
landan	London	**dillī**	Delhi
ghar	house	**kitāb**	book
hāth	hand	**nazar**	vision
namak	salt	**mirc**	pepper
ādmī	man	**aurat**	woman
jūtā	shoe	**mā̃**	mother

Most Urdu nouns ending in **-ā** are masculine and those ending in **-ī** are feminine. There are exceptions though: **ādmī** 'man' ends in

-ī and is masculine and **āpā** 'sister' ends in **-ā** and is feminine. But you have probably guessed that the meaning takes precedence over the form of the word. After all, how could the word for *mother* be other than feminine in gender? and the word man be other than masculine? These two criteria can solve the mystery of Urdu gender in nearly every case.

Agreement: adjectives and possessive adjectives

You have already come across one adjective, **acchā** 'good/fine' which ends in **-ā**. It is an inflecting adjective. By substituting the suffixes given in the box, we can produce other forms. For example:

acchā laRkā
good boy

acchī laRkī
good girl

acche laRke
good boys

acchī laRkiyā̃
good girls

The question word **kɛsā** 'how' also behaves like an adjective ending in **-ā**.

kɛsā laRkā
what kind of boy

kɛsī laRkī
what kind of girl

kɛse laRke
what kind of boys

kɛsī laRkiyā̃
what kind of girls

The Urdu equivalents of the English possessive adjectives ('my', 'our', etc.) are:

merā	my
hamārā	our
terā	your (sg., most intimate/non-honorific)
tumhāra	your (pl., fam.)
āp kā	your (pl., hon.)
us kā	his/her (further away)
un kā	their (further away)
is kā	his/her (near)
in kā	their (near)

The Urdu possessive pronouns listed above follow the pattern of adjectives which end in **-ā**.

merā laRkā	**mere laRke**
my boy	my boys
merī laRkī	**merī laRkiyā̃**
my girl	my girls

From the above examples, it is clear that adjectives ending in **-ā** agree with the nouns that follow them. Therefore, they behave like inflecting adjectives.

In English, it is the gender of the *possessor* in third person singular pronouns (i.e. '*his* girl', '*her* girl') that is marked on the possessive adjectives. Such a distinction is not made in Urdu. Notice, however, that because possessive adjectives agree with their following nouns, the form of a possessive adjective changes in accordance with the gender and the number of the *possessed* noun. Thus, the following phrases are ambiguous in Urdu:

us kā laRkā	**us ke laRke**
his/her boy	his/her boys
us kī laRkī	**us kī laRkiyā̃**
his/her girl	his/her girls

us kā laRkā means both 'his boy' and 'her boy'. Since **laRkā** 'boy' is masculine, the possessive adjective **us kā** 'his/her' takes the masculine form, regardless of whether the boy in question belongs to a man or a woman. Similarly, **us kī laRkī** can mean both 'his girl' or 'her girl'. It is the feminine gender of the word **laRkī** 'girl' which assigns gender to the possessive pronoun.

Exercises

1 How would you reply to someone who said this to you?

(a) ādāb arz.
(b) kyā hāl hɛ?
(c) as-salām 'alɛkum.
(d) mizāj kɛse hɛ̃?
(e) acchā, xudā hāfiz.
(f) sat srī akāl jī.
(g) sab xɛriyat hɛ?
(h) namaste jī.

(i) hukam kījie/farmāiye.

(j) salām.

2 Match the replies in column B with the greetings or questions in column A.

A	*B*
(a) ādāb.	Tʰīk hɛ.
(b) kyā hāl hɛ?	allāh kā shukr hɛ.
(c) āp ke mizāj kɛse hɛ̃?	ādāb.
(d) xudā hāfiz.	xudā hāfiz.
(e) sab xɛriyat hɛ?	va-'alɛkum as-salām.
(f) as-salām 'alɛkum.	meharbānī hɛ.

3 Fill in the gaps in the two conversations given below:

Conversation 1

A: as-salām 'alɛkum.

B: _____ _____.

   sab xɛriyat hɛ?

A: _____ hɛ, aur āp ke _____ kɛse hɛ̃?

B: allāh kā _____ _____.

Conversation 2

A: _____ _____.

B: ādāb arz.

   kyā _____ hɛ?

A: _____ hɛ, aur _____?

B: mɛ̃ bʰī _____ _____.

A: accʰā, _____ _____.

B: xudā hāfiz.

4 Answer the following questions.

(a)

QUESTION: kyā hāl hɛ?

ANSWER:

QUESTION: aur āp?

ANSWER:

(b)
QUESTION: āp kɛse hɛ̃?
ANSWER:

5 Give the corresponding short sentences for the following long sentences.

(a) aur āp kɛse hɛ̃?
(b) mɛ̃ bʰī Tʰīk hũ.
(c) āp kī meharbānī hɛ.
(d) āp ke mizāj kɛse hɛ̃?

2 باب دو: آپ کہاں کے رہنے کی ہیں؟
Where are you from?

By the end of this unit you should be able to:

- introduce yourself and others
- say and ask what you and others do
- say and ask where you and others work
- talk about you and your family
- ask someone's address
- refer to possessions
- use very frequent adjectives
- learn plural formation
- form the simple present tense

English prohibition?

In the following dialogues, no attempt is made to translate artificially an English word/expression into Urdu if the English word has become a natural part of the Urdu language. The original English words in the text are italicized. Their native pronunciation is given in the section 'Pronunciation of English Words'. Try to use Urdu words, if a parallel Urdu word exists.

Dialogue 1 ▣

Small talk

A young stockbroker, Bashir Ahmad, wants to meet a distinguished gentleman standing alone in a corner of a restaurant, gazing at the wall. On learning from a friend that his name is Dr Zakir Khan, Mr Ahmad approaches him. Having exchanged greetings, Bashir Ahmad undertakes the task of introducing himself

BASHIR: kahiye, āpkā ism-e-sharīf *Doctor* zākir khān hɛ na?
DR KHAN: jī hā̃, merā nām zākir khān hɛ.
           (Extending his hand to shake hands.)
BASHIR: merā nām bashīr hɛ.
DR KHAN: mil kar baRī xushī huī. āp kā pūrā nām kyā hɛ?
BASHIR: bashīr ahmad hɛ.
DR KHAN: āp kyā karte hɛ̃?
BASHIR: mɛ̃ *stock broker* hū̃. āp tibbī *Doctor* (*medical doctor*) hɛ̃?
DR KHAN: jī nahī̃, mɛ̃ tibbī *Doctor* nahī̃ hū̃. ek aur qism *Doctor* hū̃.

BASHIR: *Excuse me, you are Dr Zakir Khan, aren't you?* (lit. Your noble name is Dr Zakir Khan, isn't it?)
DR KHAN: *Yes, my name is Zakir Khan.*
BASHIR: *My name is Bashir.*
DR KHAN: *Pleased to meet (you).* (lit. Having met (you) big happiness happened.) *What is your full name?*
BASHIR: *My name is Bashir Ahmad.*

DR KHAN:	*What (work) do you do?*
BASHIR:	*I am a stockbroker. Are you a medical doctor?*
DR KHAN:	*No, I am not a medical doctor. (I) am the other (kind of) doctor* (i.e. I am a Ph.D).

Vocabulary

kɛhnā (+ne)	to say
kahiye	Excuse me!
ism (m.)	noun
sharīf	noble, honourable, respected
ism-e-sharīf (m.)	name (lit. distinguished appellation)
nām (m.)	name
na?	isn't it?
hᷠ	yes
mil kar baRī xushī huī	Pleased to meet you
tibbī (adj.)	medical
pūrā (m.; adj.)	full, complete
karnā (+ne)	to do
ek aur	another
qism	type

Notes

The -e (called **izāfat**) in **ism-e-sharīf** 'noble name' is a common grammatical feature borrowed from Persian and its meaning is explained in the Reference Grammar. However, in writing it is indicated by adding subscript **zer** to the last letter of the first compound word. The word **ism** means 'noun' and not 'name' when used independently. The polite form of asking 'What is your name?' (**āp kā nām kyā hɛ?**) is **āp kā ism-e-sharīf kyā hɛ?**

Attention-getters

The Urdu literal equivalent of the English expression 'Excuse me!' is **māf kījiye**. However, the Urdu expression actually means 'I apologize' or 'I beg your pardon'. It is not appropriate where the real intent of 'Excuse me' is to get attention. Although some English-speaking Indians and Pakistanis tend to translate directly from English, it is not the natural tendency of native speakers. The expression 'Excuse me' is best paraphrased by native Urdu speakers either as 'Please say' (**kahiye**) or 'Please listen' (**suniye**). *Do not use **māf kījiye** if you do not intend to apologize. **māf** is written as **mu'āf**.*

Set phrases

Every language employs some expressions which are often fixed and invariable. In some respects, Urdu expressions such as 'Pleased to meet you' belong to this category. For the time being, you should memorize them without going further into their composition. Also, learn their appropriate usage. They are usually used in introductions.

The mystery of what the correct subject of 'Pleased to meet you' is will become clear later when the concept of **ko** subjects (called 'dative subjects' or 'experiential subjects') is introduced. For the time being, use the expression as if it were a subjectless sentence.

Word-for-word translation

The Urdu expression for 'I am pleased to meet you' is:

mil	**kar**	**baRī**	**xushī**	**huī**
met	having	big	happiness	happened

In the above expression, the object 'you' is implied; however, for emphasis the object can be inserted.

āp se	**mil**	**kar**	**baRī**	**xushī**	**huī.**
you with	met	having	big	happiness	happened

Notice the Urdu equivalent of the English 'I am pleased to meet you' is 'I am pleased to meet with you'.

Word order with the question word 'what'

Observe the place of the question word **kyā** 'what' in the following sentences.

āp kā pūrā nām kyā hɛ?
your full name what is
'What is your full name?'

āp kyā kām karte hɛ̃?
you what work do are
'What do you do (for a living)?'

When one compares these sentences with the expression – **kyā hāl hɛ**, one might be tempted to conclude that 'anything goes' regarding the placement of **kyā** in a sentence. The following sentences strengthen this belief further because one can say the above two sentences in the following way:

āp kām kyā karte hɛ̃?
you work what do are
'What do you do (for a living)?'

The placement of **kyā** at the beginning or at the end of the sentence, or between the two verbal elements, will lead to some problems. Such placements will change the meaning of the sentences and may even sound abrupt and impolite. Therefore, the rule of thumb is to keep the question word closer to the word which is the subject of the enquiry. Usually, **kyā** is placed before the noun or the verb it modifies. If the noun phrase is modified, as the noun **nām** is in the following sentence by the two modifiers – 'your' and 'full' – rather than breaking the bond between the noun and the modifier, as in

āp kā kyā pūrā nām hɛ?

the question word is placed after the noun:

āp kā pūrā nām kyā hɛ?

In the following sentence, the noun **kām** is, however, not modified further; thus, it is better to say

āp kyā kām karte hɛ̃?

i.e. literally, 'What work do you do?' instead of

āp kām kyā karte hɛ̃?

which has some negative connotations, as does the English sentence 'Tell me, what do you actually do with your life?'

Dialogue 2 💽

Where are you from?

Two female college students on their way to Banaras from Delhi engage in a dialogue which is typical of Indian travellers whether from urban or rural areas. After asking each other their names, Fatima Banu and Sahira Dawood start enquiring about each other's family background

FATIMA: āp kahā̃ kī hɛ̃.
SAHIRA: mɛ̃ dillī kī hū̃. aur āp?
FATIMA: mɛ̃ banāras mɛ̃ rɛhtī hū̃.
SAHIRA: āp ke kitne bʰāī-bɛhɛn hɛ̃?
FATIMA: ham cār bʰāī aur do bɛhɛnē hɛ̃.
SAHIRA: merā ek bʰāī aur ek bɛhɛn hɛ.

FATIMA: *Where are you from?* (lit. Of where (= of what place) are you?)
SAHIRA: *I am from Delhi.* (lit. I am of Delhi.) *And you?*
FATIMA: *I live in Banaras.*
SAHIRA: *How many brothers and sisters do you have?* (lit. How many your brothers and sisters are?)
FATIMA: *We are four brothers and two sisters.*
SAHIRA: *I have one brother and a sister.*

Vocabulary

kahā̃	where
mɛ̃	in
dillī (f.)	Delhi (the capital city)
kī (f.)	of
banāras	Banaras (one of the oldest cities in India)
rɛhnā (**-ne**)	to live
kitnā (m.)	how many?
kitne	how many?
bʰāī (m.)	brother/brothers
bɛhɛn, āpā (f.)	sister (**āpā** is an affectionate term for elder sister)

cãr	four
do	two
ek	one

Notes

Word-for-word translation: 'Where are you from?'

The Urdu equivalent of the English 'Where are you from?' is:

āp	**kahā̃**	**kī**	**hɛ̃?**
you	where	of	are

The response to the English question in Urdu is

mɛ̃	**dillī**	**kī**	**hū̃**
I	Delhi	of	am

As we saw in the last unit, like other possessive pronouns, **kī** agrees with the number and the gender of its possessor. In the above two sentences the subject pronoun is the possessor. Since the subjects are feminine, the feminine form **kī** is used. It is not difficult to guess what would happen if the subjects were masculine. If these sentences are spoken by males, the sentences are:

āp	**kahā̃**	**ke**	**hɛ̃?**
you	where	of	are

mɛ̃	**dillī**	**kā**	**hū̃**
I	Delhi	of	am

Remember the honorific pronoun **āp** always takes the plural form.
Don't be surprised if you hear someone using **se** 'from' instead of **kā**, **ke** or **kī**:

āp	**kahā̃**	**se**	**hɛ̃?**
you	where	from	are

mɛ̃	**dillī**	**se**	**hū̃.**
I	Delhi	from	am

However, **se** is invariable whereas **kā** is variable. You will learn about invariable elements such as **se** later under the section on invariable postpositions.

Also, notice the placement of the English 'from' in the Urdu sentence.

Postpositions

The Urdu equivalents of English 'in Banaras' and 'from Delhi' are:

banāras	**mẽ**	**dillī**	**se**
Banaras	in	Delhi	from

Notice the English *pre*positions placed after the noun of the prepositional phrase. In other words, the word order of the English prepositional phrase is reversed in Urdu. Since the prepositional elements always follow the noun they modify, they are called *post*-positions in Urdu grammars.

Question words: 'where' and 'how many/much'

From the Urdu sentence 'Where are you from?' it should be obvious that the Urdu word for 'where' is **kahā̃**. Like the English question word, Urdu **kahā̃** does not change its shape. Also, it is not placed at the beginning of the sentence. Its usual place is before the verb; however, this word is rather mobile within a sentence.

The Urdu equivalent of 'how many/much' is **kitnā**. This question word agrees with its following noun in number and gender.

kitnā kām?	how much work
kitne bʰāī?	how many brothers
kitnī bɛhɛnẽ?	how many sisters

This question word is like an inflecting possessive adjective.

Dialogue 3 🔾🔾

A train journey: exchanging addresses

During the train journey, Fatima and Sahira become friends; they are ready to exchange addresses

SAHIRA:	ye merā patā hɛ.
FATIMA:	ye patā bahut lambā hɛ.
SAHIRA:	hã, baRā shɛhɛr, lambā patā.
FATIMA:	lekin, cʰoTā shɛhɛr, cʰoTā patā. (*Both laugh.*)
SAHIRA:	accʰā, pʰir milēge.
FATIMA:	jī, pʰir milēge.
SAHIRA:	*This is my address.*
FATIMA:	*This is a very long address.*
SAHIRA:	*Yes, a big city, a long address.*
FATIMA:	*But, a small city, a short address.*
SAHIRA:	*OK, (we) will meet again.*
FATIMA:	*OK, until then* (lit. *(we) will meet*).

Vocabulary

patā (m.)	address	**cʰoTā** (m.; adj.)	small, short
bahut	very	**pʰir**	again, then
lambā (m.; adj.)	long	**accʰā** (m.; adj.)	good, OK
shɛhɛr (m.)	city	**milnā** (-ne)	to meet
lekin	but	**milēge**	(we) will meet

Pronunciation

The Urdu word for 'address' is written as **patah** but is pronounced as **patā**.

Notes

Word-for-word translation

ye	patā	bahut	lambā	hɛ.
this	address	very	long	is

Notice the Urdu sentence ends with a verb and not with an adjective unlike the English 'This address is very long'.

Subject omission

The Urdu expression for 'we will meet again' is:

pʰir   milẽge.
again   will meet

The subject 'we' is implied; it is rarely spelled out. Normally such subjectless expressions are considered ungrammatical in many languages, including English; however, they are quite normal in Urdu.

Grammar

Tag question

A tag question is usually 'tagged' to a statement. The Urdu equivalent of

  You are Dr Zakir Khan, aren't you?

is very simple – just add **na** at the end of the statement. It will take care of both the positive tags (e.g. is it?, will you?, do you?, etc.) and the negative ones (e.g. isn't it?, won't you?, don't you?, etc.) which are attached to statements in English. The only difference is that English speakers will pause at the point where a comma is placed in the English sentence whereas Urdu speakers will not pause at this point. Therefore, no comma is placed between the statement and the tag. However, the tag question will receive rising intonation.

The verb 'to be'

There is a striking resemblance between the verb 'to be' in English and Urdu. Just as in English, you would not say 'you am', 'I is', 'he am', or 'they is', neither would you in Urdu. Different forms are used depending upon the person and number of the subject. The Urdu counterparts of the English verb 'to be' are given below.

	singular	plural	honorific
first person	**hū̃**	**hɛ̃**	–
	(I) am	(we) are	
second person	**hɛ**	**ho**	**hɛ̃**
	(you sg.) are	(you pl.) are	(you *hon.*) are
third person	**hɛ**	**hɛ̃**	–
	(he/she/it) is	(they) are	

It is possible to say 'you is' in Urdu, provided the Urdu singular 'you' **tū** is selected. Of course, the second person honorific pronoun (**āp**) always takes a plural form. As we mentioned in the first unit, be careful when you need to use Urdu second person pronouns. The chances are you will rarely need to use the pronoun **tū** and, thus, the singular you 'to be' form.

Present habitual actions = simple present tense

The Urdu sentences

āp	**kyā**	**karte**	**hɛ̃?**		
you	what	do	are		
mɛ̃	**banaras**	**mɛ̃**	**rɛhtī**	**hū̃**	
I	Banaras	in	live	am	

are equivalent of English 'What do you do?' and 'I live in Banaras', which refer to habitual or regularly repeated acts. Look at the verb form/phrase, and you will readily observe that there are two main parts to the Urdu verb form. The first one, usually called the 'main verb', is composed of three elements:

kar	+	**t**	+	**e**
stem 'do'	+	aspect marker	+	gender-number marker (m. pl.)
rɛh	+	**t**	+	**ī**
stem 'live'	+	aspect marker	+	gender-number marker (f. sg.)

The first element of the first part is the verb stem. The second element is the aspect marker. The aspect marker simply shows whether the act is completed or ongoing. At this point it is important to understand the difference between tense and aspect.

As mentioned above, aspect is concerned about the ongoing, repeated or completed state of the action whereas tense (present, past or future) provides information as to what point in time the action takes place. The third element of the main verb is the same masculine plural ending from the Box on page 36.

The second part of the verb is called the 'auxiliary verb'. In the two sentences, the auxiliary verb is the same form of the verb 'to be' discussed in the box on p. 53.

This verb form is referred to by various technical names. We will call it the *simple present tense*. The complete paradigm is given in the Reference Grammar.

The verb 'to have'

The Urdu expression for 'How many brothers and sisters do you have?' is:

āp ke	kitne	bʰāī-bɛhɛn	hɛ̃?
your	how many	brothers-sisters	are

Notice the Urdu sentence contains neither an equivalent of the English verb 'have' nor the subject 'you'. In Urdu, the subject takes a possessive form and the verb 'have' becomes the verb 'to be'. As we proceed further, it will become clear that many languages of the world do not have the exact equivalent of English 'have'. In Urdu such a construction is used to express inseparable or non-transferable possessions (body parts, relationships or dearly held possessions such as a job, house or shop). Transferable possessions will be dealt with later on. (Note that it is also possible to use the plural form **bɛhɛnẽ** in the above expression.)

Number and gender (plural formation of marked nouns)

Now do some detective work and work out patterns for the following nouns.

Masculine

	singular			*plural*	
bʰāī	brother		**bʰāī**	brothers	
gʰar	house		**gʰar**	houses	

hātʰ	hand	**hāt**ʰ	hands
mard	man	**mard**	men
ādmī	man	**ādmī**	men

Feminine

singular		*plural*	
bɛhɛn	sister	**bɛhɛnẽ**	sisters
kitāb	book	**kitābẽ**	books
aurat	woman	**aurtẽ**	women
zabān	language	**zabānẽ**	languages

If you think that the masculine nouns which do not end in ā remain unchanged and the feminine nouns which do not end in ī take ẽ to form plurals, you are right. The masculine nouns which depart from the normal trend, i.e. those which do *not* end in ā and the feminine nouns which do *not* end in ī, are called *marked* nouns.

	singular	*plural*
masculine	non-**ā**	-∅ (zero = unchanged)
feminine	non-**ī**	ẽ

Exercises

1 The computer has swallowed either some parts of a word or a whole word. Supply what is missing where you see the blanks.

mẽ dillī _____ hũ. me _____ cār bʰāī _____. merā cʰoT _____ bʰāī *Chicago* mẽ kām kar _____ hɛ. mer _____ do baR _____ bʰāī *inglistān* mẽ rɛht _____ _____. merā nām salman _____. mẽ *school* ja _____ hũ. mer _____ do bɛhɛn _____ bʰī _____. mer _____ vālid sāhab bʰī kām kart _____ hɛ̃. āp kah _____ rɛhte hɛ̃? āp _____ kit _____ bʰāī-bɛhɛn hɛ̃? āp _____ vāldah kyā _____ kar _____ hɛ?

2 Pair the words on the right with those on the left.

accʰā	cʰoTā
baRā	laRkī
bɛhɛn	aurat
laRkā	burā

ādmī   .   nahī̃
hã̃   bʰāī

3 The software system of our computer has imposed a strange system on the following Urdu phrases. Your job is to correct them.

se	banāras
mẽ	shɛhɛr
das	bɛhɛn
cār	bʰāīyã̃
do	ādmīyã̃
kitnā	bʰāī
zard	sāRī

4 Unscramble the following words/phrases and fill the unscrambled expression in the blank spaces on the right.

hiyeka	_____		
shīxu	_____		
bīRa xuīsh hīu	_____	_____	_____
rūpā mnā	_____	_____	
dūrās	_____		
kinte bʰīā	_____	_____	
mẽlieg	_____		

5 In this crossword puzzle there are four Urdu words from our dialogues. Find the words and circle them. The words can be found horizontally and vertically. (Note that vowels usually written with a macron are represented by double vowels here; so **ū** = **uu** in the crossword.

a	d	b	a	s	u	n	i	y	e
b	l	a	g	j	q	w	e	r	t
s	y	R	u	p	u	o	p	l	g
i	c	i	q	k	a	e	b	d	j
i	q	i	c	s	p	t	l	s	t
p	g	t	x	i	f	q	a	d	s
r	f	h	j	q	s	c	v	a	p
d	x	u	s	h	i	i	n	m	a
a	g	h	n	t	s	x	q	j	b

3 باب تین: آپ کو کیا چاہئے؟

What would you like?

By the end of this unit you should be able to:

- tell someone what you wish to get
- describe locations
- use some negotiation skills
- make reservations
- describe possessions (transferable)
- understand verb agreement with subjects and objects
- express physical states (fever, headache)

Dialogue 1 🔘🔘

Buying a shalvār qamīz

Susan Brown and Maha Ahmad go to a local shop in Liverpool called 'Habib's fabrics'. Maha Ahmad visits the shop quite frequently. After greeting each other, Maha Ahmad tells the shopkeeper that Susan is visiting from America and she wants a shalvar qamiz. Maha begins by saying to Javed Malik

MAHA: zarā naye fɛshan ke shalvār qamīz dikʰāīye.
JAVED: kaun sā shalvār qamīz cāhiye? reshmī yā sūtī?
MAHA: reshmī.
JAVED: ye dekʰiye. āj-kal is kā bahut rivāj hɛ. dekʰiye, resham kitnā accʰā hɛ!
(Javed shows a number of shalvar qamiz. Maha asks Susan about her choice.)
MAHA: susan, āp ko kaun sā shalvār qamīz pasand hɛ?
SUSAN: ye zard.
(turning to Javed to ask the price)
MAHA: is kī qīmat kyā hɛ?
JAVED: bīs pāunD (*pounds*).
MAHA: Tʰīk batāiye, ye bāhar se āyī hɛ̃.
JAVED: āj-kal itnī qīmat hɛ ... accʰā aTʰārah pāunD.
MAHA: accʰā Tʰīk hɛ.

MAHA: *Please show me a shalvar qamiz that is in fashion.* (lit. Please show me a little bit of a new fashion shalvār qamīz.)
JAVED: *What kind of shalvar qamiz (do you) want? Silk or cotton?*
MAHA: *Silk.*
JAVED: *Look at this. Nowadays it is very much in fashion.* (lit. Nowadays its very much custom is.) *See, how good the silk is!* (lit. How much good the silk is!)
MAHA: *Susan, which shalvar qamiz do you want?*
SUSAN: *(I) want this yellow (one).*
MAHA: *What is its price?*
JAVED: *Twenty pounds.*
MAHA: *Please tell (me) the right (price); she has come from abroad.* (Lit. She has come from outside.)

JAVED: *This is the price nowadays . . . OK, eighteen pounds.*
MAHA: *OK, (that) is fine.*

Vocabulary

zarā	little, somewhat	dek^hiye	Have a look.
nayā (m.; adj.)	new	āj-kal	nowadays
shalvār (m.)	loose trousers	rivāj (m.)	custom
	(worn by	āp ko	to you
	women)	pasand (f.)	choice, liking
qamīz (f.)	shirt	zard (adj.)	yellow
dik^hānā	to show	qīmat (f.)	price
dik^hāiye.	Please show.	bīs	twenty
kaun sā (m.; adj.)	which one	pāunD	pound (British
cāhiye	desire, want		currency)
resham (m.)	silk	batāiye	Please tell.
reshmī (adj.)	silk	bāhar	outside
yā	or	āyī	(she) came
sūt (m.)	cotton	itnā	this much
sūtī (adj.)	cotton	aT^hārah	eighteen
dek^hnā	to see		

Pronunciation

The word for 'want, desire' is written as **cāhiye** or **cāhie**.

Notes

Politeness

As we showed in the last unit, Urdu is a very rich language as regards politeness. When **zarā** 'little, somewhat' is used at the beginning of a request, its main function is politeness. It is almost like the English, 'I do not want to impose on you but . . .' By adding **zarā**, Urdu speakers convey the meaning, 'I want to put as little burden as possible on you by my request'. **zarā** remains invariable.

cāhnā 'want' vs. cāhiye 'desire/want'

As the English expression 'What do you want?' would be considered less polite than 'What would you like to have?', similarly in Urdu

āp   kaun sā   shalvār   qamīz   cāhtī   hɛ̃?
you   what kind of   shalvar   qamiz   want   are

would be considered less polite than

āp   ko   kaun sā   shalvār   qamīz   cāhiye?
you   to   what kind of   shalvar   qamiz   desire
(lit. What kind of shalvar qamiz is desirable to you?)

In the first sentence the subject **āp** indicates a deliberate subject whereas in the second sentence the subject **āp ko** is an experiencer one. Sometimes the politeness is achieved in Urdu by means of experiencer subjects. In other words, the verb **cāhiye** is the relatively polite counterpart of English 'want' (and Urdu **cāhnā** 'to want') because it always selects an experiencer subject. Hereafter the Urdu verb **cāhiye** will be glossed as 'want' because 'desire' is not its best translation.

For more information, see the discussion on the experiencer subject in the next unit.

Word-for-word translation

The Urdu equivalent of English 'It is very much in fashion' is

is kā   bahut   rivāj   hɛ.
its   very   custom   is

Similarly, the English expression 'This (she) is a visitor' is realized in Urdu as:

ye   bāhar   se   āyī   hɛ̃.
these (hon.)   outside   from   came   are

In other words, the Urdu expression is literally 'She has come from outside'. The past tense will be dealt with later on; for the time being memorize this sentence and learn to make number and gender changes in **āyī** (**āyā** for masculine singular subjects, **āye** for

masculine plural, and **āyī** for feminine plural) and person and
number changes in the verb form 'to be'.

Polite commands

The Urdu equivalent of English 'Please show' and 'Please see' are:

dikʰā-iye   **dekʰ-iye.**
show (imper. polite)   see (imper. polite)

The other examples of polite commands you have encountered
earlier are:

kah-iye   **sun-iye.**
say (imper. polite)   listen (imper. polite)

In short, **-iye** is added to a verbal stem to form polite commands.
It is called the 'polite imperative' in grammatical literature.

No 'please'

There is really no *exact* equivalent of the English word 'please'.
The most important way of expressing polite requests is by means
of a polite verb form, i.e. by adding **-iye** to a verb stem. Even if
one uses the word-for-word Urdu equivalent of 'please', which is
meharbānī kar ke, the verbal form with **-iye** has to be retained.
meharbānī kar ke means 'kindly' in Urdu.

Context

Note the change in meaning of Urdu **kaun sā** 'which one' in the
following two contexts: (1) when a shalvar qamiz has yet to be
shown by the shopkeeper:

kaun sā   **shalvār**   **qamīz**   **cāhiye?**
what kind of   shalvar   qamiz   want
'What kind of shalvar qamiz do (you) want?'

and (2) in the context of choosing a shalvar qamiz from a set of
suits which are shown to the customer.

āp   ko kaun sā   shalvār qamīz   pasand   hɛ?
you to   which one   shalvar qamiz   choice/liking is
'Which shalvar qamiz do (you) like?'

Subject omission

kaun sā   shalvār qamīz cāhiye?
what kind of   shalvar qamiz want
'What kind of shalvar qamiz do (you) want?'

Dialogue 2 ▣

Booking a flight

John Smith goes to the airline booking office to make a reservation for Lahore. He talks with the agent

JOHN: lahore kā ek TikaT (*ticket*) cāhiye.
AGENT: kaun se din ke liye?
JOHN: kal ke liye.
AGENT: kampyuTar (*computer*) par dekhtā hū̃, hɛ yā nahī̃.
JOHN: subā kī parvāz cāhiye.
AGENT: mere pās TikaT (*ticket*) hɛ.
JOHN: to dījiye. jahāz kab caltā hɛ?
AGENT: subā das baje.
JOHN: mere pās zar-e-naqd nahī̃ hɛ.
AGENT: to krɛDiT kārD (*credit card*) dījiye.

JOHN: *(I) want one ticket for Lahore.*
AGENT: *For which day?*
JOHN: *For tomorrow.*
AGENT: *I'll check on the computer to see if one is available. (lit.
         (It) is or not.)*
JOHN: *(I) need a morning flight.*
AGENT: *I have a ticket.*
JOHN: *Then (please) give (it to me). When does the (aero)plane
         leave?*
AGENT: *10 o'clock in the morning.*

JOHN: *I do not have cash.*
AGENT: *Then use a credit card.* (lit. give a credit card.)

Vocabulary

din (m.)	day	**dījiye.**	Please give.
ke liye	for	**jahāz**	aeroplane
kal	yesterday, tomorrow	**kab**	when (question word)
par	on	**calnā** (-ne)	to leave, to walk
dekʰnā (+ne)	to see	**das**	ten
subā	morning	**baje**	o'clock
parvāz	flight	**pās**	near, possession
to	then		(have)
denā (+ne)	to give	**zar-e-naqd**	cash

Pronunciation

In words borrowed from English, such as *compute*r and *ticket*, the English *t* is pronounced with the retroflex **T** (see the unit beginning on page 7 for the pronunciation of Urdu sounds).

Notes

Word-for-word translation

> **Lahore   kī   TikaT**
> Lahore   of (f.)   ticket (f.)
> 'a ticket for Lahore' (lit. Lahore's ticket)

The borrowed words *ticket* and *computer* are assimilated into Urdu and, consequently, are assigned feminine and masculine gender, respectively.

to 'then'

'then' is **to** (short form of **tab**), as in:

to **dijiye**
then please give

Compound and oblique postpositions

Observe the order of the English preposition in Urdu:

(noun)   postposition   postposition
kal   **ke**   **liye**
tomorrow   of   for

As we proceed further we will introduce the concept of the 'oblique' case in Urdu. You will notice, as we go on, that compound postpositions begin with either **ke** or **kī**, but *never* with **kā**. In the above expression **liye** changes **kā** → **ke**. That is, the postposition ending **ā** becomes **e**.

The oblique effect is not confined to the preceding postposition but extends to the phrase as a whole.

kaun **sā** **din**
which   day (m.)

Notice that the **sā** part of the question word 'which' agrees in number and gender with the following noun, i.e. **din** 'day' which is masculine singular. Now, if we expand this phrase by adding the Urdu compound postposition **ke liye**, we get:

kaun **se** **din**   **ke** **liye**
which   day (m.)   of   for

Now the influence of **liye** not only extends to **ke** but all the way to **se**. The way **kā** gives in to the influence of **liye** is similar to the way **sā** gives in to **se**. However, if we replace the marked noun with an unmarked noun **laRkā** 'boy', you will see a clear change.

kaun **se** **laRke**   **ke** **liye**
which   boy (m.)   of   for
'for which boy'

Although **laRkā** 'boy' changes to **laRke**, its meaning does not change. It still keeps its singular identity.

Separable or transferable possessions

In the last unit we dealt with non-transferable and inseparable possessions, i.e. expressions such as 'I have four brothers'. Let us turn our attention to separable possessions, as in:

mere pās   **zar-e-naqd**   **nahī̃**   **hɛ.**
my   near   cash   not   is
'I do not have cash.'

Similarly, in Urdu the expression 'You have a ticket' will be

āp ke   **pās**   **TikaT**   **hɛ.**
your   near   ticket   is
'You have a ticket.'

In the case of separable possessions the subject receives the **ke pās** compound postposition and, subsequently, the following changes take place. Notice **ke** makes the subject oblique masculine possessive:

mɛ̃ + ke pās → **mere pās**   'I have'
āp + ke pās → **āp ke pās**   'you have'

Dialogue 3 🔲

A visit to a doctor

Iqbal Malik is under the weather with a cold. He has a fever and a headache. He goes to his doctor, Mushtaq Mir. After exchanging greetings, Iqbal tells Dr Mir the purpose of his visit

IQBAL: DākTar (*Doctor*) sāhab, mujʰe kucʰ buxār hɛ.
DR MIR: kab se hɛ?
IQBAL: kal rāt se.
DR MIR: sar mɛ̃ dard bʰī hɛ?
IQBAL: jī hā̃. (*Putting the thermometer in Iqbal's mouth*)
DR MIR: *thermometer* lagāiye. (*After taking the thermometer from Iqbal's mouth*)

Dr Mir:	tʰoRā buxār hɛ. . . . ye davāī din mɛ̃ do bār lījiye. . . . jaldī Tʰīk ho jāẽge.
Iqbal:	*Doctor sir, I have a slight fever.* (lit. some fever.)
Dr Mir:	*Since when?* (lit. Since when is it?)
Iqbal:	*Since last night.*
Dr Mir:	*(Do you have a) headache too?*
Iqbal:	*Yes.*
Dr Mir:	*(You) have a little fever.* . . . *Please take this medicine twice a day.* (lit. Please take this medicine two times in a day.) *(You) will soon be fine.*

Vocabulary

DākTar	doctor	lagānā (+ne)	to fix, put into,
sāhab	sir		stick
mujʰe	to me	lagāiye	please fix, put
kucʰ	some		into, stick
buxār (m.)	fever	tʰoRā (m.; adj.)	little
kab	when	davāī (f.)	medicine
kal	yesterday,	do	two
	tomorrow	bār (f.)	time, turn
rāt (f.)	night	lenā (+ne)	to take
sar (m.)	head	lījiye	please take
dard (m.)	pain	jaldī	soon, quickly
sar mɛ̃ dard	headache (lit.	ho jāẽge	will become
	pain in head)		

Pronunciation

The word **sāhib** has other variants: **sāhab** and more informal **sāb**.

Notes

'Since'

The Urdu equivalent of 'since' is the postposition **se** 'from', e.g.:

kab	**se**	**kal**	**rāt**	**se**
when	since	yesterday	night	from
'since when'		'since last night'		

Dialogue 4 ▢▢

'Humour column'

Two thieves are being interrogated in a Delhi police station. The inspector is interrogating the thieves and his assistant is taking notes

INSPECTOR: tumhāra nām?
THIEF: banerjī.
(Now turning to the other)
INSPECTOR: tumhāra nām?
THIEF: chaterjī.
(Inspector talking to both thieves)
INSPECTOR: corī karte ho aur nām ke sāt^h 'jī' lagāte ho.
(turning to his assistant) in ke nām lik^hiye, baner aur chater.

INSPECTOR: *Your name?*
THIEF: *Banerji.*
INSPECTOR: *Your name?*
THIEF: *Chatterji.*
INSPECTOR: *(You) commit theft (lit. (you) steal) and then you add 'jī' to your name.*
INSPECTOR: *Write down their names, Baner and Chatter.*

Vocabulary

corī karnā (+ne)	to steal	ke sātʰ	with
likʰnā (+ne)	to write	lagānā (+ne)	to attach, to fix
likʰiye	Please write		

Note (cultural)

Some common last names in the state of Bengal end with **-jī**. However, this **jī** is not the honorific suffix as found in colloquial Urdu.

Grammar

cāhiye **and verb agreement**

In Standard Urdu **cāhiye** has a plural form **cāhiyẽ**, which is used when the subject of the sentence is plural.

> **āp ko   qamīzẽ   cāhiyẽ?**
> You to   shirts (f. pl.)   desire/want
> 'Do you want shirts?'

Simple present tense: subject-verb agreement

As pointed out earlier, the verb agrees with the subject in person, number and gender. The first part of the verb (called the 'main verb' i.e. caltā) agrees in number and gender and the second part of the verb (called the 'auxiliary verb') agrees in person and number with the subject:

> **jahāz   kab   caltā   hɛ?**
> aeroplane (m.)   when   move/walk   is
> 'When does the aeroplane leave?'
> (lit. When does the aeroplane walk/move?)

Object in English, subject in Urdu

āp	**ko**	**qamīz**	**pasand**		**hɛ?**
you	to	shirt (f.)	likeable/pleasing		is

'Do you like the shirt?'

Notice that 'Do you like . . .? is phrased in Urdu as 'Is/are . . . pleasing to you?' So the object of the English sentence appears as the subject of the Urdu sentence – 'Do you like the shirt?' becomes 'Is the shirt pleasing to you?' Recall the 'have' construction:

mere	**cār**	**bʰāī**	**hɛ̃**
my	four	brothers(m. pl.)	are

'I have four brothers.'

In the above sentence, the verb form is not **hū̃**, indicating that the verb does not agree with the English subject. The verb agrees with **bʰāī** 'brothers' and takes the plural ending, because 'brothers' *is* the subject in the Urdu construction.

mere	**pās**	**qamīzẽ**	**nahī̃**	**hɛ̃**
my	near	shirts	not	are

'I do not have shirts.'

Similary, the verb agrees with **qamīzẽ**, which is plural.
How about the expression 'I have a slight fever'?

mujʰ	**ko**	**kucʰ**	**buxār**	**hɛ**
me	to	some	fever	is

'I have a slight fever.'
(lit. I have some fever.)

Once again the subjects differ in the English and Urdu sentences.

When does the subject take a postposition?

Urdu verbs such as **pasand honā** 'to like' and **cāhiye** 'want' use the **ko** postposition with their subject. You will have to remember which verb takes which postposition with the subject. For example, you will have to remember that the English verb 'to have' takes three different postpositions with the Urdu subject:

subject postposition	*possession*
ke pās	separable, transferable
kā, ke, kī	inseparable
ko	physical states (such as fever, headache)

Exercises

1 Translate the following sentences into Urdu according to the following model. (Remember Urdu does not have articles. Therefore, the articles 'a', 'an' and 'the' cannot be translated.)

Model: **āp ko kitāb cāhiye.** 'You want a book.'
mujʰe kitāb cāhiye. 'I want a book.'

(a) I want a ticket for Jaipur.
(b) Do you want medicine?
(c) I want two houses.
(d) I want a car in the garage. (garage: use the English word)
(e) You want this beautiful shirt. (beautiful: **xūbsūrat**)

2 Fill in the blanks by making an appropriate choice from the following Urdu subjects.

merā, mere, merī, mere pās, mujʰ ko

(a) _____ ek bɛhɛn hɛ.
(b) _____ do bʰāī hɛ̃.
(c) _____ ek *computer* hɛ.
(d) _____ hāl Tʰīk hɛ.
(e) _____ ek gāRī hɛ.
(f) _____ kām cāhiye.

3 Match the parts of the sentences given on the right with the parts on the left to make a complete sentence.

mujʰ ko	gʰar mẽ kitne ādmī hɛ̃?
mere pās	kyā hɛ?
āp ke	buxār hɛ.
merā	āp ke liye hɛ.
ye xat	shɛhɛr bahut xūbsūrat hɛ.
is kī qīmat	do rupaye hɛ̃.

4 باب چار: آپ کے شوق کیا ہیں؟
What are your hobbies?

By the end of this unit you should be able to:

- talk about hobbies and interests
- talk about likes and dislikes
- manage some more expressions of health and ailments
- learn expressions with 'generally'
- form derived adjectives
- note asymmetry between English and Urdu expressions

Dialogue 1 ◼◼

What are your hobbies?

Professor James Jones is an internationally acclaimed expert on international advertising and he is being profiled in a newspaper, called 'Asian Eye', published in London. After talking about his research, the interviewer, Yaseen Malik, wants to report Professor Jones' interests to his readers

MALIK: kyā āp hindustān jāte hɛ̃?
PROF. JONES: jī hɑ̃, kaī bār.
MALIK: āp ko hindustānī kʰānā pasand hɛ?
PROF. JONES: jī hɑ̃, tandūrī murGī (tandoori chicken), Dosā (dosa) ... vɛse samosā bʰī bahut pasand hɛ.
MALIK: āp ke shauq kyā kyā hɛ̃?
PROF. JONES: mujʰ ko tɛrne kā shauq hɛ, is ke alāvah hindustānī mausīqī kā bʰī shauq hɛ.
MALIK: gāne kā bʰī?
PROF. JONES: zarūr, mere gāne se mere bacce hɛD fon (*head phone*) lagāte hɛ̃.
MALIK: vāh, vāh.

MALIK: *Do you visit India (quite frequently)?*
PROF. JONES: *Yes, quite often* (lit. several times).
MALIK: *Do you like Indian food?*
PROF. JONES: *Yes, tandoori chicken, dosas. In addition (I) like samosas very much.*
MALIK: *What are your hobbies?*
PROF. JONES: *I am fond of swimming, besides this, (I) am fond of Indian music.*
MALIK: *(Fond) of singing too?*
PROF. JONES: *Of course, my children put on head phones (because of) my singing.* (lit. (My) children put on head phones from my singing.)
MALIK: *Excellent!* (i.e. What an excellent sense of humour!)

Vocabulary

jānā (-**ne**)	to go	**shauq** (m.)	hobby, fondness, interest
kaī	several		
kʰānā (m.), (v.) (+**ne**)	food (n.), to eat (v.)	**tɛrnā** (-**ne**)	to swim
		mausiqī (f.)	music
tandūr (m.)	oven	**ke alāvah**	besides, in addition to
tandūrī (adj.)	ovenbaked		
Dosā	Indian-style savoury pancake	**gānā** (m.), (v.) (+**ne**)	song (n.), to sing (v.)
		zarūr	of course, certainly
murGī (f.)	chicken		
vɛse	otherwise, in addition	**par**	on, at
		vāh	ah! excellent! bravo! super!

Notes

The experiencer subject

The Urdu equivalent of the English 'I am fond of swimming' is:

mujʰ ko tɛrne kā shauq hɛ
me to swimming of fondness is

In English 'I' is the subject of the sentence; however, in Urdu the equivalent of English 'I' is **mujʰ ko** 'to me'. The nominative subjects (e.g. 'I') denote volitional/deliberate subjects as in English 'I met him'. The experiencer (**ko**) subjects are non-volitional/non-deliberate, as in English 'I ran into him'. In other words, sentences like the following are expressed in a slightly different fashion:

English	*Urdu*
I am fond of swimming.	The fondness of swimming is *to me*.
You want a ticket.	The desire of a ticket is *to you*.
I have a fever.	A fever is *to me*.
She likes this book.	The choice of this book is (i.e. experienced by) *to her*.

In Urdu the verb 'to be' does not agree with the experiencer subject. For agreement purposes, **shauq** 'fondness' becomes the element of agreement.

There are two other terms for experiential subjects – dative subjects and **ko** subjects. We will call them experiencer subjects in this book.

Verbal nouns (infinitive verbs)

Now observe the status of the word 'swimming' in the English sentence:

I am fond of swimming.

The word 'swimming' functions like a noun in the above sentence. As a matter of fact, one can replace it with a noun, e.g. 'I am fond of chocolate'. The only difference is that 'chocolate' is a noun to begin with and 'swimming' is derived from the verb 'swim' by adding '-ing' to it. Such nouns are called verbal nouns or gerunds. We will call them verbal nouns throughout this book.

Urdu does not differentiate between verbal nouns and infinitive forms. Examples of Urdu verbal nouns or infinitive forms are given below:

verb stems		*verbal nouns/infinitive verbs*	
kar	do	**kar***nā*	to do/doing
ā	come	**ā***nā*	to come/coming
jā	go	**jā***nā*	to go/going
dekʰ	see	**dekʰ***nā*	to see/seeing
batā	tell	**batā***nā*	to tell/telling
tɛr	swim	**tɛr***nā*	to swim/swimming
kʰā	eat	**kʰā***nā*	to eat/eating
gā	sing	**gā***nā*	to sing/singing
likʰ	write	**likʰ***nā*	to write/writing

You will have discovered by now that the only counterpart of the English infinitive 'to' (as in 'to leave') and the verbal noun marker '-ing' (as in 'leaving') in Urdu is **-nā**. It is like English '-ing' in the sense that it follows a verbal stem rather than the English infinitive marker 'to', which precedes a verbal stem.

Oblique verbal nouns

Remember the influence of a postposition on the words in a phrase. See the section on 'Compound and oblique postpositions' in case you have forgotten it.

Now consider the Urdu counterpart of the English 'of swimming' as in 'I am fond of swimming':

tɛrne   kā
swimming   of

Under influence from the postposition **kā**, the Urdu verbal noun **tɛrnā** 'swimming' undergoes a change exactly like the noun **laRkā**. Thus, it becomes **tɛrne**. Study the following sentences carefully. Do you see the same change?

mujʰ ko   gāne   kā   shauq   hɛ.
me   to   singing of   fondness is
'I am fond of singing.'

mujʰ ko   kʰāne   kā   shauq   hɛ.
me   to   eating   of   fondness is
'I am fond of eating.'

āp   ko   filmẽ   dekʰne kā   shauq   hɛ.
you   to   films   seeing of   fondness is
'You are fond of watching films.'

āp   ko   kʰāne   kā   shauq   hɛ.
you   to   eating   of   fondness is
'You are fond of eating.'

'Yes-no' questions with 'kyā'

In Unit 1, we showed you how to change a statement into a 'yes-no' question with merely a change in intonation. Optionally, one can place **kyā** in front of a statement and form a 'yes-no' question out of it. (Yes, it is the same word **kyā** which means 'what'!) Even if **kyā** is placed at the beginning of a sentence, rising question intonation is imperative. Since it is difficult to show intonation in writing, **kyā** is more prevalent in writing and its omission is common in speaking.

The statement

āp   hindustān   jāte   hε̃.
you   India   go   are
'You go to India.'

becomes a 'yes-no' question with the mere addition of **kyā** in front of it:

kyā   āp   hindustān   jāte   hε̃?
Q   you   India   go   are
'Do you go to India?'

You do not need any verb forms at the beginning of a yes-no question in Urdu.

Repetition of question words

The repetition of a question word is quite common in Urdu. In many languages of South East Asia repetition indicates plurality. Almost the same is true in Urdu.

āp ke   shauq   kyā   kyā   hε̃?
your   interests/hobbies   what   what   are
'What are your interests/hobbies?'

In English you cannot repeat the question word 'what' even if you know that the person in question has many interests. However, the repetition of **kyā** has a 'listing' function and, thus, asks the person to give a list of interests which are more than one according to the speaker.
  Similarly, if someone asks in Urdu

āp   kahā̃   kahā̃   jāte   hε̃?
you   where   where   go   are
'What places do you go to?'

the speaker has reason to believe that the listener goes to more than one place.

Dialogue 2 ▭

Indian films

India is the largest producer of films in the world. More films are produced by the Bombay film industry than by Hollywood. Therefore, it is no wonder that Urdu/Hindi films are often the topic of social conversation and are an excellent source of learning agreement-disagreement, likes and dislikes and social and political thoughts. In this dialogue, the topic of discussion is Indian films. The participants are Akbar Ali and Sajid Rahim. Sajid has seen the film badmāsh (villain). He is ready to express his delight over it

SAJID: badmāsh merī pasanddīdah film hε.

AKBAR: vo kεse?

SAJID: gāne bahut accʰe hε̃, kahānī aur adākārī bʰī shāndār hε.

AKBAR: hindustānī filmε̃ to mujʰ ko bilkul pasand nahī̃. sirf *formula.*

SAJID: lekin ye *formula* film nahī̃, is kā andāz aur hai.

AKBAR: sab hindustānī filmε̃ ek sī hotī hε̃, laRkā laRkī se miltā hε, donõ mε̃ ishq hotā hε, pʰir badmāsh ātā hε . . .
          (Sajid: interrupting Akbar)

SAJID: aur donõ kī shādī hotī hε. jī nahī̃, ye εsī film nahī̃.

AKBAR: to maGrib kī naqal hogī.

SAJID: to āp ke xayāl mε̃ sirf maGribī filmε̃ accʰī hotī hε̃?

AKBAR: mε̃ ye nahī̃ kεh rahā hū̃, purānī hindustānī filmε̃ accʰī hotī hε̃.
          (Mushtaq Ahmad patiently listens to this discussion and intervenes by saying)

MUSHTAQ: film kī bāt par jʰagRā kyõ?

SAJID: *'Badmash' is my favourite film.*

AKBAR: *How come?*

SAJID: *(The) songs are very good; (the) plot and acting are great too.*

AKBAR: *I dislike Indian films – (they are) only formula (films).*

SAJID: *But this (one is) not a formula film. Its style is different.*

AKBAR: *All Indian films are alike – a boy meets a girl, both fall in love* (lit. love happens in both), *then a villain comes.* . . .

SAJID: *And, both get married. This is not such a film.*

AKBAR: *Then it must be an imitation of Western (films)* (lit. of the West).

SAJID: *(Do) you think only Western films are (generally) good?* (lit. In your opinion only Western films are (generally) good.)

AKBAR: *I'm not saying that* (lit. this)*; the old Indian films are good.*

MUSHTAQ: *Why argue over the topic of films?* (lit. Why (wage a) battle over the topic of films? implying that the topic of films is not worthy of such a serious discussion.)

Vocabulary

badmāsh (m.)	villain	**hotī hɛ̃**	generally happen, generally take place (pl.)
pasanddīdā	favourite		
vo kɛse	how come?		
kahānī (f.)	story	**hogī**	will be
adākār (m./f.)	an actor/actress	**ɛsā**	such
adākārī	acting	**maGrib** (m.)	west; the West
shāndār	splendid, great	**maGribī**	western; Western
nāpasand	dislike	**naqal** (f.)	copy, fake, imitation
aur	and, more, other, else		
		xayāl (m.)	opinion, view
andāz (m.)	style	**sirf**	only
ek-sā	alike	**kɛhnā** (+**ne**)	to say
ishq (m.)	love	**purānā**	old (inanimate)
shādī (f.)	marriage	(m.; adj.)	
honā (-**ne**)	to be	**bāt** (f.)	matter, conversation, topic
hotī hɛ	generally happens, generally takes place (sg.)	**jʰagRā** (m.)	a quarrel, battle
		kyõ	why

Pronunciation

The Urdu word for 'opinion' can be pronounced in two ways: **xyāl** and **xayāl**. The Urdu word for 'copy' is pronounced as **naqal** or **naql**. The word for 'villain' is written as **badm'āsh**, but is pronounced as **badmāsh**. (Remember the discussion on **mu'āf** and **māf**?)

Notes

filmē

The English word 'film' is assimilated into Urdu. It is no longer treated as a foreign word in the language; therefore, it has gender. From the plural ending **ē**, you can predict its gender. It is, of course, feminine.

Negative markers: nahī̃, nā

The short version of **nahī̃** 'not' is **nā**.

With polite orders **nā** is used instead of **nahī̃**. However, observe the use of **nā** with polite orders ('polite imperatives'.)

nā   dījiye.
not   please give
'Please don't give' (me any/it etc.).

It is also used with the word **nā**pasand 'dislike'. However, with nouns it is not as productive as with polite commands. For example, you cannot make the word 'dissatisfaction' using **nā** with the Urdu equivalent of 'satisfaction'.

aur as an adjective or adverb

is kā   andāz   aur   hɛ.
its   style   *different*   is

The conjunction 'and' in Urdu expresses a range of meanings when used either as a predicate as in the above sentence or as an adjective, below:

aur cāy dījiye.
more tea please give
'Please give me (some) more tea.'

ek aur sāRī dikʰāiye.
one *other* saree please show
'Please show (me) another saree.'

aur is the equivalent of English 'different', 'more', 'else'. Observe another frequent expression with **aur:**

aur kucʰ cāhiye?
else some want
'(Do you) want something else?'

Note the difference in word order.

ek-sā 'same', 'alike'

sab hindustānī filmẽ ek sī hotī hɛ̃.
all Indian films one -ish (generic) BE are
'Generally, all Indian films are alike.'

The **-sā** is like English '-ish' (e.g. boyish). Therefore, the Urdu sentence is the literal equivalent of English, 'generally all Indian films are one-ish'.

'Generally' and the 'to be' verb

There is no separate exact word equivalent to English 'generally' in Urdu. It is the verb **hotī** which contributes to this meaning. Compare the last sentence above with the following:

sab hindustānī filmẽ ek sī hɛ̃.
all Indian films one -ish are
'All Indian films are alike.'

Notice the slight difference in the two conjugations of **honā** 'to be':

generic				non-generic
ho + **t**	+ **ī**		**hɛ̃**	**hɛ̃**
be + aspect + number, gender			are	are

It is the generic conjugation which expresses the English word 'generally' in Urdu. The verb agrees with the subject. Now observe two other examples of the generic BE in Urdu:

> **donõ   mẽ   ishq   hotā   hɛ.**
> both   in   love (m.)   (generic) BE   is
> 'Generally, love blossoms (lit. happens) between the two.'

> **donõ   kī   shādī   hotī   hɛ.**
> both   of   marriage (f.)   (generic) BE   is
> 'Generally, their marriage (lit. the marriage of both) takes
>   place.'

hotā agrees with **ishq** 'love', which is masculine singular in Urdu, whereas **hotī** agrees with **shādī** 'marriage'. Similarly, **hɛ** agrees with its respective subjects.

Direct object ko or se

The English expression 'boy meets girl' in Urdu is:

> **laRkā   laRkī   se   miltā   hɛ.**
> boy   girl   with   meet   is
> 'Boy meets girl.'

> **laRkā   laRkī   ko   dekʰtā   hɛ.**
> boy   girl   object   see   is
> 'The boy sees the girl.'

Notice the English animate object 'girl' is followed by a postposition, either **se** or **ko**. Usually, the most frequent object postposition is **ko**. But some verbs such as 'meet' and the verbs of communication (e.g. 'ask', 'say', 'speak', even 'love'!) are exceptions – they take **se** instead of **ko**.

Remember only animate objects take **ko.** Inanimate objects do not take an object marker.

laRkā gʰar dekʰtā hɛ.
boy house see is
'The boy sees the house.'

The object **gʰar** 'house' is not marked with **ko** because it is an inanimate noun. More details are given in the Reference Grammar.

Word-for-word translation

maGrib kī naql hogī.
West of copy be-will
'(The film) will be an imitation of the West.'

The verb formation is as follows:

ho + **g** + **ī**
be + future tense + number gender

Text 1

'Tell me why' column

Very often we are asked how Indians and Pakistanis say 'I love you'. In this 'Tell me why' column you will get the answer to this question in three sequential segments and in question–answer exercise form.

I savāl: kyā hindustānī log kɛhte hɛ̃: 'I love you'?
  javāb: (a) ā̃kʰõ se, lekin alfāz se nahī̃.
    (b) sirf alfāz se.

  sahī javāb: (a).

  Question: Do Indians say: 'I love you'?
  Answer: (a) By eyes, but not with words.
    (b) Only with words.

  Correct answer: (a).

II savāl: kyā hindustānī log alfāz se kabʰī kɛhte hɛ̃: 'I love you'?

javāb: (a) kabʰī nahī̃
          (b) kabʰī kabʰī.

sahī javāb: (b)

Question: Do Indians ever say in words: 'I love you'?
Answer: (a) Never.
          (b) Sometimes.

Correct answer: (b).

III   savāl: hindustānī log alfāz se kɛse kɛhte hɛ̃: 'I love you'?
       javāb: (a) mɛ̃ tum se ishq kartā hū̃.
                  (b) mujʰ ko tum se ishq hɛ.

Tʰīk javāb: (b).

Question: How do Indians say in words: 'I love you'?
Answer: (a) I love you.
          (b) Love with you is to me.

Correct answer: (b).

Vocabulary

log (m.)	people	**alfāz** (pl.)	words
ā̃kʰ (f.)	eye	**sirf**	only
ā̃kʰõ	eyes	**kabʰī**	ever
(f. pl.,oblique)		**kabʰī nahī̃**	never
se	from, with, by	**kabʰī kabʰī**	sometimes
lafz (m.)	word		

Note

'I love you' prohibition

If one has to say 'I love you' in words, it is better to express it by means of the experiencer subject construction rather than by the non-experiencer deliberate subject. The following expression is almost vulgar:

mɛ̃	tum	se	ishq	kartā	hū̃.
I	you	with	love	do	am

Therefore, the expression 'I love you' is best expressed in the following words:

mujʰ	ko	tum	se	ishq	hɛ.
me	to	you	with	love	is

However, nowadays 'I love you' is becoming quite popular but it would never be used in writing.

Repetition and pluralization

The repetition of the adverb **kabʰī** gives the plural meaning 'sometimes'.

Oblique plural nouns

Notice the influence of a postposition on plural nouns:

	masculine		*feminine*	
singular	**lafz**	word	**ā̃kʰ**	eye
plural	**alfāz**	words	**ā̃kʰẽ**	eyes

The plural nouns yield to the pressure of the postposition and take the ending **õ**.

alfāz	se	by words
ā̃kʰõ	se	by eyes

Dialogue 3 ▢▢

What do you eat for breakfast?

Irshad Ali visits his doctor in London. He complains about his stomach problems. Apparently, he is suffering from indigestion. The doctor begins by enquiring about his eating habits

DOCTOR: Irshad sāhab, nāshte mẽ āp kyā kʰāte hɛ̃?
IRSHAD: das samose.

DOCTOR: aur, kyā pīte hɛ̃?

IRSHAD: mujʰe cāy bahut accʰī lagtī hɛ. subā cāy bahut pītā hū̃.

DOCTOR: āp ko jism kī bimārī nahī̃. dimāG kī bimārī hɛ. is liye āp *psychiatrist* ke pās jāiye.

DOCTOR: *Irshad sahab, what do you eat for breakfast? (lit. What do you eat in breakfast?)*

IRSHAD: *Ten samosas.*

DOCTOR: *And, what (do you) drink?*

IRSHAD: *I like tea a lot. (In the) morning (I) drink a lot of tea. (lit. To me a lot of tea feels good.)*

DOCTOR: *You do not have (any) physical illness. (You) have a mental illness. Therefore, you (should) go to the psychiatrist.*

Vocabulary

nāshtah (m.)	breakfast	**subā** (f.)	morning
pīnā (+ne)	to drink	**jism** (m.)	body
cāy (f.)	tea	**bimārī** (f.)	illness
mujʰe	(to) me	**dimāG** (m.)	brain
lagnā (+ko)	to seem, to be applied	**isliye**	therefore, so, thus, because of this
accʰā lagnā (+ko)	to like		

Notes

acchā lagnā 'to like'

You have already learned expressions such as:

mujʰ ko cāy pasand hɛ.
to   me   tea   liking   is

Another common way of saying the same expression is:

mujʰ ko cāy accʰī lagtī hɛ.
me   to   tea (f.)   good   feel   is
'I like tea.' (lit. Tea feels good to me.)

Word formation: derived adjectives

Do some detective work and see how English adjectives such as 'silk' are formed in Urdu:

nouns		adjective	
resham	silk	**reshmī**	silk
sūt	cotton (crop)	**sūtī**	cotton (as in cotton clothes)
naql	copy/imitation	**naqlī**	fake
asl	fact	**aslī**	real, genuine
pākistān	Pakistan	**pākistānī**	Pakistani
kashmīr	Kashmir	**kashmīrī**	Kashmiri

If you think that the addition of *ī* at the end of the word makes it an adjective, you are right. Notice that all the nouns (and place names) in the list above end in a consonant. You cannot derive an adjective by adding *ī* to nouns ending in a vowel. For example, the expressions 'from Delhi' or 'from Agra' cannot be reduced to one-word adjectives by the addition of *ī*. Only the postposition **se** can rescue the expressions.

Now, observe how words such as 'physical' and 'mental' are formed in Urdu:

jism	**kī**	**bimārī**		**dimāG**	**kī**	**bimārī**
body	of	illness (f.)		brain	of	illness (f.)

'physical/bodily illness'   'mental illness'

The possessive construction is used instead. Is it possible to reduce **jism kī** and **dimāG kī** to the *ī* types of adjectives? Yes, of course!

jismānī bimārī   **dimāGī bimārī**
'physical/bodily illness'   'mental illness'

Always remember, though, that word formation can be quite tricky.

'Go to the doctor'

You have observed that English 'to' is usually **ko** in Urdu. However, the English expression 'Go to the psychiatrist' is:

psychiatrist **ke pās jāiye.**
psychiatrist of near please go

In other words, the Urdu expression is phrased as 'Please go near the psychiatrist'. The compound postposition **ke pās** is used instead of **ko**. Similarly, the Urdu sentence 'Please go to the doctor' will be:

doctor **ke pās jāiye.**

Contractive e pronoun forms

mujʰe is the short form of **mujʰ ko**.

Exercises

1 Choose any word from the following six columns and form at least seven sentences. You can choose a word from the columns as many times as you like.

mujʰ	ko	paRʰnā	kā	shauq	hɛ
āp		gāne	ke	pasand	hɛ̃
		kyā			
		tɛrne			
		kʰāne			
		kyā-kyā			

2 Read the following statements and then answer the question about each statement. Your answer should be in Urdu.

(a) Statement : John is fond of dancing and singing. (hint: dancing = **nācnā**)
Question: gāne ke alāvah John ko kyā pasand hɛ?
Answer:

(b) Statement: Judy loves to write stories and poems? (hint: poem = **nazm** (f.))
Question: Judy ko kyā kyā shauq hɛ̃?
Answer:

(c) Statement: Sanjida's likes and dislikes are given below:

likes	*dislikes*
to eat samosas	to eat chicken
vegetarian food	non-vegetarian
stories	poetry (hint: poetry = **shāirī** (f.))
Indian music	Western music

Question: Sanjida ko kyā kyā nāpasand hε?

Answer:

(d) Question: Sanjida ko kyā kyā pasand hε/hε̃?

Answer:

3 There are two possible interpretations of the following sentences. Uncover their ambiguity by translating them into English.

(a) John ko kʰānā pasand hε.
(b) John ko gāna pasand hε.

a1:
a2:

b1:
b2:

4 Write two things which children do not like about their parents.

5 How many ways can you find to say 'I like swimming' in Urdu?

5

باب پانچ: آپ چُھٹیوں میں کیا کریں گے؟

What are you going to do during the holidays?

By the end of this unit you should be able to:

- talk about your own and others' plans
- compare people and objects
- develop paraphrasing skills
- express desires
- use the future tense
- express ability/capability
- use progressive tense forms

Dialogue 1 ▣

I want to go to India

Shabir Khan is planning to spend his Christmas holiday in India. He knows that December and January are excellent months to visit India. Summers are hot and they are followed by the monsoon. He goes to an Indian travel agent in London to make his travel plans

AGENT: mɛ̃ kyā xidmat kar saktī hū̃?
SHABIR: hindustān ke liye TikaT (*ticket*) cāhiye?
AGENT: sirf apne liye?
SHABIR: xāndān ke liye.
AGENT: kitne log hɛ̃?
SHABIR: cār – do baRe aur do bacce.
AGENT: baccõ kī umar bārah sal se kam hɛ?
SHABIR: laRkī kī umar bārah sāl hɛ aur laRke kī cʰe sāl.
AGENT: kab jānā cāhte hɛ̃?
SHABIR: *Christmas* ke dino mɛ̃.
AGENT: is vaqt bahut *rush* hotā hɛ, *ticket* mɛhɛ̃ge hõge.
SHABIR: koī bāt nahī̃.

AGENT: *What can I do (for you)?* (lit. What service can I do?)
SHABIR: *I need a ticket for India.*
AGENT: *Only for yourself?*
SHABIR: *For the family.*
AGENT: *How many people are (there in the family)?*
SHABIR: *Four – two adults and two children.*
AGENT: *Is the age of the children less than twelve?*
SHABIR: *The girl is twelve and the boy (is) six.* (lit. The age of the girl is twelve years and (the age) of the boy (is) six years.)
AGENT: *When do (you) want to go?*
SHABIR: *During Christmas.* (lit. During Christmas days.)
AGENT: *It's a very busy time.* (lit. There's a rush this time.) *The ticket will be expensive.*
SHABIR: *It does not matter.*

Vocabulary

xidmat (f.)	service	**kam**	less
saknā	can, be able to	**cāhnā**	to want
apnā	one's own	**mẽ**	in, during
xāndān (m.)	family	**vaqt** (m.)	time, season
umr (f.)	age	**mɛhɛ̃gā** (m.; adj.)	expensive
sāl (m.)	year	**koī**	some, any,
se	than, from, by		someone, anyone

Pronunciation

The word for 'age' is written as **umar** but is pronounced **umr**.

Notes

saknā 'can'

The expression 'What can I do (for you)?' is expressed as:

mẽ	**kyā**	**xidmat**	**kar**	**saktī**	**hū̃?**
I (f. sg.)	what	service	do	can	am

Notice the placement of **saknā** 'can/to be able to' which is like any other verb in Urdu. It is conjugated in different tenses.

Consider one more example.

mẽ	**bol**	**saktā**	**hū̃.**
I (m. sg.)	talk	can	am

'I can talk.'

The form **saktā hū̃** agrees with the subject and the real (as opposed to modal or auxiliary) verb **bol** 'talk' precedes **saktā hū̃**.

apnā 'one's own'

apnā is a possessive pronoun which means 'one's own'. English possessive adjectives can be translated either as regular possessives or with the **apnā** form. Observe the distinction Urdu makes in this regard:

> **merā nām John hε.**
> my name John is
> 'My name is John.'

> **mɛ̃ apnā nām likʰtā hũ̃.**
> I own name write am
> 'I write my name.'

In other words, English 'my' can be said in two ways in Urdu: **merā** or **apnā**. The possessive pronoun does not show any relationship to the subject of the sentence, whereas **apnā** shows this relationship. In the second sentence, the possessed thing **merā nām** belongs to the subject of the sentence; therefore, **merā** changes to **apnā**. In other words in the English combinations such as 'I ... my', 'we ... our', the possessive pronoun becomes **apnā** in Urdu.

subject		possessive	possessive changes to
mɛ̃	...	merā	
ham	...	hamārā	
tū	...	terā	
tum	...	tumhārā	
āp	...	āp kā	apnā
vo	...	us kā	.(**vo ... us kā** must refer to the same person)
vo (pl.)...		un kā	(**vo ... un kā** must have the same referent)

Prediction: In Urdu the **mɛ̃ ... merā** type of combination cannot be used in a simple sentence. In the third person, the **vo ... us kā** (**vo ... un kā**) combination cannot be used if the possessed thing and the possessor subject refer to the same person:

> **vo apnā kām kartā hε.**
> he own job do is
> 'He (i.e. John) does his (i.e. John's) work.'

However, if in the English sentence 'he' refers to John and 'his' refers to Bill, then **apnā** will not be used. When the subject possessor and the possessed thing are not identical, possessive pronouns are used.

vo   us kā   kām   kartā   hɛ.
he   his   job   do   is
'He (i.e. John) does his (i.e. Bill's) work.'

apnā is masculine singular. Its two other number-gender variants
are **apne** (m. pl.) and **apnī** (f.). In dialogue 1, in

sirf   apne   liye?
only   own   for

the subject **āp** is implied. Because of the following postposition,
apnā becomes oblique.

Comparative/superlative se 'than'

While learning Urdu you do not need to memorize different comparative forms such as 'good, better, best'. Only the postposition
se is used to make a comparison:

baccõ   kī   umar   bārah   se   kam   hɛ̃.
children   of   age   twelve   than   less   are
'The children's ages are less than twelve.'

se is used after the standard/object of comparison which is 'twelve'.
Also, the adjective follows the postposition. Similarly:

john   firoz   se   accʰā   hɛ.
John   Firoz   than   good   is
'John is better than Firoz.'

Thus, the word order of the comparative phrase 'better than Firoz'
is just reversed in Urdu, i.e. 'Firoz than good'.

Superlatives are expressed by choosing **sab** 'all' as the object of
comparison. The English sentence 'John is best' will be expressed
as 'John all than good is', as in:

john   sab   se   accʰā   hɛ.
John   all   than   good   is
'John is the best.'

Again notice the Urdu word order – 'all than good'. The sense of this
construction is: 'From (*se*) all (the others) John is (the) good (one)'.
The adjective can be further modified by words, indicating
degree, such as **zyādā** 'more':

john firoz se zyādā accʰā hɛ.
John Firoz than more good is
'John is much better than Firoz.'

cāhnā 'to want'

Notice the word order of the English sentence 'you want to go':

āp jānā cāhte hɛ̃.
you to go want are
'You want to go.'

The infinitive form 'to go' precedes the verb **cāhnā** 'to want'. The verb **cāhnā** is conjugated. Study one more example:

vo nācnā cāhtī hɛ.
she to dance want is
'She wants to dance.'

Dialogue 2 ▮▮

Thinking about India

On the same day Shabir Khan runs into his colleague Al Nasiri. They start talking about the Christmas break. Al Nasiri has caught Shabir off-guard, lost in his own world and attracts Shabir's attention by saying:

AL NASIRI: bʰaī, kis duniyā mẽ ho? kyā soc rahe ho?
SHABIR: hindustān ke bāre mẽ soc rahā tʰā.
AL NASIRI: kyõ, sab Tʰīk hɛ na?
SHABIR: hā̃, *Christmas* kī cʰuTTiyõ mẽ hindustān jā rahā hū̃.
AL NASIRI: akele yā xāndān ke sātʰ?
SHABIR: bīvī bacce, yānī pūrī *tribe* ke sātʰ.
AL NASIRI: hā̃ bʰāī, nahī̃ to bīvī talāq de degī. kahā̃ jāoge?
SHABIR: dillī, āgrā aur jaipur.
AL NASIRI: āgrā kɛse jāoge?
SHABIR: havāī jahāz se.
AL NASIRI: havāī jahāz se jānā bekār hɛ.

SHABIR: kyõ?

AL NASIRI: havaī jahāz se rel gāRī mẽ kam vaqt lagtā hɛ.

AL NASIRI: *Well, in what world are you? What are you thinking?*

SHABIR: *I was thinking about India.*

AL NASIRI: *Why, everything is alright, isn't it?*

SHABIR: *Yes (everything is fine); (we) are going to India during the Christmas holidays.*

AL NASIRI: *Alone or with the family?*

SHABIR: *Wife, children, that is, with the whole **tribe**.*

AL NASIRI: *Yes, brother; otherwise, (your) wife will divorce you. Where will (you) go?*

SHABIR: *Delhi, Agra and Jaipur.*

AL NASIRI: *How will (you) go to Agra?*

SHABIR: *By plane.*

AL NASIRI: *(It is) useless to go to Agra by plane.*

SHABIR: *Why?*

AL NASIRI: *(It) takes less time (to go to Agra) by train than by plane.*

Vocabulary

bʰaī	hey, well (excl.)	yānī	that is, in other words
kis	which		
duniyā (f.)	world	nahī̃ to	otherwise
socnā (+ne)	to think	talāq (m.)	divorce
ke bāre mẽ	about, concerning	talāq denā (+ne)	to divorce
tʰā	was		
sab	all	havā (f.)	air, wind
cʰuTTī (f.)	holiday, leave	jahāz (m.)	a ship, vessel, plane
akelā (m.; adj.)	alone	bekār	useless
xāndān (m.)	family	gāRī (f.)	train, vehicle, cart
ke sātʰ	with, together	rel gāRī (f.)	(railway) train
bīvī (f.)	wife	vaqt (m.)	time
		lagnā (-ne)	to take, to cost

Notes

bʰai 'hey' vs. bʰāi 'brother'

The short vs. long vowel can make a considerable difference in meaning. A case in point is the contrast between **bʰai** and **bʰāi**. The former is used as an exclamatory marker to express surprise, happiness, etc. The latter (**bʰāi**) is a kinship term and you will recall that it means 'brother'. However, in Urdu, it can be used as an address for a friend, stranger, shopkeeper both for young and old. Sometimes in very informal circumstances, it can even be used for women who are familiar to the speaker. Our advice is not to use it for women.

kyā 'what', kaun 'who' and kis 'what, who'

kis is the oblique singular counterpart of both **kyā** 'what', and **kaun** 'who'.

kyā duniyā	what world
kis duniyā mẽ	in what world

For details see the Reference Grammar.

Compound postpositions

You have come across postpositions of one and two elements. Here is a compound postposition consisting of three elements. Remember not to use compound postpositions with **kā**.

ke bāre mẽ   'about, concerning' (lit. in regard to)

Observe the usage of this postposition:

hindustān ke bāre mẽ	about India
kahānī ke bāre mẽ	about the story
laRkõ ke bāre mẽ	about the boys (**laRkõ** = boys, obl. pl.)

Past tense: the verb 'to be'

The Urdu forms for English 'was' and 'were' are:

	masculine		*feminine*	
singular	tʰā	was	tʰī	was
plural	tʰe	were	tʰī̃	were

As in English, these forms agree with their subject. The only difference is that in Urdu they agree in gender as well as number.

Progressives

So far you will have observed that Urdu verbs consist of either one unit (e.g. polite commands) or two units (e.g. the simple present). Now, you have an opportunity to familiarize yourself with a verb which has three units:

mɛ̃	hindustān	ke bāre mɛ̃	soc	rahā	tʰā.
I	India	about	think	-ing	was

'I was thinking about India.'

The Urdu equivalent of English 'was thinking' is *soc rahā tʰā*. The Urdu verb is broken into three units: 'verb stem' (**soc**), '-ing' (**rahā**), 'was' (**tʰā**). The only difference between Urdu and English is that in Urdu '-ing' is a separate word and the auxiliary 'was' ends the verbal string. The tense used above is called either 'past progressive' or 'past continuous'. We will call it the *past progressive*.

Like an adjective ending in **-ā**, **rahā** has three variants: **rahā** (m. sg.), **rahe** (m. pl.) and **rahī** (f.).

In order to form the present progressive, as in English, the auxiliary 'was' is replaced by present forms such as 'am', 'is', 'are'. The same is true in Urdu. Just substitute the present 'to be' forms and you will get the present progressive. For instance:

mɛ̃	hindustān	ke bāre mɛ̃	soc	rahā	hū̃.
I	India	about	think	-ing	am

'I am thinking about India.'

The future tense

The English future tense consists of two verbal units, whereas it is only one unit in Urdu. You came across an example of an Urdu future tense in Unit 3:

ham pʰir milẽge.
we again meet-will
'We will meet again.'

tum kahā̃ jāoge?
you where go-will
'Where will you go?'

The Urdu verb forms can be broken up in the following manner:

mil + **ẽ** + **g** + **e**
stem + person (**āp**) + future 'will' + number-gender (m. pl.)

jā + **o** + **g** + **e**
stem + person (**tum**) + future 'will' + number-gender (m. pl.)

jā + **ū̃** + **g** + **ī**
stem + person (**mɛ̃**) + future 'will' + number-gender
(f. sg./pl.)

The postposition ko 'to' with locations

āp *Christmas* kī chuTTiyõ mẽ hindustān jā rahe hɛ̃.
you Christmas of holiday in India go -ing are
'You are going to India in the Christmas holiday.'

The postposition **ko** is dropped in Urdu in expressions such as 'to India'.

Dialogue 3 ▨

A train to Agra

Al Nasiri and Shabir Khan continue to discuss the best ways of getting to Agra. Finally, Al Nasiri convinces Shabir Khan to take a train to Agra

AL NASIRI: āgrā ke liye sab se accʰī rel gāRī tāj express hɛ.
SHABIR: tāj express kahā̃ se caltī hɛ?
AL NASIRI: nayī dillī se, subā sāt baje.

SHABIR:	aur vāpas āne ke liye?
AL NASIRI:	vohī gāRī shām ko vāpas ātī hɛ.
SHABIR:	lekin ham log rāt ko tāj mɛhɛl dekʰnā cāhte hɛ̃.
AL NASIRI:	hɑ̃, tāj rāt ko aur bʰī xūbsūrat lagtā hɛ.
SHABIR:	to ek rāt āgrā rukēge, agle din dillī vāpas āēge.
AL NASIRI:	cɑ̃dnī rāt, tāj mɛhɛl aur bīvī sātʰ . . . mazā kījiye.

AL NASIRI:	*The best train for Agra is the Taj Express.*
SHABIR:	*Where does the Taj Express leave from?*
AL NASIRI:	*From New Delhi, at seven o'clock in the morning.*
SHABIR:	*And for the return journey? (lit. And to come (back)?)*
AL NASIRI:	*The same train comes back (to New Delhi) in the evening.*
SHABIR:	*But we* (lit. *we* people) *want to see the Taj Mahal at night.*
AL NASIRI:	*Yes, the Taj looks even more beautiful at night.*
SHABIR:	*Then, we will stay (for a) night (in) Agra; the next day (we) will return to Delhi.*
AL NASIRI:	*A moon-lit night, the Taj Mahal and (your) wife by your side . . . (do) enjoy yourselves!*

Vocabulary

nayā (m.; adj.)	new		**tāj mɛhɛl**	the Taj Mahal
subā (f.)	morning			(lit. Crown
sāt baje	seven o'clock			Palace)
vāpas	back		**aur bʰī**	even more
vāpas ānā (-ne)	to come back		**lagnā** (+ko)	to seem, to appear
vo	that, he, she, they		**ruknā** (-ne)	to stop
vohī (**voh**+**hī**)	same, that very		**aglā** (m.; adj.)	next
shām (f.)	evening		**din** (m.)	day
rāt (f.)	night		**cɑ̃d** (m.)	moon
tāj (m.)	crown		**cɑ̃dnī**	moon-lit
mɛhɛl (m.)	palace		**mazā karnā**	to enjoy
			(**+ne**)	

Pronunciation

mɛhɛl is also pronounced as mɛhl.

Notes

Time expressions

subā/savere	in the morning
dopɛhɛr ko	at noon
shām ko	in the evening
rāt ko	at night

With the exception of **subā/savere**, the postposition **ko** is uniformly used with other time adverbs.

Further information on time and other number expressions can be found in the English–Urdu glossary.

Emphatic particle, hī 'only, right, very'

The particle of exclusion is **hī** 'only'. The English word 'same' is equivalent to 'that very' in Urdu. It can be used with nouns, pronouns and adverbs. It is usually used as a separate word except with those pronouns and adverbs which end in -**h**. The pronouns and adverbs undergo contraction before *hī*:

pronoun		*particle*	*emphatic pronoun*	
vo (vah)	he/she/that	+ **hī**	= **vohī**	that very, same
ye (yah)	this	+ **hī**	= **yahī**	this very

adverb		*particle*	*emphatic adverb*	
vahā̃	there	+ **hī**	= **vohī̃**	right there
yahā̃	here	+ **hī**	= **yahī̃**	right here

Irregular commands

Recall that polite commands are formed by adding -**iye** to a stem. The following four stems are irregular because they undergo a change with -**iye**.

stem		irregular stem	polite command	
kar	do	**kīj**	**kīj-iye**	Please do.
de	give	**dīj**	**dīj-iye**	Please give.
le	take	**līj**	**līj-iye**	Please take.
pī	drink	**pīj**	**pīj-iye**	Please drink.

Text 1

An ancient folk tale: 'To build castles in the air'

This is a folk tale about a poor beggar from ancient times. He was a miser and used to save the flour that he got from his clients in a ceramic pitcher. He used to guard the pitcher jealously and kept it next to his bed. One day he began to day-dream:

1 ek din mulk mē qāhat paRegā.
2 mē āTā becū̃gā.
3 aur kuc^h jānvar xarīdū̃gā.
4 to mē amīr banū̃gā.
5 ek din merī shādī hogī.
6 p^hir merā baccā hogā.
7 ab mē ārām se kitābē paR^hū̃gā.
8 baccā mere pās āyegā.

1 *One day (there) will be a famine in the country.*
2 *I will sell the flour.*
3 *And will buy some animals.*
4 *Then I will become rich.*
5 *One day I'll get married* (i.e. my marriage will take place).
6 *Then, I will have a child.* (lit. My child will happen.)
7 *Now, I will read books in comfort.*
8 *The child will come to me.* (lit. come near me)

(At this point he continues to dream that he will ask his wife to take away the child. Because she is busy she won't be able to hear him. Therefore, he will kick her. Thinking this, he actually kicks and hits the pitcher. The pitcher falls over and breaks. With this, the castle he has built in the air vanishes.)

Vocabulary

mulk (m.)	country	**xarīdnā** (+**ne**)	to buy
qāhat	famine	**amīr**	rich
āTā (m.)	flour	**bannā** (-**ne**)	to become
becnā (+**ne**)	to sell	**ārām** (m.)	comfort
kuc^h	some	**paR^hnā** (-**ne**)	to study, to read
jānvar (m.)	animal	**paRnā**	to occur

Exercises

1 You land at Karachi Airport and while going through immigration, the officer asks you the following questions in Urdu. First, translate the questions into English and then answer the questions in Urdu.

OFFICER: āp kā nām?
YOU:
OFFICER: āp pākistān mẽ kitne din rahẽge?
YOU:
OFFICER: kahā̃-kahā̃ jāẽge?
YOU:
OFFICER: pākistān mẽ patā kyā hɛ?
YOU:
OFFICER: vāpas kab jāẽge?
YOU:
OFFICER: koī Gɛr qānūnī (illegal) sāmān hɛ?
YOU:

2 There are a few incorrect verbs in the following passage. Pick them out and replace them with the right verbs.

mẽ āp ke liye kyā karnā saktā hɛ? ham āgrā jā cāhtā hɛ. āgrā kitnī dūr hẽ? bahut dūr nahī̃, lekin āp kab jā rahā hɛ? ham kal jāegā. gāRī subā dillī se calte hɛ. kyā āp gāRī se jā cāhtā hẽ?

3 The words in the following sentences are in the wrong order. Re-arrange them in the right order.

azīz manzūr:

tumhārā milā xat. paRʰ kar xushī huī. tum rahe kab ā ho? kal mɛ̃
Chicago hũ jā rahā. *Chicago* bahut sheher hɛ baRā. mɛ̃ *Chicago*
se havāī jahāz (*aeroplane*) jāũgā. lekin mɛ̃ jānā cāhtā havāī jahāz se
nahī̃ hũ. gāRī mujʰe pasand hɛ se zyādā havāī jahāz. bāqī sab hɛ
Tʰīk.

> tumhārā dost,
>
> iqbāl

4 Here are some answers. What were the questions? (Wherever
needed, the object of enquiry is in italics.)

Q:
A: mɛ̃ *Chicago* jā rahī hũ.
Q:
A: mɛ̃ yahã̄ *sāt din* rahū̃gā.
Q:
A: mɛ̃ *apnā* kām kar rahā hũ.
Q:
A: jī hã̄, cāy bahut pasand hɛ.
Q:
A: mere *cār bʰāī* hɛ̃.

5 If you won a million pounds, what would you do? Use the
following words or phrases in your answer in Urdu.

das lākʰ	million
bādshā	king
malikā	queen
nāv	boat
rolsa rāyas	Rolls Royce
xarīdnā	to buy
duniyā	world
safar karnā	to travel
hīrā	diamond
xushī se	with happiness
pāgal ho jānā	to become crazy
naukrī karne jānā	to return to the job

6 This fast-talking robot is programmed for the 'me' generation. Could you change his speech to suit the 'we' generation. Note the gender of robot is masculine in Urdu.

mɛ̃ *robot* hũ. mɛ̃ *California* se hũ. mɛ̃ urdū bol saktā hũ. mɛ̃ urdū samaj^h b^hī saktā hũ. mɛ̃ urdū gāne gā saktā hũ. merī yādasht (*memory*) bahut tez hɛ. mɛ̃ har savāl pūc^h saktā hũ aur har javāb de saktā hũ. yānī har kām kar saktā hũ. mɛ̃ hameshā kām kar saktā hũ. mɛ̃ kab^hī nahī̃ t^haktā hũ. mere pās har savāl kā javāb hɛ. lekin masāledār k^hānā nahī̃ k^hā saktā.

6   باب چھ: آپ نے کل کیا کِیا؟
What did you do yesterday?

By the end of this unit you should be able to:

- talk about past events/actions
- use time adverbials with full clauses
- talk about topics dealing with 'lost and found'
- learn to express sequential actions
- employ some more very frequent expressions

Dialogue 1 ▣

Someone has picked my pocket

Nadia Ali is on her way to Edinburgh to take up graduate studies.
She lands at Heathrow Airport in London. As she prepares to take
her flight on to Edinburgh, she gets the horrifying feeling that her
passport and traveller's cheques have been stolen. She makes a reverse
charge call to her family in Lahore. She gets in touch with her father,
Haider Ali, who is anxiously waiting to hear of her arrival in Great
Britain

HAIDER: hɛllo.
NADIA: hɛllo, abbā jān, mɛ̃ Nadia bol rahī hū̃.
HAIDER: kahā̃ se bol rahī ho?
NADIA: landan (*London*) se.
HAIDER: kyõ, abʰī eDinbaro (*Edinburgh*) nahī̃ pahũcī̃?
NADIA: nahī̃.
HAIDER: kyā bāt hɛ? pareshān lag rahī ho. sab Tʰīk-Tʰāk hɛ na?
NADIA: mɛ̃ to Tʰīk hū̃, lekin merā safar nāmah (*passport*), mere
pɛse aur Trɛvlarz (*traveller's*) cheques kʰo gaye.
HAIDER: kyā!
NADIA: ɛsā lagtā hɛ ke kisī ne merī jeb kāT lī.
HAIDER: sac!
NADIA: hā̃.

HAIDER: *Hello.*
NADIA: *Hello, Dad, it's Nadia.* (lit. I am Nadia speaking.)
HAIDER: *Where are you calling from?*
NADIA: *From London.*
HAIDER: *Hey, haven't you reached Edinburgh yet?* (lit. Why, you
did not reach Edinburgh yet?)
NADIA: *No.*
HAIDER: *What is the matter? (You) seem to be upset. Everything*
is fine, isn't it?
NADIA: *I'm fine, but my passport, money and traveller's cheques*
are lost.
HAIDER: *What!* (lit. What! I do not believe it!)
NADIA: *It appears that somebody picked my pocket.*

HAIDER: *Really?* (lit. truth!)
NADIA: *Yes.*

Vocabulary

hɛllo	hello	**kʰonā** (+**ne**)	to lose
jān (f.)	darling, life	**kʰo jānā** (-**ne**)	to be lost
abbā jān	father	**gaye** (m. pl)	went
abʰī	right now	**kyā!**	What! I do not
pahũcnā (-**ne**)	to reach, to arrive		believe it!
bāt (f.)	matter	**kisī**	someone
kyā bāt hɛ?	What is the	**ne**	agent marker in
	matter?		the past tense
pareshān (adj.)	troubled, worried	**jeb** (f.)	pocket
sab	all	**kāTnā** (+**ne**)	to cut
Tʰīk-Tʰāk	fine	**jeb kāTnā**	to pick pocket
to (particle)	then, as regards	**ɛsā**	such, it
safar nāmah	passport, an	**sac!**	It can't be true!
(m.)	account of a		Really?
	journey		

Notes

The perfective form (the simple past)

We have introduced the simple past tense forms of the verb 'to be'. Now, observe the Urdu equivalent of English 'Haven't you reached Edinburgh yet?':

(tum)	**abʰī**	**eDinbaro**	**nahī̃**	**pahũcī̃?**
you	right now	Edinburgh	not	reached (f. pl.)

Although the Urdu verb **pahũcī̃** is translated as 'reached', it has no intrinsic tense reference as words such as **hɛ** 'is' and **tʰā** 'was'. It simply shows that the action or situation is *completed*. The act may be completed in present, past or future tense. Usually, adverbs such as 'yesterday' and 'tomorrow' and the verb form of the verb 'to be' provide the tense information.

Now recall the suffixes given in the box on page 36 and do some detective work regarding the feminine forms.

verb stem	*perfective form*	
pahŭc reach	**pahŭcā**	masculine singular
	pahŭce	masculine plural
	pahŭcī	feminine singular
	pahŭcī̃	feminine plural

Yes, feminine plural forms for the first time compete with masculine forms and have their distinct plural identity. The Urdu pronoun **tum** always takes the plural form.

Now observe another perfective form from the above dialogue:

kisī	**ne**	**merī**	**jeb**	**kāṭī.**
someone	(agent)	my	pocket (f.)	cut (f. sg.)

'Someone picked my pocket.' (lit. Someone cut my pocket.)

You will notice two things that are different from the previous sentence: (1) the use of the postposition **ne**, and (2) the verb agreement. The postposition **ne** occurs with those subjects which have transitive verbs in the perfective form. Notice that verbs such as 'come', 'go' and 'reach' are intransitive whereas verbs such as 'cut', 'write', 'do' and 'buy' are transitive. The Urdu word for English 'someone' is **koī**. Because of the postposition **ne**, the subject pronoun **koī** becomes **kisī** (oblique). Also, remember verbs do not agree with those subjects that are followed by a postposition. Instead of agreeing with the subject, the verb agrees with the object **jeb** 'pocket', which is feminine singular in Urdu. For details on perfective forms see the Reference Grammar.

Because perfectives mark a situation or action as *completed*, they are usually associated with the past tense.

'Went': an irregular verb

The past tense of the English verb 'to go' is irregular – 'went' rather than 'goed'. It is also irregular in Urdu in the perfective form. Here are the Urdu equivalents of the English 'went':

verb stem	*perfective form*		
jā go	**gayā**	went	(m. sg.)
	gaye	went	(m. pl.)
	gayī	went	(f. sg.)
	gayī̃	went	(f. pl.)

Because Urdu and English belong to the same language family, what is remarkable is that the English 'g' of the verb stem 'go' shows up in the Urdu irregular form and then it takes the Urdu perfective suffixes. The sound 'y' intervenes in the two vowels.

The other three important verbs which are irregular in the past are the following: **lenā** 'to take', **denā** 'to give' and **pīnā** 'to drink'.

stem	*masculine*		*feminine*	
	singular	*plural*	*singular*	*plural*
le take	**liyā**	**liye**	**lī**	**lī̃**
de give	**diyā**	**diye**	**dī**	**dī̃**
pī drink	**piyā**	**piye**	**pī**	**pī̃**

Word-for-word translation

mere	**pɛse**	**aur**	***Trɛvlarz***	**cheques**	**kʰo**	**gaye.**
my	money	and	traveller's	cheques	lost	went

'My money and traveller's cheques (are) lost.'

Notice the clustering of the two verbs **kʰo** 'be lost' and **gaye** 'went' (m. pl.). This clustering of the real verbs is a special property of Urdu. They are called 'compound verbs'. We will deal with this class of verbs later on in the book. For the time being observe such verb clustering and memorize the sentence given above.

Echo words

You have already come across the word **Tʰīk** 'fine, correct'. In the phrase **Tʰīk Tʰāk**, the second word **Tʰāk** does not have any meaning of its own. It just echoes the first word by making a slight vowel change in it. The meaning added by the echo word is 'etc.', 'and all that' or 'other related things/properties'. Therefore, **Tʰīk Tʰāk** means 'fine etc'. Very often the first consonant is changed in the Urdu echo words, e.g. *k*ām *v*ām 'work etc.', *n*ām *v*ām 'name etc.'. The most preferred consonant change is by means of **v**.

Dialogue 2 ▢▢

My passport is lost

Nadia Ali continues to talk with her father, Haider Ali about the incident. She informs her father that she has filed a report at the airport and that American Express will issue her with new traveller's cheques but not without her passport. She urgently needs some money to be sent to her, and in the meanwhile she goes to the Pakistani High Commission in London. At the High Commission, she talks to an officer

NADIA: merā safar nāmah kʰo gayā hɛ. nayā safar nāmah cāhiye.
OFFICER: kab kʰo gayā?
NADIA: āj, taqrīban pā̃c gʰanTe pɛhle.
OFFICER: āp ko mālūm hɛ ki kahā̃ kʰo gayā?
NADIA: jī hā̃, *Heathrow* havāī aDDe par.
OFFICER: kɛse?
NADIA: jab daftar-e-hijrat se bāhar āyī, to mere pās tʰā. pʰir, eDinbaro (*Edinburgh*) kī parvaz ke liye dūsre Tarmīnal (*terminal*) gayī, tab bʰī tʰā. jab kaunTar (*counter*) par pahū̃cī, to dekʰā, safar nāmah, TikaT, pɛse, aur Trɛvlarz *cheques purse* mẽ nahī̃ tʰe.
OFFICER: *police* ko riporT (*report*) kī?
NADIA: jī hā̃, ye dekʰiye.
OFFICER: accʰā ye savāl nāmah bʰariye, ek-do mahīne mẽ nayā safar nāmah āp ko milegā.
NADIA: is se jaldī nahī̃ mil saktā?
OFFICER: jī nahī̃ pɛhle bayān pākistān jāyegā aur safāī ke bād hī safar nāmah mil saktā hɛ.
NADIA: shukriyā.
OFFICER: koī bāt nahī̃.

NADIA: *I have lost my passport.(I) need a new passport.*
OFFICER: *When was (it) lost?*
NADIA: *About five hours ago today.*
OFFICER: *Do you know where (it) was lost?*
NADIA: *Yes, at Heathrow Airport.*
OFFICER: *How?*
NADIA: *When I came out of Immigration, I had (it). (lit. then*

(it) was near me.) *Then (I) went to the other terminal (to catch) the flight for Edinburgh; even then I had (it). When I reached the counter, then (I) noticed (my) passport, ticket, money and traveller's cheques were not in (my purse).*

OFFICER: *(Did you) report (this) to the police?*

NADIA: *Yes, look at this (referring to the police report.)*

OFFICER: *OK. Fill out this form. In one or two months you will receive a new passport.*

NADIA: *Can't (I) get (it) earlier than that?* (lit. Can't (I) get it before than this?)

OFFICER: *No, first the report will go to Pakistan and only after clearance, can (you) get (it).*

NADIA: *Thanks.*

OFFICER: *You are welcome.* (lit. (it) is no matter.)

Vocabulary

safar nāmah (m.) passport

taqrīban about, approximately

gʰanTā (m.) hour

pɛhlā (m.; adj.) first

pɛhle (at) first, ago, previously

mālūm honā (+ko) to know, to be known

havāī aDDā (m.) airport

jab (relative pronoun) when

daftar-e-hijrat (m.) immigration office

parvāz (f. sg.) flight

savāl nāmah (m. sg.) form, questionnaire

bāhar out, outside

ānā (-ne) to come

  āyī (f. sg.) came

dūsrā (m.; adj.) second, other, another to then

dekʰnā (+ne) to see, to look at, to notice

  dekʰiye please see, look at, notice

bʰarnā (+ne) to fill

  bʰariye please fill, please fill out

ek-do one or two

mahīnā month

milnā (-ne, +ko) to meet, to get, to be available, to receive

  milegā (m.; sg.) will get

jaldī quickly

bayān (m. sq.) report

  bayān denā (+ne) to report

(ke) bād	after, later	shukriyā	thanks
safāī (f.)	clearance, (legal) defence		

Pronunciation

The word for 'to be known' in Urdu is written as **ma'lūm** but is pronounced as **mālūm**.

Notes

mālūm honā vs. jānnā 'to know'

Consider the word-for-word translation of the Urdu equivalent of the English expression 'Do you know . . .?' in our dialogue.

āp   ko   mālūm   hɛ . . .?
you   to   known   is
'Do you know . . .?'

The Urdu sentence is similar to English 'Is it known to you. . .?' The only difference is that Urdu **āp ko** is still the subject. Remember the discussion in Unit 3, Urdu verbs distinguish between non-volitional and volitional verbs. The verb **mālūm honā** points to that type of knowing or knowledge which is non-volitional or unintentional in nature. The verb **jānnā** can also be translated as 'to know' but the difference is that **jānnā** refers to the act of knowing which is volitional and some effort or research has gone into that knowledge. As pointed out earlier, volitional verbs do not take dative **ko** marking with their subjects. Observe the following volitional counterpart of **mālūm honā**.

āp   jāntī   hɛ̃ . . .?
you (f.)   know   are
'Do you know . . .?'

Notice that the verb agrees with the subject **āp** which is feminine in our dialogue. In the former sentence **āp ko** is the subject and the verb does not agree with it. We will detail the question of agreement again in this unit. In the former sentence the verb agrees with the object **ye** 'this', which is masculine singular, and that is why the verb takes the singular form **hɛ**.

Similarly, you have already come across two different usages of the verb **milnā** 'to meet' and **milnā** 'to get, to obtain'.

> **ham   milége**
> we   meet-will
> 'We will meet.'

The understood subject in Urdu for 'you will get the passport' is supplied below:

> **āp   ko   safar nāmah   milegā.**
> you   to   passport   get-will
> 'You will get the passport.'

The English verbs such as 'to get' or 'to obtain' are treated as unintentional acts in Urdu. That explains why the Urdu subject is followed by the postposition **ko**. Can you predict the element which the verb **milegā** agrees with? No more suspense; it agrees with the object **safar nāmah** (*passport*) which is masculine singular in Urdu.

The ne construction

If we add the understood subjects to the following two expressions

> **to   dekʰā**
> then   saw

> **police   ko   bayān   diyā?**
> police   to   report   give

the complete sentences will be

> **to   mɛ̃   ne   dekʰā.**
> then   I   (agent)   saw
> 'Then I saw.'

> **āp   ne   *police*   ko   bayān   diyā?**
> you   (agent)   police   to   report (m.)   gave (m. sg.)
> 'Did you report to the police?'

The postposition **ne** is attached to the subject. Without the post-position the sentences would be ungrammatical. However, observe the following sentences:

> **jab   mɛ̃   daftar-e-hijrat   se   bāhar   āyī.**
> when   I (f. sg.) Immigration   from   out   came (f. sg.)
> 'When I came out of Immigration.'

> **mɛ̃   dūsre   Tarminal   gaī.**
> I (f. sg.)   other   terminal   went (f. sg.)
> 'I went to the other terminal.'

The above two sentences do not require the postposition **ne** because verbs such as 'come' and 'go' are intransitive. The post-position **ne** is restricted to *transitive verbs in the perfective form.* In the first example above, the verbs 'to see' and 'to report' are transitive and are used in the perfective form; therefore, the postposition **ne** is required with the subject.

The pronominal forms with the **ne** postposition are as follows:

nominative pronouns	*ne pronouns*	
mɛ̃	**mɛ̃ ne**	I
ham	**ham ne**	we
tū	**tū ne**	you (sg.)
tum	**tum ne**	you (pl.)
āp	**āp ne**	you (hon.)
vo	**us ne**	she, he, it; that
vo (pl.)	**unhõne**	they; those
ye	**is ne**	this
ye (pl.)	**inhõne**	these

Notice that the third person pronouns change as a result of **ne**. If you are learning the script, it is written as one word with the third person plural pronouns.

The **ne** forms of the question pronoun are: **kis ne** 'who' (sg.) and **kinhõne** 'who' (pl.).

Complex verbs

As in English, in Urdu, a noun can be turned into a verb. The only difference is that the noun has to be anchored in verbs such as **karnā** 'to do' and **honā** 'to be'. This is a very productive process which allows Urdu to take nouns from languages such as Sanskrit and Persian and turn them into verbs. English has not been spared either. So, you can take English nouns such as the following and turn them into verbs:

English nouns	Urdu verb		complex verb	
fax	**karnā** 'to do'	*fax* **karnā**	'to fax'
telephone	**karnā**	Tɛlīfon **karnā**	'to telephone'

As a matter of fact, even English adjectives and verbs can be used to generate Urdu complex verbs:

English adjectives/verbs	Urdu verb	complex verb	
recover	**honā**	*recover* **honā**	'to recover'
choose	**karnā**	*choose* **karnā**	'to choose'

This construction can be extremely useful in those situations where one fails to recall the Urdu verb. For example, if you fail to recall the Urdu verb **paRʰnā** 'to read/study', do not give up that easily; you can custom-make the verb *study* **karnā** from English – 'study'. We will call Urdu anchor verbs such as **karnā** and **honā** 'transformers'.

The omission of 'to'

Remember that we pointed out earlier the English preposition in expressions such as 'I went to the other terminal'. In Urdu no postposition is used with the destination. Therefore, it is not appropriate to substitute Urdu **ko** for English 'to'.

ek-do   mahīne   mẽ
one-two   month   in
'in one or two months'

Dialogue 3 🔘

Buying handicrafts

John Kearney has visited the Indian subcontinent once and he loves Indian handicrafts. John wants to buy a few decorative pieces for his new house. An international fair is being held in London. He visits the Indian pavilion and there he speaks to Nazir Ahmad, who is in charge of the handicrafts section

JOHN: mɛ̃ ne hāl hī mɛ̃ ek nayā makān xarīdā hɛ, isliye mɛ̃ kuc^h sajāvaT kī cīzɛ̃ xarīdnā cāhtā hū̃.

NAZIR: nayā makān xarīdne par mubārak ho, hamāre pās bahut hī xūbsūrat dastkāriyā̃ hɛ̃, ummīd hɛ ke āp ko koī cīz pasand āyegī.

JOHN: mɛ̃ ne kashmīrī dastkāriyõ kī xūbsūrat kārīgarī ke bāre mɛ̃ bahut sunnā hɛ. āp muj^he kuc^h cīzɛ̃ dik^hā saktɛ̃ hɛ̃?

NAZIR: hā̃ zarūr, ye dek^hiye sāhab kashmīrī qālīn.

JOHN: kyā cīz hɛ! ye to muj^he bahut hī pasand āyā. kyā vo pashmīne kā shāl hɛ?

NAZIR: kamāl hɛ! āp ne itnī dūr se kɛse pahcānā?

JOHN: darasal mere ek azīz dost ke pās ɛsī hī shāl t^hī. vo pic^hle mahīne ek gāRī ke hādise mɛ̃ guzar gaye.

NAZIR: ye baRe afsos kī bāt hɛ.

JOHN: *I have recently bought a new house, so I want to buy a few decorative* (lit. decoration) *pieces.*

NAZIR: *Congratulations on buying a new house. We have beautiful handicrafts here and I hope you find something you like.*

JOHN: *I have heard a lot about the beautiful artistic quality of Kashmiri handicrafts. Could you please show me a few things.*

NAZIR: *Certainly. Take a look at this Kashmiri carpet.* (lit. Please see (sir) this Kashmiri carpet.)

JOHN: *What a beautiful (thing) carpet! I like it very much. Is that a pashmina (woollen) shawl (over there).*

NAZIR: *Amazing! How did you recognize it from so far away?*

JOHN: *Actually, one of my very good friends had such a shawl. Last month, he died in a car accident.*

NAZIR: *I am sorry (to hear) that.* (lit. This is a matter of great sorrow.)

Vocabulary

hāl (m.)	state, present time	**saknā** (-ne)	to be able to, can
hāl mē̃	recently	**zarūr** (adv.)	certainly
nayā	new	**sāhab**	Mr, sir
makān (m.)	house	**qālīn** (f.)	a woollen carpet
xarīdnā (+ne)	to buy	**pashmīnā** (adj.)	woollen (made of
isliye	therefore		a specific
kucʰ	some		variety of
sajāvaT	decoration		Kashmiri wool
cīz (f.)	thing		which is very
mubārak	auspicious		light)
mubārak ho	congratulations	**shāl** (f.)	a shawl
hamārā	our	**kamāl** (m.)	perfection
ke pās	have	**itnī** (adj.)	this much
xūbsūrat (adj.)	beautiful	**dūr** (adj.)	far
dastkārī (f.)	handicrafts	**pahcānnā** (+ne)	to recognize
ummīd (m.)	hope	**darasl** (adv.)	actually
pasand ānā (-ne)	to like	**azīz** (adj.)	dear
kārīgar (m.)	an artisan	**εsā**	like this
kārīgarī (f.)	artistic work	**pic**ʰ**lā**	last
ke bāre mē̃	about (postposition)	**mahīnā** (m.)	month
bahut	a lot, very	**hādsah** (m.)	accident
sunnā (+ne)	to hear	**guzarnā** (-ne)	to pass
dikʰ**ānā** (+ne)	to show	**guzar jānā** (-ne)	to pass away, to die
		afsos (m.)	sorrow

Notes

Very frequent expressions: word-for-word translation

Consider how the following four very frequent English expressions are phrased in idiomatic Urdu:

English	*Urdu*		
Congratulations.	**mubārak**	**ho.**	
	blessed/happy	be, (subjunctive)	
	'(You) be happy.'		
That's really something!	**kyā**	**cīz**	**hɛ.**
	what	thing (f.)	is
	'What a thing.'		
That's amazing.	**kamāl**	**hɛ.**	
	amazing	is	
	'(It) is amazing.'		
I am sorry to hear that.	**ye** **afsos**	**kī** **bāt**	**hɛ.**
	this sorrow	of matter (f.)	is
	'This is a matter of sorrow.'		

Exercises

1 Re-arrange the following words to make correct sentences in Urdu.

mere dost, vo tʰe accʰe kitne din! mɛ̃ socā ne vo rahẽge din hameshah. vo bacpan din ke tʰe. mɛ̃ tʰā hameshah kʰeltā aur nāctā tʰā. har xūbsūrat cīz tʰī. har tʰā din nayā aur har rāt andāz kā apnā tʰā. din ab vo nahī̃ rahe.

2 Circle the correct form of the subject and the verb in the following sentences. Hint: the gender of the Urdu word bayān 'report' is masculine.

(a) (mɛ̃ ne/ mɛ̃) vahā̃ (gaye/gayī).

(b) (vo/us ne) mujʰ ko (batāyā/batāye).

(c) (ham/ham ne) gʰar (āyā/āye).
(d) (tum/tum ne) gʰar der se (pahŭce/ pahŭcā).
(e) (vo /vo ne/unhõne) *police* ko bayān (dī/diyā/diye).
(f) (āp/āp ko/āp ne) ye kitāb kab (milā/mile/milī).

3 Activity: asking about your family histories
First talk about your family history making use of the cues to make questions.

Examples: **xāndān** 'family'/**kahā̃ se/ā** 'come'
āp kā xāndān kahā̃ se āyā?
vāldɛn 'parents/**paidāish** birth/**ho** 'be, happen'
āp ke vāldɛn kī paidāish kahā̃ huī?

Hint: arranged marriage = **vāldɛn kī pasand kī shādī**. The verb 'to be married' = marriage to take place/happen, younger/older = small/big.

(a) parents/where/born   (e) how old/marriage
(b) parents/when/born   (f) arranged marriage/love marriage
(c) rich or poor   (g) mother younger than your father.
(d) marriage/when/happen

4 Make questions from the following statements. The object of the enquiry is indicated by the italicized words in the statements.

Examples: shādī ke bād mere vāldɛn *inglistān* (*England*)
gaye.
shādī ke bād mere vāldɛn kahā̃ gaye?

merā xāndān *das sāl pɛhle* yahā̃ āyā.
merā xāndān kitne sāl pɛhle yahā̃ āyā?

(a) kal *John* kī sālgirah tʰī.
(b) *John* ke xāndān ne ek dāvat di.
(c) vo dāvat *shām ko* huī.
(d) John ko *dāvat* ke bāre mẽ mālūm nahī̃ tʰā.
(e) ye *surprise* dāvat tʰī.
(f) *kal* John kī sālgirah tʰī.

7 باب سات: کیا آپ اُردو بول سکتے ہیں؟

Can you speak Urdu?

By the end of this unit you should be able to:

- talk about your skills
- give advice
- express obligation
- observe compound verbs
- use emphatic and persuasive forms

Dialogue 1 🔲

You can speak Urdu

Imran Khan takes a bus from Southall to the centre of London, the West End. He puts the money into the slot of the fare box. The bus driver, who is a white blue-eyed Englishman, utters something and Imran Khan understands it as 'West End eh', and he replies 'yes' and sits down. As he settles down, he thinks that what he heard was not English but Urdu. A bit puzzled, he does not want to rule out that what he actually heard was the Urdu language. In fact, the driver had asked, **West End jānā hɛ**? *So Imran Khan asks*

IMRAN:	māf kījiye, āp ne kyā kahā?
DRIVER:	mɛ̃ ne pūchā ke āp ko *West End* jānā hɛ.
IMRAN:	are! āp to bahut acchī urdū bol sakte hɛ̃.
DRIVER:	hã, thoRī thoRī urdū bol letā hū̃.
IMRAN:	urdū āp ne kahã̄ sīkhī?
DRIVER:	dusrī jaŋg-e-azīm ke vaqt mɛ̃ bartānvī (British) fauj mɛ̃ sipāhī thā. us vaqt hindustān mɛ̃ sīkhī.
IMRAN:	abhī bhī acchī urdū ātī hɛ.
DRIVER:	kāfī arse se ek hindustānī dukān mɛ̃ kām kar rahā hū̃ isliye urdū nahī̃ bhūlī.
IMRAN:	ye to bahut acchā hɛ, nahī̃ to yahã̄ hindustānī bhī urdū bhūl jāte hɛ̃.
DRIVER:	ye bāt to sac hɛ.

IMRAN:	*Excuse me, what did you say?*
DRIVER:	*I asked if you have to go to the West End.* (lit. I asked that you have to go to the West End.)
IMRAN:	*Hey, you speak Urdu very well.* (lit. You can speak very good Urdu.)
DRIVER:	*Yes, (I) speak a little Urdu.* (lit. I take speak little Urdu.)
IMRAN:	*Where did you learn Urdu?*
DRIVER:	*During World War II, I was a soldier in the British Army. (I) learned (it) in India at that time.*
IMRAN:	*Even now you know Urdu well.* (lit. Even now good Urdu comes (to you).)

DRIVER: *I have been working in an Indian store for a long time; so (I) haven't forgotten Urdu.*

IMRAN: *This is very good; otherwise even Indians forget Urdu here.*

DRIVER: *This is true.*

Vocabulary

to	as regards (particle)	**bartānvī** (f.)	British
tʰoRā	little, few	**bartānyā**	Great Britain
bolnā (+/-**ne**)	to speak	**fauj** (f.)	army
bol lenā (+**ne**)	to speak for one's benefit	**sipāhī** (m.)	soldier
		abʰī bʰī	even now
bol letā hū̃	(I can) speak/ manage/get by.	**kāfī**	enough, sufficient
		arse se	time
sīkʰnā (+**ne**)	to learn	**bʰūlnā** (+/-**ne**)	to forget
jaŋg-e-azīm	world war	**nahī̃ to**	otherwise
arsā (m.)	time	**yahā̃**	here

Notes

Formulaic expression: māf kījiye 'forgive/ excuse me'

The English expression 'excuse me' has a number of uses. We pointed out earlier in Unit 2 that when the main function of 'excuse me' is to get attention, then it is paraphrased as 'please say' or 'please listen'. In this dialogue, Imran did not hear the driver at first and then asked him to repeat his statement; therefore, this calls for an apology. Thus, Imran appropriately uses **māf kījiye**. The first part of the expression **māf** 'pardoned' is the short adjectival form of the noun **māfī** 'forgiveness' which is used with the verb **karnā** 'to do'. (Remember the previous unit.) So this expression is like other conjunct verbs you have encountered in earlier dialogues:

noun	verb
māf	karnā
pasand	karnā

The polite imperative form of **māf karnā** is **māf kījiye**. The subject **āp** and the object **mujʰ ko** 'me' are implied.

The internal obligative: mujʰ ko jānā hɛ 'I have to go'

The Urdu counterpart of the English expression 'You have to go to the West End' is:

āp   ko   *West End*   jānā   hɛ.
you   to   West End   to go   is
'You have to go to the West End.'

Obligation is expressed by the infinitive form followed by the verb 'to be'. The subject is always the experiencer subject with the **ko** postposition. In the above sentence the verb 'to be' is in the present tense. This gives the following structure:

subject +**ko**	infinitive verb	verb 'to be'	
	jānā	**hɛ**	is
		tʰā	was
		hogā	will be

Examples:

āp ko *West End* jānā hɛ.	'You have to go to the West End.'
āp ko *West End* jānā tʰā.	'You had to go to the West End.'
āp ko *West End* jānā hogā.	'You will have to go to the West End.'

In the case of an intransitive verb, the verb always stays masculine singular. The reason for this is that the verb cannot agree with a subject because it has to be followed by the postposition **ko** and there is no object to agree with either.

Three ways to say you can . . .

In the dialogue, you will have noticed three different ways of saying 'can speak Urdu':

āp	urdū	acc^hī	bol	sakte		hɛ̃
you	Urdu	good	speak	can	(pres.)	are

'You can speak good Urdu.'

Notice the placement of **saknā** in the Urdu sentence. The subject is nominative as in English. The verb agrees with a subject. It is **saknā** which receives the tense conjugation and it is preceded by the stem of the verb.

The second way is:

mɛ̃	t^hoRī	t^hoRī	urdū	bol	letā		hū̃.
I	little	little	Urdu	speak	take	(pres.)	am

'I can speak a little Urdu.'

This type of expression is used to express 'partial competence' and it usually has quantifiers such as **t^hoRā** 'a little/few' with it. Notice the clustering of the two verbs – **bol** 'speak' and **lenā** 'to take'. It is the second verb which carries the tense/aspect. These types of verb are called 'compound' verbs. We will discuss these verbs in detail later. For the time being just memorize this expression.

The third way is like saying 'Urdu comes to you', as in

āp	ko	ab^hī	b^hī	urdū	ātī		hɛ.
you	to	now	even	Urdu	come	(-pres.)	is

'Even now you know Urdu', *or* 'Even now you know (how to speak) Urdu.'

(lit. Urdu even now comes to you.)

In this construction the verb is **ānā** 'to come' and the subject is an experiencer subject. Remember that experiencer subjects are marked with the postposition **ko**. The verb agrees with 'Urdu', which is feminine singular. Unless otherwise modified with a quantifier denoting meagreness, this construction expresses 'full' or 'near complete' competence in a skill.

This construction – 'Urdu comes to you' – is restricted to skills such as swimming or playing a musical instrument. It cannot be used in expressions such as 'I know John'.

Compare the following two sentences:

us   ko   tɛrnā   ātā   hɛ.
he/she   to   to swim   come (pres.)   is
'(S)he knows (how to) swim.' (lit. Swimming/to swim comes to him/her.)

The verb agrees with **tɛrnā** which is masculine singular.

mɛ̃   John   ko   jāntā   hū̃.
I   John   (object)   know (pres.)   am
'I know John.'

However, one cannot say 'John comes to me.'

Focus, emphasis and word order

In the dialogue, Imran asks the driver:

urdū   āp   ne   kahā̃   sīkʰī?
Urdu   you   (agent)   where   learned
'Where did you learn Urdu?'

The normal word order is as follows:

āp   ne   urdū   kahā̃   sīkʰī?
you   (agent)   Urdu   where   learned
'Where did you learn Urdu?'

Since the Urdu language is the centre of the discussion, 'Urdu', which is the object of the sentence, is moved to the beginning of the sentence. If you have a recording, you will hear a slight emphasis on the word 'Urdu'. In other words, an element of a sentence can be pulled out of its normal place in a sentence and placed at the beginning of a sentence to express focus or emphasis.

The Particle to 'as regards'/'as far as (. . .) is concerned'

We came across the use of **to** in the sense of 'then'. However, observe that in the following two examples, **to** follows a constituent rather than appearing in clause-initial position in a 'when – then' type of sentence:

āp	to		bahut	acc^hī	urdū	bol	sakte	hɛ̃.

āp to bahut acc^hī urdū bol sakte hɛ̃.
you as regards very good Urdu speak can (pres.) are
'As far as you're concerned, you can speak very good Urdu.'

ye to bahut acc^hā hɛ.
this as regards very good is
'As far as this is concerned, it is very good.'

The particle **to** is another way of expressing emphasis but **to** can also imply some sense of exclusion. The first sentence says, 'As far as you're concerned, you can speak very good Urdu' and implies that 'Others (from your group) cannot speak very good Urdu'.

Compound verb: b^hūl jānā 'to forget'

Observe another example of a compound verb in dialogue 1:

yahā̃ hindustānī b^hī urdū b^hūl jāte hɛ̃.
here Indians also Urdu forget go (pres.) are
'Here even Indians forget their Urdu.'

The two verbs are clustered together – **b^hūl** and **jānā;** they share the job of expressing meaning. **b^hūl**, which is the first verb, is in the form of a stem and conveys the main meaning, whereas **jānā** carries the tense but does not convey its literal meaning of 'going'. We will detail this class of verbs later.

Dialogue 2 ▣

Can you write Urdu?

Imran Khan and the driver continue to talk with each other. The topic of the discussion is still the Urdu language . . .

IMRAN: kyā āp ko urdū lik^hnī ātī hɛ?

DRIVER: zyādā nahī̃. fauj mẽ kab^hī kab^hī lik^hnī paRtī t^hī lekin ab koī zarūrat nahī̃.

IMRAN: urdū mẽ kyõ lik^hnā paRtā t^hā?

DRIVER: *secret codes* aur pɛGāmõ ke liye – xāskar *Europe* jāne vāle pɛGāmõ ke liye. *West End* mẽ kuc^h kām hɛ?

IMRAN: bijlī kā *bill* denā tʰā. āj fursat milī, to socā ke xud vahā̃ jāū̃.
DRIVER: to vo daftar āne vālā hɛ ... asal mẽ aglā *stop* hɛ.
IMRAN: accʰā, xudā hāfiz.
DRIVER: xudā hāfiz.

IMRAN: *Do you know (how to) write Urdu?* (lit. Does to write Urdu come to you?)
DRIVER: *Not much. In the army I had to write* (it) *occasionally* (lit. sometimes) *but now (there) is no need (to write in Urdu).*
IMRAN: *Why did (you) have to write in Urdu?*
DRIVER: *For secret codes and messages, especially for messages going to Europe. Do (you) have work* (i.e chores or tasks to carry out) *in the West End?*
IMRAN: *(I) need to pay the electricity bill.* (lit. I need to give the electricity bill.) *(I) have (some) free time today, so I thought I would go myself* (i.e. in person).
DRIVER: *Well, (in that case), that office is about to come up* (i.e we are about to reach that office) *... in fact, (it) is the next stop.*
IMRAN: *OK. Goodbye.*
DRIVER: *Bye.*

Vocabulary

likʰnā (+ne)	to write	**kām honā** (+ko)	to have work
zyādā (invariable)	more	**bijlī** (f.)	electricity,
kabʰī	ever		lightning
kabʰī-kabʰī	sometimes	**fursat** (f.)	free time, spare
paRnā	to fall, to lie down,		time, leisure
	in compound	**xud**	oneself
	verbs 'to have to'	**jānā** (-ne)	to go
zarūrat (f.)	need, necessity	**jāū̃**	(I) should go
pɛGām (m.)	message	**daftar** (m.)	office
xāskar	especially,	**āne vālā**	'the one who is
	particularly		about to
jāne vāle	'the ones' or		come'
	'those who	**asl mẽ**	in fact, in reality
	are going'	**aglā** (m.; adj.)	next

Notes

Variation: urdū likʰnī ātī hɛ **or** urdū likʰnā ātā hɛ

In the Standard Urdu-speaking area, the verb and the preceding infinitive form agree with the object in number and gender, whereas in the southern Urdu-speaking area both remain invariable, i.e. masculine singular:

Standard Urdu	*Southern Urdu*
āp ko urdū likʰnī ātī hɛ.	**āp ko urdū likʰnā ātā hɛ.**
'You know how to write Urdu.'	'You know how to write Urdu.'
āp ko xatūt likʰne hɛ̃.	**āp ko xatūt likʰnā hɛ̃.**
you to letters (m. pl.) to write are	you to letters (m. pl.) to write are

However, the following sentence in our dialogue,

bijlī	**kā**	*bill*	**denā**	**tʰā.**
electricity	of	bill (m. sg.)	to give	was

'(I) needed to pay the electricity bill.'

remains the same in both dialects because, in Standard Urdu, agreement is with *bill* which is masculine singular.

mujʰ ko jānā paRtā hɛ **'I have to go'**

When the obligation to do something is felt to be an external compulsion rather than an internal need, the infinitive is followed by the verb *paRnā* instead of the verb *honā*. The literal meaning of *paRnā* is 'to fall', however, one of the translations of this word is 'to have to'.

Compare:

internal

āp	**ko**	**urdū**	**likʰnī**	**hɛ.**
you	to	Urdu (f. sg.)	write (f. sg.)	is

'You need to write Urdu.'

external

āp	**ko**	**urdū**	**likʰnī**	**paRtī**	**hɛ.**
you	to	Urdu (f. sg.)	to write (f. sg.)	has to (lit. fall) (f. sg.)	is

'You have to write Urdu.'

In eastern Urdu the infinitive and the verb form will be in the masculine singular form, i.e. **likʰnā hɛ** and **likʰnā paRtā hɛ**, respectively.

Now, take a look at the use of the external obligative in our dialogue:

fauj	**mẽ**	**kabʰī kabʰī**	**likʰnī**	**paRtī**	**tʰī.**
Army	in	sometimes	to write (f. sg.)	has to lie down (f. sg.)	was

'I had to write (it) sometimes in the Army.' (i.e. I had to write Urdu sometimes in the Army.)

The omitted subject **mujʰ ko** 'to me' is experiencer and the object is 'Urdu'. The tense is the past habitual. If the act of compelled writing was carried out only once, the verb **paRnā** would have been in the simple past, i.e. **paRī** and the adverb **kabʰī-kabʰī** would have to be dropped.

Be careful not to confuse **paRnā** 'to lie down' and **paRʰnā** 'to read/study'.

Negative words: 'nobody', 'nowhere', 'never', etc.

Have a look at the Urdu expression 'I no longer need to write Urdu':

ab	**koī**	**zarūrat**	**nahī̃.**
now	some	need	not

'I no longer need (to write Urdu).'

The negative words such as 'nobody', 'nowhere', 'never', are simply derived from their positive counterparts and the negative particle **nahī̃** is placed in its original position, i.e. right before the verb:

koī	'someone' ...	**nahī̃**	=	no one, nobody
kahī̃	'somewhere' ...	**nahī̃**	=	nowhere
kabʰī	'ever' ...	**nahī̃**	=	never

The immediate future: the vālā construction

The **vālā** construction conveys a range of meanings when used with nouns, adjectives, verbs and adverbs. Here, we will examine the cases in which **vālā** follows an infinitive verbal form and thus marks 'immediate future' tense:

> **vo   daftar   āne   vālā   hɛ.**
> that   office (m. sg.) to come about   is
> 'That office is about to come up.' (i.e. 'We are about to reach that office')

The many faces of **vālā** become evident from the following two facts: (1) it acts like a postposition and (2) it agrees with the subject in number and gender in the fashion which is typical of an adjective ending in -**ā**. Now, observe one more example of such usage:

> **rel gāRī̄   jāne   vālī̄   tʰī̄.**
> train (f. sg.) to go   about   was
> 'The train was about to go/leave.'

It might be puzzling to see how **vālā** can still be considered as an example of 'immediate future'. However, in this example, **vālā** still renders 'immediate future' with reference to the past. In short, the structure of the 'immediate future' construction in Urdu is as follows:

Subject (nominative) + stem + **ne** + **vālā** + verb 'to be'
vālī
vāle

The vālā construction

In comparison with the examples in the previous section, observe the position of **vālā** in the following phrase. Here, its best literal translation is the English agentive suffix -'er':

> *Europe* **jāne   vāle   pɛGāmõ   ke liye**
> Europe to go   -er   messages   for
> 'for messages going to Europe.' (lit. for the Europe go-er messages)

Can you predict the meaning of the following phrases?

kʰelne vālā
paRʰne vālī

The meaning is 'player' and 'reader', respectively. In the former a masculine singular head (e.g. boy) is implied, whereas a feminine singular head (e.g. girl) is implied in the latter.

The meaning of the **vālā** phrase is often clear from the context. For example, the phrase

dillī   vālā
Delhi   -er

means 'the person who lives in Delhi'. However, if the phrase is used in the context of a train or vehicle, it can mean either 'the train which goes/is going to Delhi' or a vehicle 'which is made in Delhi'.

'I have some work' and 'Are you free?'

kyā   āp   ko   *West End*   mẽ   kucʰ   kām   hɛ?
what   you   to   West End   in   some   work   is
'Do you have some work (i.e. chores or tasks to carry out) in the West End?'

āj   mujʰ   ko   fursat   milī.
today   me   to   free/spare time (f.)   got
'Today I was free.'

English expressions such as 'I am busy' and 'I am free' are paraphrased as 'to me the work is' and 'to me the free/leisure/spare time is'. Similarly, the best way to ask, 'Are you free?' is:

āp ko fursat hɛ?

and for 'Are you busy?':

āp ko kām hɛ? *or* **āp masrūf hɛ̃?**

The subjunctive

The subjunctive expresses the idea of a possibility. Expressions with words like 'perhaps', suggestions (e.g. Shall we go?) or permission (e.g. May I come in?) usually employ the subjunctive.

mɛ̃	ne	socā	ke	xud	vahā̃	*jāū̃.*
I	(agent)	thought	that	self	there	*go* (subjunctive)

'I thought that (I) would go there myself.'

Verbs such as **cāhnā** 'to want', **socnā** 'to think' (which are called non-factive verbs) and **jānnā** 'to know' (which belongs to the class of factive verbs) use a subjunctive verb form in their subordinate clause, i.e. *jāū̃.*

Subjunctives are very simple to form. Take any future form and just drop the future ending, i.e. **gā, ge** and **gī**. For instance, the corresponding subjunctive form of **ham milẽge** 'we will meet', **tum jāoge** 'you will go' and **mɛ̃ jāū̃gī** 'I will go' are **ham milẽ** 'we might meet', **tum jāo** 'you (should) go', and **mɛ̃ jāū̃** (with rising intonation) 'May I go?', respectively. Note that the precise meaning of the subjunctive will depend on the context and intonation.

xud 'oneself'

The emphatic pronoun **xud** is very similar to English emphatic pronouns, 'myself', 'yourself', etc. with the difference that the Urdu form **xud** remains invariable whereas the English emphatic pronouns vary according to their subject. In

mɛ̃ ne socā ke *mɛ̃ xud* **vahā̃ jāū̃.**

the emphatic form will always remain unchanged even if the subject of the subordinate clause changes.

Dialogue 3 💿

I am ill

Professor John Ryder has gone on his second research trip to rural India. He reaches his village at the beginning of the monsoon season. Although he has taken all precautions and injections before leaving for India, he awakens one night with high fever and diarrhoea. He calls Dr Naim's residence. Dr Naim's wife picks up the phone

JOHN: hɛllo, kyā DāKTar nāīm hɛ?

MRS NAIM: jī nahī̃, koī zarūrī bāt hɛ?

JOHN: merī tabīyat bahut xarāb hɛ.
MRS NAIM: ek marīz ko dekʰne gaye hɛ̃.
JOHN: kitnī der mẽ vāpas āyẽge?
MRS NAIM: mere xayāl mẽ jaldī ā jāyẽge. mujʰe apnā Tɛlīfon (*telephone*) *number* aur patā de dījiye. āte hī unhẽ bʰej dũgī.
JOHN: bahut bahut shukriyā.

JOHN: *Hello, is Dr Naim (there)?*
MRS NAIM: *No, is (it) something urgent?*
JOHN: *(I) am very ill.* (lit. My condition/health is very bad.)
MRS NAIM: *He has gone to see a patient.*
JOHN: *When will he be back?* (lit. In how much period of time will he return?)
MRS NAIM: *I think (he) will come (back) soon.* (lit. In my opinion (he) will come back soon.) *Please give me your address and phone number. As soon as he returns, (I) will send him (to see you).*
JOHN: *Thank you very much.*

Vocabulary

zarūrī	important, urgent, necessary	**mujʰe**	to me
		patā (m.)	address
tabīyat (f.)	health, disposition	**de denā** (+**ne**)	to give (compound verb)
xarāb	bad		
marīz (m.)	patient	**de dījiye**	please give (compound verb)
der (f.)	delay, time (period of, slot of)		
		āte hī	as soon as (he) comes
vāpas ānā (-**ne**)	to return		
vāpas āyẽge (pl.)	will return	**unhẽ** (obl.)	him
		bʰejnā (+**ne**)	to send
xayāl (m.)	opinion, thought	**bʰej denā** (+**ne**)	to send (compound verb)
jaldī	quickly		
ā jānā (-**ne**)	to come (compound verb)	**bʰej dũgī**	(I) will send (compound verb)
ā jāyẽge	will come (compound verb)	**shukriyā**	thank you, thanks

Notes

The present and past perfective forms

> **vo   ek   marīz   ko   dekʰne   gaye   hɛ̃.**
> he   one   patient   (obj.)   to see (obl.)   went   are
> 'He has gone to see a patient.'

> **kyā   āp   kabʰī   āgrā   gaye   hɛ̃?**
> what   you   ever   Agra   went   are
> 'Have you ever been (lit. gone) to Agra?'

> **hā̃,   mɛ̃   gayā   hū̃.**
> yes   I   went   am
> 'Yes, I have been (there).' (lit. Yes, I have gone (there).)

> **hā̃,   do   sāl   pɛhle   mɛ̃   gayā   tʰā.**
> yes   two   years   ago   I   went   was
> 'Yes, I went (there) two years ago.' (lit. Yes, two years ago, I
>   had gone (there).)

By adding 'to be' to the present forms (**hū̃** 'am', **hɛ** 'is', **hɛ̃** 'are'
and **ho** 'are' (you), and past forms (**tʰā** 'was', **tʰe** 'were', **tʰī** 'was'
and **tʰī̃** 'were') to the perfective form, one can get present and
past perfective forms, respectively. The present perfect indicates
completed action which has relevance for the present situation and
the past perfective indicates relevance to the past. Note that in the
first and last sentences given above English will use the simple
perfective but Urdu will use the present and past perfective, respectively. The past perfect in English is viewed with reference to an
event in the past, as in 'When I was in Agra, he had already come'.

Compound verbs

We have already remarked on compound verbs in Urdu. Observe
another example from your dialogue:

> **mere   xayāl   mɛ̃   vo   jaldī   ā   jāyẽge.**
> my   opinion   in   he (hon.)   soon   come   go-will
> 'I think he will come (back) soon.'

Notice the two verbs **ā** 'come' and **jā** 'go' are clustered in the verb phrase. However, the sentence does not mean 'he will come and go'. **ā** describes the action of coming and **jānā** 'to go' carries the tense.

The compound verb **ā jāyẽge** is composed of two units: the main verb **ā** 'come', is in the stem form and is totally dependent on the second unit, i.e. the helping verb – **jā** 'go' – for the tense information. The other roles the helping verb plays are described below:

1 jānā as a helping verb
As we already know, the literal meaning of **jānā** is 'to go'. As a helping verb, it refers to the transformation of a state or action, completeness or finality.

simple verbs		*compound verbs*		
ānā	to come	**ā**		to come back, arrive
kʰānā	to eat	**kʰā**		to eat up
pīnā	to drink	**pī**	**jānā**	to drink up
samajʰnā	to understand	**samajʰ**		to understand fully
honā	to be	**ho**		to become
bʰūlnā	to forget	**bʰūl**		to forget completely

2 denā as a helping verb
The literal meaning of **denā** is 'to give'. As a helping verb, **denā** conveys that the action is done for the benefit of someone other than a subject of a sentence. In the dialogue, Mrs Naim first asks for John's address and telephone number. The expression she uses is the following sentence:

> **mujʰe apnā Tɛlīfon *number* aur patā de dījiye.**
> 'Give me your telephone number and address.'

and then says:

> **āte hī unhẽ bʰej dū̃gī.**
> 'As soon as he comes, I will send him.'

The compound verbs **de denā** and **bʰej denā** are used to highlight the beneficiary of the actions. The simple corresponding verbs **denā** 'to give' and **bʰejnā** 'to send' are unable to emphasize the beneficiary. In the first sentence, the direct beneficiary of the action is Mrs Naim herself and in the second sentence John is the beneficiary of Mrs Naim's action of sending Dr Naim to his house.

3 lenā as a helping verb

The verb **lenā** means 'to take'. You can now predict its meaning as a helping verb. It conveys 'doing for oneself', i.e. for the benefit of the subject. For example, in answer to the request for the telephone number and address, John could have answered:

accʰā, likʰ līered.
OK   write   take (imper.)
'Please, write (it) down (for your benefit).'

The compound verb **likʰ lenā** stresses Mrs Naim as being the direct beneficiary of the action of writing down the address and telephone number.

In the previous dialogue, we saw the other meaning (i.e. partial competence) of **lenā** when used as a helping verb with verbs denoting skills.

te hī 'as soon as'

The addition of **te hī** to the verbal stem gives the meaning of 'as soon as', as in:

āte hī   unhẽ   bʰej dū̃gī.
come-as soon as   him (hon.)   send   give-will
'I will send him as soon as (he) comes (back).'

Pitfalls

Compare and contrast the Urdu phrase with its English translation:

mere xayāl mẽ ...   I think ...

The Urdu equivalent is either **mere xayāl mẽ** 'in my opinion' or **mere xayāl se** 'with my opinion'. The Urdu verb **socnā** 'to think' is not acceptable in this context, as in the following sentence:

mẽ   soctā   hū̃
I   think (pres.)   am

The English verb 'to think' has two meanings: (1) it refers to the process of thinking, as in 'I will think of something'; and (2) it expresses an opinion, as in 'I think he is a nice man'. In the latter sense, it is paraphrased as 'In my opinion he is a nice man'. The failure to distinguish between the two types of 'think' is the source of many common errors by English learners of Urdu as a second language.

Compound verbs

It is important to understand the shades in meaning conveyed by compound verbs. For example, if a student goes to a professor and requests a letter of recommendation (i.e. a reference), it makes a significant difference which of the below the student uses. A letter of recommendation in Urdu is **sifārshī xat**.

sifārshī xat	lik^{h}iye.	
sifārshī xat	lik^h	dījiye.
sifārshī xat	lik^h	lījiye.

Even if the polite forms are used in all three expressions, the only appropriate choice is the second. The first and last ones have the potential of offending the professor. The first one is polite, but still a command, and the last one claims the professor to be the direct beneficiary of the act of writing a letter of recommendation.

Similarly, be gentle and sensitive with the use of 'must'/'need' and 'can'.

Coping skills

If you are unsure which form to use, compound or simple verb, the best thing you can do is to spell out the beneficiary **mere liye** 'for me' with simple verbs.

Exercises

1 Circle the appropriate choice of the subject in the following sentences and then translate the sentences into English.

(a) (mɛ̃/muj^h ko/mɛ̃ ne) sitār ātā hɛ.

(b) kyā (āp/āp ko/āp ne) tɛr sakte hɛ̃?

(c) (us ko/vo /us ne) kahā̃ jānā hɛ?

(d) (vo/unhõne/un ko) mausīqī kab sīkʰī?

(e) vo *salesman* hɛ. (us ko/us ne/vo) bāhar jānā paRtā hɛ.

(f) John ko bahut kām hɛ. isliye (vo/us ko/us ne) koi fursat nahī̃ hɛ.

2 Complete the following sentences by supplying the missing parts of the verb.

(a) Bill ko jaldī hɛ kyõki uskī gāRī das minute mẽ jā _____
    _____ hɛ.

(b) *Driver* jaldī karo, mere dost kā jahāz a _____ _____ hɛ.

(c) sardī kā mausam tʰā, jaldī baraf gir _____ _____ tʰī.

(d) dāvat ke liye mɛhmān pahū _____ _____ hɛ̃.

(e) shām kā vaqt tʰā, andʰerā ho _____ _____ tʰā.

(f) āp kabʰī hindustān ga _____ hɛ̃?

3 Match the duties given on the left with the professions given on the right.

(a) ustād   us ko gāRī calānī hɛ.

(b) *Doctor*   us ko kapRe dʰone hɛ̃.

(c) gulūkar   us ko paRʰānā hɛ.

(d) *Driver*   us ko likʰnā hɛ.

(e) dʰobī   use marīz ko dekʰnā hɛ.

(f) musannif   us ko gānā hɛ.

4 Circle the appropriate helping verb in the following sentences.

(a) kyā āp mere liye sifārshī xat likʰ (lẽge/dẽge)?

(b) rāt āyī aur andʰerā ho (gayā/āyā) tʰā.

(c) mẽ urdū nahī̃ paRʰ saktā, āp ye xat paRʰ (lījiye/dījiye).

(d) vo tʰoRā tʰoRā tɛr (saktā/letā/ātā) hɛ.

(e) us ko bahut accʰā nācnā (saktā/letā/ātā) hɛ.

(f) mẽ āp kī bāt bilkul bʰūl (āyā/gayā).

5 Write five sentences about the things you hated doing during your childhood, but which you had to do. The following sentence can serve as a model.

Model:

bacpan	**mẽ**	**mujʰe**	**pālak**	**kʰānī**	**paRtī**	**tʰī.**
childhood	in	to me	spinach (f.)	eat-to	lay (pres.)	was

'During my childhood, I had (lit. used) to eat spinach.'

8 باب آٹھ: مُجھے چیک تبدیل کروانے ہیں
I need to get some cheques cashed

By the end of this unit you should be able to:

- use causative verbs
- use the present participial forms
- learn more about compound verbs, subjunctives and expressing obligation
- use conditionals
- highlight contrast
- persuade someone
- advise and caution someone

Dialogue 1 🔲

Be careful what you eat

Finally, Dr Naim reaches John Ryder's house. It is about eleven o'clock at night

JOHN: ādāb arz DākTar nāīm.

DR NAIM: ādāb, ryder sāhab. is bār kaī sāl ke bād mulāqāt huī.

JOHN: jī hā̃, koī pā̃c sāl bād.

DR NAIM: tashrīf rakʰiye accʰā, pɛhle batāiye, tabīyat kɛsī hɛ?

JOHN: tabīyat to accʰī nahī̃, nahī̃ to itnī rāt ko āp ko taklīf na detā.

DR NAIM: taklīf kī bāt kyā hɛ? ye to merā farz hɛ. xɛr, buxār kitnā hɛ?

JOHN: jab ek gʰanTe pɛhle mɛ̃ ne *thermometer* lagāyā, to ek sau do *degree* tʰā. ab shāyad kucʰ zyādā ho.

DR NAIM: accʰā, zarā pʰir *thermometer* lagāiye.
(After taking John's pulse and temperature Dr Naim says)

DR NAIM: buxār tʰoRā baRʰ gayā hɛ. dast bʰī hɛ̃?

JOHN: jī hā̃, do gʰanTe mɛ̃ sāt-āTʰ bār Gusl xāne gayā.

DR NAIM: picʰlī bār āp ne bahut samose kʰāye tʰe, aur is bār?

JOHN: shām ko kucʰ ām kʰāye.

DR NAIM: merī salāh māniye ek-do mahīne tak āp kucʰ parhez kījiye, samose aur ām band. mɛ̃ ek Tīkā lagātā hū̃ aur ye davāī lījiye. do goliyā̃ har do gʰanTe ke bād. to kal subā apnī tabīyat ke bāre mɛ̃ batāiye. mɛ̃ āp ke Tɛlīfon kā intzār karū̃gā. accʰā ab ārām kījiye. xudā hāfiz.

JOHN: bahut bahut shukriyā, DākTar sāhab, xudā hāfiz.

JOHN: *Hello* (lit. 'I greet you respectfully'), *Dr Naim.*

DR NAIM: *Hello Mr Ryder, (we) meet again after several years.* (lit. This time (our) meeting happened after several years.)

JOHN: *About five years.*

DR NAIM: *Please be seated. OK. First, tell (me), how you are feeling?* (lit. How is (your) disposition?)

JOHN:	*As regards my health, I am not feeling well; otherwise I would not have bothered you so late at night.*
DR NAIM:	*Not at all!* (lit. Why talk about trouble?) *This is my duty. Well, how high is the fever?*
JOHN:	*An hour ago when I took my temperature* (lit. an hour ago when put the thermometer), *it was 102 degrees. Now it might be slightly higher.*
DR NAIM:	*OK, (let's) take (your) temperature again.* (lit. Again put the thermometer (in your mouth).)
DR NAIM:	*The fever has increased slightly; (do you) have diarrhoea too?*
JOHN:	*Yes, (I) have been to the bathroom about seven or eight times in the past two hours.*
DR NAIM:	*You ate a lot of samosas last time – what about this time?*
JOHN:	*In the evening (I) ate some mangoes.*
DR NAIM:	*Please take my advice. For about one or two months exercise some caution* (lit. do some abstinence). *No more samosas and mangoes.* (lit. samosas and mangoes closed.) *I (will) give you an injection and (give you) this medicine. Two pills every two hours. Then let me know tomorrow morning how you feel. OK. Now (please) get some rest. Goodbye.*
JOHN:	*Many many thanks, doctor. Goodbye.*

Vocabulary

ādāb (m.)	salutation, greetings	**tashrīf rak^{h}nā** (+**ne**)	to be seated
arz (f.)	request	**tashrīf lānā** (-**ne**)	to honour with one's presence, come, welcome
is bār	this time		
sāl (m.)	year		
ke bād	after	**intzār** (m./f.)	wait
mulāqāt (f.)	meeting	**(kā/kī) intzār karnā** (+**ne**)	to wait
mulāqāt honā (-**ne**)	to meet		
		pɛhle	first
tashrīf (f.)	honouring (a term signifying respect)	**itnā** (m.; adj)	so much/many, this much/many
		rāt (f.)	night

taklīf (f.)	trouble, bother	**mahīnā** (m.)	month
taklīf denā (+**ne**)	to bother	**parhez** (m.)	abstinence
		x se parhez karnā (+**ne**)	to abstain, avoid
farz (m.)	duty		
lagānā (+**ne**)	to fix, to apply	**band**	closed
shāyad	perhaps	**band karnā** (+**ne**)	to close
baRnā (-**ne**)	to increase, to advance	**band honā** (-**ne**)	to close
dast (m.)	diarrhoea	**Tīkā lagānā** (+**ne**)	to give an injection/ a shot
Gusl xānā (m.)	bathroom		
ām (m.)	mango; as adj. common, general	**davāī/davā** (f.)	medicine
		golī (f.)	tablet, pill; bullet
salāh (f.)	advice	**ārām** (m.)	comfort, rest
salāh mānnā (+**ne**)	to accept/take advice	**ārām karnā** (+**ne**)	to rest
salāh lenā (+**ne**)	to seek/take advice	**xudā hāfiz**	goodbye

Notes

'We meet again after several years'

Another way of saying 'We meet again after several years' in Urdu is something like 'Our meeting took place after several years'.

kaī	sāl	bād	hamārī	mulāqāt	huī.
several	years	after	our	meeting (f.)	happened.

Politeness

Note the use of **tashrīf rakʰiye** instead of **bɛTʰiye** 'please sit'. As in English, while receiving a guest, we will usually say 'Please have a seat', or 'Please be seated', rather than 'Please sit'. Similarly it is more polite and much warmer to use **tashrīf rakʰiye** rather than **bɛTʰiye**, particularly in more formal contexts. In English if the verb 'sit' is used, it is modified in some form, e.g. 'Please sit down for a while'; the same is true of the Urdu verb **bɛTʰ** 'sit'. If it is used, it needs to be preceded by the polite form of the verb **ā** 'come' (e.g. **āiye bɛTʰiye** 'Please come (and) sit', or followed by the tag question (e.g. **bɛTʰiye na** 'Please sit down, won't you?').

'To wait for x'

The Urdu equivalent of the English 'I was waiting for you' is:

mɛ̃	**āp kā**	**intzār**	**kar**	**rahā**	**tʰā.**
I	your	wait (m.)	do	-ing	was

i.e. 'I was waiting for you.'

The conditional

The Urdu sentence in our dialogue is as follows:

itnī	**rāt**	**ko**	**mɛ̃**	**āp**	**ko**	**taklīf**	**na**	**detā.**
so much	night	at	I	you	to	bother	not	give
								would have

'(otherwise) I would not have bothered you so late at night.'

The above sentence is a part of the 'if' clause which is implied.

agar	**tabīyat**	**Tʰīk**	**hotī**	**to ...**
if	disposition	fine	were	then ...

'If I were feeling fine ...'

Notice the simple present form without the auxiliary verb is used in such conditional sentences. The 'if' clause implies that the condition has not been fulfilled; therefore, the action expressed by the 'then' clause did not take place. Consider, another example of conditionals:

agar	**vo**	**ātā,**	**to**	**mɛ̃**	**jātā**
if	he	come (pres.)	then	I	go (pres.)

'If he had come, I would have gone.'

agar	**vo**	**kitābẽ likʰtī,**	**to**	**ham**	**bahut**	**xush**	**hote.**
if	she	books write (pres.)	then	we	very	happy	be
							(pres.)

'Had she written books, we would have been very happy.'

Thus, the English verb forms such as 'had come' and 'would have gone' are translated, not as a past tense forms, but with the present imperfective without an auxiliary verb.

Formulaic expression

The Urdu expression

taklīf	kī	bāt	kyā	hɛ
bother	of	matter	what	is

is not a question sentence, it is rhetorical. It is equivalent to the English expressions 'don't bother' or 'don't mention'. Thus, the Urdu question word **kyā** is like 'not' in the expression above. The verb is always in the simple present rather than in the imperative as in English.

The negative particle: na

We have already come across **nahī̃** 'not'. Another Urdu negative particle is **na**, which occurs in constructions such as 'neither ... nor', conditionals and polite imperatives. (See Unit 9, dialogue 1 for more details.)

The subjunctive

ab	buxār	kucʰ	zyādā	ho.
now	fever (m. sg.)	some	more	be (subjunctive)

'The fever might be slightly higher.'

Since the context is the probable increase in fever, the verb 'to be' is in the subjunctive in Urdu. The verb agrees with **buxār** 'fever'. Although **ho** might appear to be in the simple present tense, it is not, since **tum** is not the subject in the above sentence.

'Accept my advice'

In Urdu the English expression, 'Take my advice' is paraphrased as 'Accept my advice'.

merī   salāh   māniye.
my   advice (f.)   accept (imperative)
'Please accept my advice.'

The use of the verb **lenā** 'take' would produce an odd sentence in Urdu.

Dialogue 2 ▣

Lost in Delhi

Philip Rosenberg is lost in Delhi's city centre. He knows that somewhere in the vicinity there is a Thomas Cook office where he could cash some traveller's cheques. In fact, he visited that office just two days ago, but he cannot remember its address. He asks a stranger where it is

PHILIP: yahā̃ qarīb koī *Thomas Cook* kā daftar hɛ? mɛ̃ do
              din pɛhle vahā̃ gayā tʰā, lekin āj nahī̃ mil rahā.
STRANGER: āp ko patā mālūm hɛ?
PHILIP: mɛ̃ patā hī to bʰūl gayā.
STRANGER: (*Pointing to the street*) mere xayāl mɛ̃ aglī saRak par
              Thomas Cook kā daftar hɛ.
PHILIP: (*Seemingly puzzled*) vo saRak to xūbsūrat hɛ, log use
              aglī saRak kyõ kɛhte hɛ̃?
STRANGER: aglī urdū kā lafz hɛ aŋgrezī kā nahī̃. 'aglī' kā matlab
              aŋgrezī mɛ̃ 'next' hɛ.
PHILIP: bahut xūb.
              (*Philip goes to the cashier's window at the Thomas
              Cook office.*)
              mujʰe kucʰ *traveller's cheque cash* karvāne hɛ.
CASHIER: kaun se sikkõ (*currency*) mɛ̃ hɛ̃?
PHILIP: bartānvī pāunDz (*pounds*). zar-e-mubādilah kī sharah
              (*Exchange rate*) kyā hɛ?
CASHIER: ek bartānvī pāunD (*pound*) pacās rupaye kā hɛ.
              (*Philip signs the cheques and the cashier gives him the
              equivalent amount in rupees.*)
              kul do sau *pounds*. ye rahe āpke das hazār rupaye.
              gin lījiye.
PHILIP: Tʰīk hɛ̃. shukriyā.

PHILIP:	*(There) is a Thomas Cook office nearby. Two days ago I went there. But today I cannot find (it).*
STRANGER:	*Do you know the address?*
PHILIP:	*I have forgotten the address.* (lit. As regards the address, I forgot.)
STRANGER:	*I think* (lit. in my opinion) *the Thomas Cook office is on the next* (i.e. **aglī**) *street.*
PHILIP:	*That street is a beautiful one. Why do people call it 'ugly'?*
STRANGER:	*'aglī' is an Urdu word, not English. In English the meaning of 'aglī' is 'next'.*
PHILIP:	*(That's) great!*
PHILIP:	*I need to get some traveller's cheques cashed.*
CASHIER:	*In which currency are they?*
PHILIP:	*In British pounds. What is the exchange rate?*
CASHIER:	*One British pound to fifty rupees.*
CASHIER:	*A total of two hundred pounds. Here are your ten thousand rupees. Please count it (for your own sake).*
PHILIP:	*That's fine. Thanks.*

Vocabulary

qarīb (adv.)	nearby		
daftar (m.)	office	**sikkah** (m.)	currency
milnā (+**ko**)	to find, to receive	**zar-e-mubādilah**	foreign exchange
aglā (m.; adj.)	next	**sharah** (f.)	rate
lafz (m.)	word	**kul**	total
aŋgrezī (f.)	the English language	**sau**	hundred
aŋgrez (m.)	the English	**rɛhnā** (-**ne**)	to live
matlab (m.)	meaning	**rahe**	lived, are
bahut xūb	Great! Splendid!	**hazār**	thousand
tabdīl karnā (+**ne**)	to cash, to exchange	**ginnā** (+**ne**)	to count
tabdīl karvānā (+**ne**)	to get someone to cash/exchange	**gin lenā** (+**ne**)	to count (for one's benefit)
		shukriyā	thanks

Notes

milnā **find**

In the preceding units we came across three important uses of the verb, **milnā** – namely 'to meet', 'to run into', and 'to be available'. Now, observe another use of this verb in the following sentence in your dialogue. Also, note its word-for-word translation:

> **lekin   āj   nahī̃   mil   rahā.**
> but   today   not   find   -ing
> 'But today (I) cannot find (it).' (lit. But today I am not finding it.)

When the verb **milnā** is used to express the meaning 'find', it uses **ko**. If we insert the implied subject in the above sentence, the Urdu subject will not be nominative **mɛ̃**, but **mujʰ ko** or **mujʰe**.

> **lekin āj mujʰe daftar nahī̃ mil rahā.**

Notice that the verb does not agree with the subject. Instead, it agrees with the object which is **daftar** 'office' in the above sentence. The gender of **daftar** is masculine. Did you notice the missing element of the verb phrase?

Negation and auxiliary verb deletion

Notice the element of the verb that is missing from the above sentence:

> **lekin āj mujʰe daftar nahī̃ mil rahā hɛ.**

The auxiliary verb **hɛ** can be optionally deleted in negative sentences. Only the auxiliary verbs of the simple present and present progressive tenses are subject to this optional deletion. Observe some examples:

positive sentences		*negative sentences*	
mɛ̃ jātā hū̃	I (m.) go	**mɛ̃ nahī̃ jātā hū̃**	I (m.) do not go
		mɛ̃ nahī̃ jātā	I (m.) do not go
mɛ̃ jā rahā hū̃	I (m.) am going	**mɛ̃ nahī̃ jā rahā hū̃**	I (m.) am not going
		mɛ̃ nahī̃ jā rahā	I (m.) am not going

tum jātī ho	you (f.) go	**tum nahī̃ jātī ho**	you (f.) do not go
		tum nahī̃ jātī	you (f.) do not go
tum jā rahī ho	you (f.) are going	**tum nahī̃ jā rahī ho**	you (f.) are not going
		tum nahī̃ jā rahī	you (f.) are not going

Causative verbs

We came across some related verbs such as the following in the previous dialogues. Note the slight change in form and meaning:

paRʰ	study, read	**paRʰā**	teach	**paRʰvā**	have someone teach
kar	do	-		**karvā**	have someone do
lag	seem, be attached	**lagā**	attach	**lagvā**	cause to be attached, have attached

You might already have observed the same base stem in the three verb forms. At first glance it becomes clear that the verb forms in the two right columns share the verb stem in the left-most column adding either the suffix **ā** or **vā**, as in:

paRʰ + **ā** = **paRʰā** cause someone to read, teach
paRʰ + **vā** = **paRʰvā** to have x teach y

The two suffixes **ā** and **vā** form causative verbs. The meaning expressed by them can be translated as follows: **ā** expresses 'make someone do something' whereas **vā** means 'have x make y do something'. The English verb 'teach' is a causative verb in Urdu, but in most cases causative verbs cannot be translated into English that easily. Observe the following examples:

mɛ̃	**kahānī**	**paRʰtā**	**hū̃.**
I	story	read (pres.)	am

'I read a story.'

mɛ̃ john ko kahānī paRʰ*ætā*   hū̃.
I   John to   story   read (caus.ā-pres.) am
'I read John a story', *or* 'I teach John a story.'

mɛ̃ john ko islām se kahānī paRʰ*vætā*   hū̃.
I   John to Islam by story   read (caus. vā-pres.) am
'I make Islam read a story to John.'

Notice that the causative verbs with **vā** always have an indirect agent (e.g. **Islam se** 'by Islam').

Did you notice the use of the causative verb in our dialogue? The following sentence contains a causative verb:

mujʰe kucʰ *traveller's cheque* tabdīl karvāne   hɛ̃.
me   some traveller's cheques cash do (caus. vā-inf.) are
'I need to (have someone) cash some traveller's cheques.'

In this sentence the indirect agent (someone) is implied by the causative verb with the suffix **-vā**.

'lenā' as a helping verb

When the cashier hands over the rupees to Philip, he says:

gin   lījiye
count   take (imper.)
'Please (you) count (for your own benefit).'

Had he used the simple verb form instead of the compound verb (i.e. **giniye**), the beneficiary of the action of counting would have remained unspecified. The helping verb **le** indicates the subject as the beneficiary.

Text 1

ek log dāstān *'A folk tale'*

Indian and Pakistani folk tales are rich in conventional wisdom and cultural values. Here is a sample of a folk tale from one region

1 ek gāõ mē ek cor qɛd xāne se bʰāg gayā.
2 pulis (*police*) vālā us ko pakaRne ke liye dauRā.
3 itne mē gāõ vālõ ne bʰāgte cor ko pakaR liyā.
4 pulis vālā zor zor se cīx rahā tʰā, 'pakRo, mat jāne do'.
5 ye sunte hī gāõ vālõ ne cor ko cʰoR diyā.
6 jab pulis vālā gāõ vālõ ke pās pahũcā,
7 to us ko bahut Gussah āyā.
8 Gussah mē us ne gāõ vālõ se pūcʰā,
9 tum ne cor ko kyõ cʰoR diyā?
10 gāõ vālõ ne javāb diyā,
11 āp ne hī kahā, 'pakRo mat, jāne do.'

1 *In a village, a thief ran away* (i.e. escaped) *from jail.*
2 *A policeman ran to catch him* (lit. ran for catching)
3 *In the meantime the villagers caught the escaping* (lit. running) *thief.*
4 *The policeman was shouting very loudly, 'Catch (him), don't let (him) go'.*
5 *As soon as the villagers heard this, they let the thief go* (lit. left the thief).
6 *When the policeman reached the villagers* (lit. reached near the villagers),
7 *He became very angry.*
8 *In anger he asked the villagers* (lit. asked from the villagers)
9 *Why did you let the thief go?*
10 *The villagers answered,*
11 *You yourself said, 'Don't catch (him), let (him) go.'*

Vocabulary

log	people	**pulis vālā** (m.)	policeman
dāstān (f.)	story	**dauRnā** (-ne)	to run
lok dāstān (f.)	folk tale	**itne mē**	meanwhile
gāõ (m.)	village	**gāõ vālā** (m.)	villager
qɛd xānā (m.)	jail	**bʰāgte** (pres.	running
bʰāgnā (-ne)	to run	participle)	
bʰāg gayā	to run away	**cor** (m.)	thief
(compound verb)			

pakaRnā (+**ne**)	to catch, to grasp, to hold	**sunte hī** (**sun** + **te hī** participle)	as soon as (someone) heard
pakaR liyā (compound verb)	caught (for one's benefit)	**cʰoRnā** (+**ne**)	to leave
		cʰoR diyā (compound verb) (+**ne**)	left (for someone else's sake)
zor se	loudly		
cīxnā (-**ne**)	to scream, to shout	**Gussah** (m.)	anger
		pūcʰnā (-**ne**)	to ask
mat	not (*see notes*)	**javāb** (m.)	answer
jāne do (compound verb)	let (someone) go	**javāb denā** (+**ne**)	to answer, reply

Pronunciation

Compare the pronunciation of the stem **pakaR** 'catch' in the following three verbal forms.

pak*a*Rne ke liye	in order to catch
pak*a*R liyā	caught (for their own benefit)
pakRo!	catch!

Notes

Present participle

In the third line of the folk tale we came across the expression

itne	mẽ	gāõ	vālõ	ne	bʰāgte	cor
this much	in	village	-er (pl. obl.)	agent	running	thief

ko pakaR liyā.
to   catch   took
'In the meanwhile (lit. in this much (time)), the villagers
   caught the thief.'

The phrase **bʰāgte cor ko** is the oblique form of the simple present participial phrase:

bʰāgtā	(huā)	cor.
run + pres. ppl.	happened	thief (m. sg.)

'the running boy', *or* 'the boy who is/was/will be running.'

The composition of the first element is as follows:

bʰāg +	t	+ ā
run +	present +	masculine singular

You have probably guessed by now that this is the same form that we came across in simple present tense formation. The only difference is that the auxiliary verb is absent.

The second element is the same form as the simple past tense form of the verb **honā**. Remember the forms **huā, hue, huī** and **huī̃**. The last form (i.e. the feminine plural **huī̃**) does not appear in the participial construction. Why does it fail to appear? Because it is optional.

Now compare the participial form with the present tense verb form.

present participle	*simple present tense*
bʰāgtā cor	**cor bʰāgtā hɛ.**
'The running thief'	'The thief runs.'

In the present participial form the verb form ceases to function like a real verb and begins to behave like an adjective. Verbal adjectives which are formed from the simple present tense are called 'present participles'. They are like adjectives ending in -ā, but they are derived from verbs.

Like adjectives ending in -ā, these agree in number or gender with the following noun. For example:

bʰāgtā laRkā the running boy   **bʰāgtī laRkī**   the running girl
bʰāgte laRke the running boys   **bʰāgtī laRkiyā̃** the running girls

The main function of the present participial clause is to denote *action in progress*.

Notice that, like adjectives, present participles do not have any inherent tense reference to time, as is clear from the English translation. The tense is usually supplied by the main verb form in the sentence. If in the third line the verb 'caught' is changed to the present and the future tense, the tense reference of the participial form 'running' will change to present and future, respectively. That is why the alternative English translation of **bʰāgtā cor** contains three possible tense references.

The negative particle: mat

We have encountered two negative particles – **nahī̃** and **na** – in an earlier unit. A third negative marker **mat**, is primarily restricted to familiar and impolite imperatives. In prohibitive expressions the use of **mat** is particularly noteworthy.

Ambiguity and pausing

pakRo	**mat**	**jāne**	**do**
catch	not	go (obl. inf.)	give

(See Text 1, p. 152.) The translation of the verb phrase **jāne do** is 'to allow to go' or 'to let go'. The familiar imperative form of the verb **pakaRnā** is **pakRo**, which means 'catch'. Depending upon the pause, the meaning changes. The pause is indicated by the comma.

pakRo	**mat,**	**jāne**	**do.**
catch	not,	go (obl. inf.)	give

'Don't catch (him), let (him) go.'

But if the pause is immediately after **pakRo**, then the negative particle **mat** negates the second verb, as in

pakRo,	**mat**	**jāne**	**do.**
catch,	not	go (obl. inf.)	give

'Catch (him), don't let (him) go.'

Word order and contrastive negation

We mentioned earlier that the negative particle is usually placed before the verb. Thus, normally the Urdu equivalent of English 'Don't catch (him, it)' will be:

mat	**pakRo.**
not	catch (imper. fam.)

'Don't catch (him, it).'

However, the contrastive function is highlighted by placing the negative particle after the verb. This is the reason why **mat** is placed after **pakRo** in the expression:

pakRo mat, jāne do.
'Don't catch (him); let (him) go.'

With the other reading, 'Catch (him), do not let (him) go', there is no contrast. Therefore, the negative particle appears in its normal position before the verb.

Text 2

ek sher *'A couplet'*

Here is a sample of the opening lines of an old Urdu romantic song. In the song, the lover is imploring his beloved to never forget him. However, the approach is an indirect one. Therefore, rather than saying directly not to forget him, he says

1 **ye rātẽ, ye mausam, ye hãsnā, hãsānā**
2 **mujʰe bʰūl jānā, inhẽ na bʰulānā.**

1 These nights, this ambience (lit. weather or season), this laughter and making (each other) laugh,
2 (You can) forget me, but never make them forget.

Vocabulary

rāt (f.)	night	**bʰūlna** (-**ne**)	to forget
mausam (m.)	weather, season	**bʰūl jānā** (com-	to forget
hãsnā (-**ne**)	to laugh	pound verb)	completely
hãsānā (+**ne**)	to make	**bʰulānā** (+**ne**)	to make some-
	someone laugh		one forget

Exercises

1 Match the words or phrases given in the following three columns to make appropriate Urdu sentences.

āiye,	kī bāt kyā	rakʰiye
taklīf	tashrīf	hẽ
shāyad	āp kā intzār	kām zyādā ho
vo	arz	hɛ
ādāb	āp ko daftar mẽ	kar rahī tʰī.

2 Circle the appropriate form of the verbs.

(a) māf kījiye, mẽ *cheque* bʰejnā (bʰūl liyā/bʰūl gayā/bʰūl diyā).
(b) mẽ ne kʰānā (kʰā liyā/kʰā paRā/kʰā diyā).
(c) āp kā buxār (baRʰ liyā/baRʰ gayā/baRʰ diyā).
(d) āp ne kucʰ javāb nahī̃ (liyā/diyā/āyā/gayā).
(e) āp merī salāh mān (lījiye/dījiye/āiye).

3 Which job description matches the job?

(a) ustād   imāratẽ banvātā hɛ.
(b) DākTar (*doctor*)   kapRe sītā hɛ.
(c) *cashier*   kʰānā pakātā hɛ.
(d) darzī   Tīkā lagātā hɛ.
(e) xānsāmā   *cheque* tabdīl kartā hɛ.
(f) *driver*   shāgirdõ ko paRʰātā hɛ.
(g) *civil engineer*   gāRī calātā hɛ.

4 Akram and Sajid are brothers. Akram believes in self-help and does everything on his own. Sajid, on the other hand, gets someone to do his work. Write about Sajid according to the model given below:

akram ne apnā kām kiyā.   Akram did his (own) work.
sājid ne akram se apnā kām   Sajid had Akram do his work.
karvāyā.

(a) AKRAM: akram ne gāRī calāī.
    SAJID:
(b) AKRAM: akram xat likʰegā.
    SAJID:

(c) AKRAM: akram gʰar banā rahā hɛ.
   SAJID:
(d) AKRAM: akram kahānī paRʰā rahā tʰā.
   SAJID:
(e) AKRAM: akram beTī ko jagātā hɛ.
   SAJID:

5 Fill out the appropriate present participial form according to the model given below.

calnā: **mɛ̃ caltī gaRī mɛ̃ caRʰā.**
bʰāgnā: **mɛ̃ ne bʰāgte kutte ko dekʰā.**

(a) hāsnā: mujʰe vo _____ laRkī bahut pasand hɛ.
(b) kʰelnā: _____ bacce bahut xūbsūrat lag rahe tʰe.
(c) gānā: _____ ciRiyā uR rahī tʰī.
(d) sitār bajānā: _____ ādmī bahut accʰā hɛ.
(e) tɛrnā: _____ macʰliyõ ko dekʰo.
(f) ronā: DākTar ne _____ bacce ko Tīkā lagāyā.

6 The pacman has attacked the following text. Consequently, some elements of the text have been chewed up. Your task is to supply the postpositions or the missing parts of the verb in those places where the three-bullet symbol is left by the pacman.

mɛ̃ *railway station* par apne dost • • • intzār kar rahā tʰā. tʰoRī der bād rel gāRī āyī aur merā dost gaRī se utrā. ham bahut xush ho kar mile. is martabā pãc sāl ke bād hamārī mulāqāt • • •. tʰoRī der bād mɛ̃ ne kahā, 'is martabā bahut der ke bād yahã āye ho.' usne javāb • • •, 'accʰī bāt tʰī ke gāRī der se āyī, agar gāRī der se na • • •, to mɛ̃ āj bʰī na • • •.'

9 باب نو: فارچون کُکی میں کیا لِکھا ہے؟

What's written in the fortune cookie?

By the end of this unit you should be able to:

- learn past participles
- use participles as adverbs
- use the construction 'neither . . . nor'.
- form purpose clauses
- learn more about Indian and Pakistani food (particularly curries)
- use the passive construction
- learn more on repetition

Text 1

Money will come soon

Once two friends went to eat in a Chinese restaurant. After they had eaten, the waiter brought Chinese fortune cookies. Let's see what happened

1 ek din do dost kʰānā kʰāne ke liye ek cīnī taʿām xāne gaye.
2 kʰāne ke bād bɛrā *'fortune cookies'* lāyā.
3 donõ ne apnī apnī *'fortune cookie'* ko kʰolā aur apnī apnī qismat ke bāre mẽ kucʰ paRʰā.
4 pʰir ek dost ne dūsre se pūcʰā, 'kāGaz par kyā likʰā hɛ?'
5 likʰā hɛ – 'jaldī pɛsā āne vālā hɛ.'
6 ye to baRī xushī kī bāt hɛ.
7 to koī lāṬrī (*lottery*) xarīdī hɛ?
8 nahī̃, lekin kal apnā zindgī kā bīmā karvāyā hɛ.

1 *One day two friends went to eat in a Chinese restaurant.*
2 *After eating (i.e. after they finished eating), the waiter brought (them) fortune cookies.*
3 *(They) both opened their fortune cookie(s) and read (something) about their fate/s.*
4 *Then, one friend asked the other friend, 'What is written on the paper?'*
5 *(It) is written 'Money is about to come soon.'*
6 *That's good news* (lit. This is a matter (lit. talk) of great happiness).
7 *Did (you) buy a lottery ticket?*
8 *No, but yesterday, I bought life-insurance.* (lit. I have caused someone to do the life insurance.)

Vocabulary

dost (m.)	friend	**cīnī**	Chinese
kʰānā (m.)	food	**taʿām xānā** (m.)	restaurant
kʰānā (+**ne**)	to eat	**bɛrā** (m.)	waiter
kʰāne (ke liye)	(in order) to eat	**lānā** (-**ne**)	to bring
cīn	China	**donõ**	both

kʰolnā (+**ne**)	to open	**jaldī**	quickly, hurry
qismat (f.)	fortune, fate, destiny	**pɛsā** (m.)	money; one hundredth of a rupee
kāGaz (m.)	paper	**āne vālā honā**	to be about to come
likʰnā (+**ne**)	to write	**zindgī** (f.)	life
likʰā hɛ	(it) is written	**bīmā** (m.)	insurance

Notes

Purpose clauses and deletion

In the last unit, we came across the following expression:

pulis (*police*)	**vālā**		**us ko**	*pakaRne*		**ke liye**	**dauRā**
police	one/man		him	to catch (obl.)		for	ran

'The policeman ran *to catch* him.'

Now compare it with the opening line of Text 1:

ek	**din**	**do**	**dost**	**kʰānā**	*kʰāne*		**ke liye**	**ek**
one	day	two	friends	food	to eat (obl.)		for	one

cīnī	**ta'ām xāne**	**gaye.**
Chinese	restaurant	went

'One day two friends went to a Chinese restaurant *to eat* food.'

Note that the italicized infinitive phrases in the English translations, such as 'to catch' and 'to eat', are not translated as simple infinitives in Urdu like **pakaRnā** and **kʰānā**. The simple infinitive phrase would give an ungrammatical sentence in Urdu. As is clear from the Urdu expression **pakaRne ke liye** 'to catch', the Urdu equivalent of 'to catch' is 'in order to catch' and so, the postposition **ke liye** 'for', 'in order to' follows the infinitive phrase **pakaRnā**. Remember the influence of the postposition on the noun which makes **pakaRnā** change to **pakaRne**.

What determines the retention or deletion of the postposition? The answer lies in the main verb of the sentence, here, **dauRā** 'ran' and **gaye** 'went'. If the main verb is a motion verb, it is possible to drop the postposition, here, **ke liye**. The first sentence could read:

pulis (*police*) **vālā us ko** *pakaRne* **dauRā.**

If we replace the main verb in the above sentence by a static (non-motion) verb, the postposition must be retained, as in

pulis (*police*) **vālā us ko** *pakaRne ke liye* (**kʰaRā**) **hɛ.**
'The policeman is (there) to catch him.'

Removing the postposition would be ungrammatical. Therefore, the following sentence would be unacceptable:

*__pulis__ (*police*) **vālā us ko** *pakaRne* **hɛ.**

apnī apnī; 'both'

In Unit 4, we demonstrated that repetition expresses intensity. In line 3 of the text the feminine form of the reflexive pronoun **apnā** is repeated:

donõ	**ne**	**apnī**	**apnī**	*fortune cookie*	**ko**	**kʰolā.**
both	(agent)	self	self	fortune cookie	(obj.)	opened

'Both opened their respective fortune cookies.'

apnī is repeated to convey that both opened their respective cookies.

The past participle: adjectival and adverbial use

In Unit 8 we introduced present participles. Compare the phrase **bʰāg*te* cor ko** 'the running thief' with **bʰāg*e* cor ko**. The latter is called a past participial form and can be translated into English as 'the escaped thief'.

Now compare the present forms and their corresponding past participial forms and the difference in meaning conveyed by the two forms:

present participle		*past participle*	
bʰāg*tā* huā cor	the running thief	**bʰāg*ā* huā cor**	the escaped thief
bol*tī* huī laRkī	the speaking girl	**bol*ī* huī bāt**	the spoken matter
likʰ*te* hue laRke	the writing boys (the boys who are/were/will be writing)	**likʰ*e* hue alfāz**	the written words

Note the composition of the past participial form:

stem	+ *past participial marker*
bʰāg	+ **ā**
run	+ past, masculine singular
bol	+ **ī**
speak	+ past, feminine singular
likʰ	+ **e**
write	+ past, masculine plural

You have probably guessed by now that past participles are formed in the same way as the simple past tense. The only difference is that the feminine singular form is used for both singular and plural forms for past participles.

The second element (optional) remains the same in both present and past participial forms, i.e. **huā, hue** and **huī**.

As stated earlier, in participles the verb form ceases to function like a real verb and begins to behave like an adjective. Therefore, verbal adjectives which are drawn from the simple past tense are called 'past participles'. They are like adjectives ending in **ā** but they are derived from verbs. Like adjectives ending in **ā**, they agree in number or gender with the following noun. Note the gender-number agreement in the above examples.

Unlike the present participle, which denotes *action in progress*, the past participle indicates a *state*. Note the difference in meaning between the present participle and its corresponding past participial form:

present participle	*past participle*
bɛTʰtā huā laRkā	**bɛTʰā huā laRkā**
'the boy who is (in the process of) sitting'	'the seated boy'
sotī huī laRkiyã	**soī huī laRkiyã**
'the girls who are (in the process of) sleeping'	'the sleeping girls'

Adverbials

So far we have discussed the adjectival use of participles. When placed before a verb participial forms mark adverbial usage. Note the translation of the sentence given in quotes in line 4:

kāGaz par kyā *likʰā* hɛ?
paper on what written is
'What is written on the paper?'

Superficially it appears as if **likʰā hɛ** is the present perfect form of the verb **likʰ** which should be translated as 'has written'; but that is not the case. The main verb is **hɛ**, while **likʰā** is the past participial form used as an adverb without the optional element **huā**. In short:

likʰā hɛ = *likʰā huā* hɛ

Since the main verb is **hɛ** and **likʰā** is the past participle, the translation is 'is written' rather than 'has written'. The insertion of the optional element distinguishes it from the present perfect form of the verb **likʰ**. By contrast, the verb phrase in line 7 **xarīdī hɛ** is a real present perfect form of the verb **xarīd** 'buy'; therefore, its literal translation is 'has bought'.

Dialogue 1 ▣

Spice up your life

Mr and Mrs Bill Hassett, who are visiting India for the first time, are invited by Bill's Indian partner for dinner. Bill's partner's wife, Fatima Ahmad, asks her guests about the type of food they would prefer. Bill suggests to his wife they spice up their lives and try some spicy food. So he tells Fatima Ahmad

BILL: hindustānī *curry* abʰī tak ham ne nahī̃ kʰāyī.
FATIMA: āp ko masāledār kʰānā pasand hɛ yā *curry* ?
BILL: donõ mẽ farq kyā hɛ?
FATIMA: amrīkā mẽ *curry* ek qism ke kʰāne kā nām hɛ lekin hindustān mẽ ye bāt nahī̃ hɛ.

BILL: hamāre yahā *curry* kā matlab 'koī masāledār hindustanī kʰānā' hε.

FATIMA: hindustān mē na to *curry* hameshah masāledār hotī hε aur na hī hindustān mē *curry powder* aksar biktā hε. *Curry* aksar tarī vālī hotī hε aur ye gosht, sabzī, maccʰlī yā pʰal kī banī hotī hε.

BILL: are! masāle ke baGεr *curry* – ye to ham ne kabʰī nahī sunā.

FATIMA: to ab āp ko kaun sī *curry* pasand hε?

BILL: ām ke ām aur guTʰlīyõ ke dām. *Curry* ke bāre mē kucʰ mālūm ho gayā. aur aslī *curry* cakʰne kā mauqā bʰī mil jāyegā. accʰā, ham ko tez masāledār gosht kī *curry* bahut pasand hε.

(They laugh at the unexpected turn of the conversation; the proverb has added a lighter touch to the conversation and they continue to talk ...)

To be continued, stay tuned ...

BILL: *So far, in India, we have not eaten any curry.*

FATIMA: *Do you like spicy food or curry?*

BILL: *What is the difference between the two?*

FATIMA: *In America, curry is the name of a dish but this is not the case in India.*

BILL: *In America* (lit. in our place) *curry is any spicy Indian dish.*

FATIMA: *In India, curry is neither always spicy, nor is curry powder usually sold (commercially). Curry is usually liquid and (it) is made of meat, vegetables, fish or fruit.*

BILL: *Wow! Curry without spices. We've never heard of that (before).*

FATIMA: *So, which curry do you like?*

BILL: *(This is like) the best of both worlds! (Now) I have come to know about curry and will (also) get an opportunity to taste a genuine curry. Well, we really like very spicy meat curry.*

Vocabulary

curry (f.)	curry (*see notes*)	**ke baGɛr**	without
masālah (m.)	spice	**kabʰī**	ever
masāledār (adj.)	spicy	**kabʰī nahī̃**	never
yā	or	**ām** (m.; adj.)	mango (n.);
farq (m.)	difference		common (adj.)
hamāre yahā̃	at our place	**guTʰlī** (f.)	stone (of a fruit)
	(house, country,	**dām** (m.),	price
	etc.)	**qīmat** (f.)	
na ... na	neither ... nor	**ām ke ām aur**	the best of both
matlab (m.)	meaning	**guTʰlīyõ ke**	worlds
hameshah	always	**dām**	
aksar	often, usually	**mālūm honā**	to be known, to
tar	wet	**(+ko)**	become known
tarī (f.)	liquid		(to)
gosht (m.)	meat	**aslī**	real, genuine
sabzī (f.)	vegetable	**cakʰnā** (+ne)	to taste
maccʰlī (f.)	fish	**mauqā** (m.)	opportunity
pʰal (m.)	fruit	**tez**	fast, quick, sharp,
bannā (-ne)	to be made		strong
banī	made		

Notes

Curry powder/curry

In Urdu the English word 'curry' simply does not exist. It is part of the vocabulary of English-educated bilingual speakers. The Urdu word **kaRʰī** is restricted to a vegetarian curry which is made from gram flour. Urdu speakers are unlikely to use the term 'curry' to refer to the dishes mentioned above. Urdu speakers will specify the degree of spiciness and qualify a dish with words such as **sālan** or **tarī vālī sabzī** or **tarī vālā gosht**. Curry is actually a blend of ground herbs and spices adapted by British settlers in India from the traditional spice mixtures of Indian cuisine.

Focus and word order

The normal word order of the opening sentence of the above dialogue is as follows:

ham	ne	hindustānī	*curry*	abʰī tak	nahī̃ kʰāyī.
we	(agent)	Indian	curry	yet	not ate

'We have not eaten Indian curry yet.'

The time adverb and object are placed at the beginning of the sentence because they are being singled out for emphasis.

hindustānī	*curry*	abʰī tak	ham	ne	nahī̃ kʰāyī.
Indian	curry	yet	we	(agent)	not ate

'As yet, it is Indian curry (that) we have not eaten.'

'Neither . . . nor' and emphatic particles

Note the use of the emphatic particles with **na . . . na** 'neither . . . nor'. Also, observe the placement of the phrase **hindūstān mē** in the 'neither' and 'nor' clause:

hindustān	mē	na	to		*curry*	hameshah	masāledār
India	in	not	(emp.part.)		curry	always	spicy
hotī	hε		aur	na	hī	hindustān	mē
be (pres.)	is (aux.)		and	not	(emp. part.)	India	in
curry powder	aksar	biktā			hε.		
curry powder	often	be sold (pres.)			is		

'As regards curry in India, it is neither always spicy nor is curry power often sold in India.'

The emphatic particles **to** and **hī** are more intimately tied to 'curry' and 'curry powder', respectively, as shown:

hindustān	mē	na	*curry*	to		hameshah	masāledār
India	in	not	curry	(emp. part.)		always	spicy
hotī	hε		aur	na	hindustān mē	*curry powder*	
be (pres.)	is (aux.)		and	not	India in	curry powder	
hī		aksar	biktā		hε.		
(emp. part.)		often	be sold (pres.)		is		

Past participles: adverbial

Can you find the past participle in the following sentence?

ye	gosht,	sabzī,	maccʰlī	yā	pʰal	kī
this	meat	vegetable	fish	or	fruit	of

banī		hotī		hɛ.	
make (past. ppl.)		be (pres.)		is (aux.)	

Yes, **banī** is the past participial form of the verb **bannā** 'to be made'. It can be followed by the optional element **huī**. However, in the following sentence:

ham	ne	kabʰī	nahī̃	sunā	tʰā.
we	(agent)	ever	not	heard	was

'We had never heard of (it).'

sunā is not a past participle. In combination with the auxiliary **tʰā**, it is the past perfect form of the verb **sunnā** 'to hear/listen to'.

Compound verbs with jānā 'to go'

As explained in Unit 7, the helping verb **jānā** expresses 'transformation' and/or 'finality or completeness'. Both semantic shades can be seen in the following sentence:

curry	ke bāre mẽ	mālūm	ho	gayā	aur	aslī	*curry*
curry	about	known	be	went	and	genuine	curry

cakʰne	kā	mauqā	bʰī	mil	jāyegā.
taste	of	opportunity	also	get	go-will

'(I) have come to know about curry and will get an opportunity to taste genuine curry.'

In this compound verb construction, the helping verb **jānā** 'to go' loses its literal meaning.

'The opportunity of'

Note the word-for-word translation of the English expression, 'We will get the chance to taste genuine curry'.

ham	ko	asli	*curry*	cakʰne	kā	mauqā		mil
we	to	genuine	curry	taste	of	opportunity		get

jāyegā.
go-will

The expression 'to get the opportunity of doing X' requires the experiencer subject; therefore, the subject **ham** 'we' is followed by the postposition **ko**. Since the Urdu verb never agrees with the subject which is followed by a postposition, the verb in the above sentence agrees with **mauqā** 'opportunity' which is masculine singular. Also, the genitive **kā** agrees with **mauqā**.

Dialogue 2 ▭

āg! āg! *'Fire! Fire!'*

The next week, Mr and Mrs Bill Hassett come to the Ahmad's residence for dinner. They converse with each other on a wide variety of subjects. Finally, the delicious smell of the food begins to over-power their conversation. In the meanwhile, the hostess, Fatima, announces that the dinner is served

BILL: vāh! vāh! shāndār xushbū ā rahī hε, aur intazār karnā mushkil hε.

FATIMA: āiye, to kʰānā shuru kiyā jāye. ye hε, āp kī pasand – tez mirc vālī murGī kā sālan.
(Bill takes a lot of curry while Mrs Hassett takes only a little bit. After taking the first substantial bite)

BILL: *(Fanning his mouth)* Ohhh . . . āg! . . . āg!

FATIMA: kyõ kyā huā?

BILL: ye to *curry* nahī̃ hε! ye to ātash fishā̃ hε!! aur mε̃ apnā āg bujʰāne kā sāmān bʰī nahī̃ lāyā.

FATIMA: āg bujʰāne kā sāmān ye hε – agar bahut mircε̃ lag rahī hε̃ to kucʰ dahī lījiye.
(After a while Bill's mouth cools down.)

BILL: sac, amrīkā (America) mε̃ tez masāledār kʰānā itnā tez nahī̃ hotā.

FATIMA: hã̃, ye to hindustān hε. yahã̃ 'tez' kā matlab 'bahut tez' hɛ. ham log bahut tez kʰāte hɛ̃ lekin hindustān mẽ sabʰī log itnā tez kʰānā nahī̃ kʰā sakte.

BILL: Galat-fahamī dūr karne ke liye āp kā shukriya. mẽ ab samajʰ gayā ki 'tez' xatarnāk lafz hɛ.

BILL: *Well! Well! there is a splendid fragrance (of food); I can't wait* (i.e. I cannot wait more).

FATIMA: *Please come, let's start eating* (lit. eating should be started). *This is your favourite – hot chicken curry* (lit. sharp pepper one chicken curry).

BILL: *Ohhh! Fire! Fire!*

FATIMA: *Why? What's the matter?* (lit. What happened?)

BILL: *This is not **curry**! This is a volcano! and I did not bring my fire extinguisher.*

FATIMA: *Here is (your) fire extinguisher – if (it) is very hot, then take some yogurt* (lit. if very much pepper is striking (you)).

BILL: *True, in America spicy food is not so spicy.*

FATIMA: *Yes, this is India* (lit. As regards this, this is India.). *Here, 'hot' means 'very hot'. We eat very hot food, but not all people can eat such hot (food) in India.*

BILL: *Thanks for dispelling this misunderstanding. Now I (fully) understand* (lit. now I understood) *that 'tez' is a dangerous word.*

Vocabulary

vāh! vāh!	Well! Well! bravo!	**āg** (f.)	fire
shāndār	grand, splendid	**ātish** (f.)	fire
xushbū (f.)	fragrance (lit. happy smell)	**ātish fishā̃** (m.)	volcano
		bujʰānā (+**ne**)	to extinguish
shurū karnā (+**ne**)	to begin	**sāmān** (m.)	baggage, goods, stuff, tools
shurū kiyā jāye	should be started	**lānā** (-**ne**)	to bring
mirc (f.)	chilli peppers	**dahī** (m./f.)	yogurt
murGī (f.)	chicken	**sac** (m.)	truth, true
sālan (m.)	curry (authentic)	**itnā**	this/so much/ many
oh	exclamation of pain/sorrow	**Galat**	wrong, incorrect

Galat-fahmī (f.)	misconception, misunderstanding	**xatrah** (m.)	danger
dūr	far, distant	**xatarnāk**	dangerous
dūr karnā (+ne)	to dispel, to eliminate	**lafz** (m.)	word

Notes

Ambiguity

The following expression in the opening line of the above dialogue is ambiguous:

aur intzār karnā mushkil hɛ.
and wait to do difficult is
'(It) is difficult to wait any longer' or 'And, (it) is difficult to wait.'

In other words, **aur** can be interpreted as either a conjunction marker or a modifier of **intzār**.

The passive construction

The English expression, 'Let's begin eating' is paraphrased as 'eating should be done':

kʰānā shurū kiyā jāye.
eating begin did go (subjunctive)

The verb phrase is in the passive subjunctive form. The passive is formed by using the main verb in the past form with the helping verb **jānā** 'to go', which undergoes tense conjugation.

	passive	
main verb (past form)	*helping verb (**jānā** + tense)*	
kiyā	**jāye**	should be done
paRʰā	**jātā hɛ**	is read
paRʰā	**gayā**	was read
paRʰā	**jāyegā**	will be read
bolā	**jā rahā hɛ**	is being spoken/told

Just as the agent in a passive construction is indicated with 'by' (e.g. 'the man was bitten by the dog'), so in Urdu it is indicated with *se* 'from'. Here is a list of pronouns with the postposition **se**.

mɛ̃	+ **se**	= **mujʰ se**	by me	**ham**	+ **se**	= **ham se**	by us
tū	+ **se**	= **tujʰ se**	by you	**tum**	+ **se**	= **tum se**	by you
				āp	+ **se**	= **āp se**	by you (hon.)
vo	+ **se**	= **us se**	by him/her	**vo** (pl.)	+ **se**	= **un se**	by them

Since the passive subject is always followed by the postposition **se**, the passive verb can never agree with it; instead it agrees with the object, as in:

mujʰ	**se**	**kitāb**	**paRʰī**	**gayī.**
me	by	book (f.)	read (past-f.)	(passive) go + past-f.-sg.

'The book was read by me.'

If the feminine object **kitāb** 'book' is replaced by the masculine object **xat** 'letter', the passive verb form will be in the masculine singular form:

mujʰ	**se**	**xat**	**paRʰā**	**gayā.**
me	by	letter (m.)	read (past-m.)	(passive) go+past-m.-sg.

'The letter was read by me.'

One important difference between Urdu and English is that intransitive as well as transitive verbs can be made passive in Urdu, while only transitive verbs can be made passive in English. See the Reference Grammar for more details.

The omitted subject

agar	**(āp**	**ko)**	**bahut**	**mircẽ**	**lag**	**rahī**	**hɛ̃**	**to**
If	(you	to)	very	pepper	strike	-ing	are	then

(āp)	**kucʰ**	**dahī**	**lījiye.**
(you)	some	yogurt	take

The omitted subject of the first clause is experiencer, while it is nominative in the second clause.

The past participle and the passive construction

You will have realized by now that there is no neat correspondence between passives in English and Urdu. The English passive construction can be paraphrased in one of the following three ways:

(1) – those instances where English and Urdu both use the passive construction to express the idea. For example, English expressions such as 'it is said' and 'it is heard' will be translated by means of Urdu passive, as in:

> **kahā**   **jātā**   **hɛ.**
> say (past)   (passive)   go (pres.)   is
> '(It) is said.'

> **sunā**   **jātā**   **hɛ.**
> hear (past)   (passive)   go (pres.)   is
> '(It) is heard.'

(2) – English passives are sometimes translated as past participle forms in Urdu. Consider sentence 4 in text 1 of this unit.

> **kāGaz   par   kyā   likʰā**   **hɛ?**
> paper   on   what   written (past. ppl.)   is
> 'What is written on the paper?'

Compare the English sentence with its corresponding Urdu sentence. The Urdu sentence does not use the passive construction. The past participial form of the verb **likʰnā** is used instead.

(3) – some Urdu intransitive verbs are translated as passive in English:

intransitive		*transitive*	
biknā	to be sold	**becnā**	to sell
bannā	to be made	**banānā**	to make
kʰulnā	to be opened	**kʰolnā**	open

Since English does not have intransitive verbs corresponding to those in Urdu, the Urdu intransitive verbs are best translated by means of the English passive. For example, a common billboard sign in India is:

> **yahā̃   kitābẽ   biktī**   **hɛ̃.**
> here   books   be sold (pres.)   are
> 'Books are sold here.'

In Urdu, the intransitive verb **biknā** is conjugated in the simple present tense. Thus, the Urdu sentence is in its active form as opposed to the passive form in English.

Negation and auxiliary deletion

The present auxiliary verb is dropped with negative sentences in the following two sentences:

| **amrīkā** | **mẽ** | **tez** | **masāledār** | **kʰānā** | **itnā** | **tez** |
| America | in | sharp | spicy | food | so much | sharp |

| **nahī̃ hotā** | **(hɛ).** |
| not be (pres.) | is (aux.) |

'In America spicy food is not as spicy.'

| **lekin** | **hindustān** | **mẽ** | **sabʰī** | **log** | **itnā** | **tez** |
| but | India | in | all + **hī** | people | so much | sharp |

| **kʰānā** | **nahī̃** | **kʰā** | **sakte** | **(hẽ).** |
| food | not | eat | can (pres.) | are |

'But in India not everybody can eat such spicy food.'

Exercises

1 Match the places with the purpose for which people visit them. Then complete the sentences according to the model presented below:

| *place* | | *purpose* | |
| **kutubxānā** | library | **kitābẽ paRʰne** | to read books |

sentence
log kutubxānā kitābẽ paRʰne ke liye jāte hẽ.
'People go to the library to read books.'

Do not attempt to translate the English locations into Urdu.

	place	*purpose*
(a)	laundromat	pīne (i.e. **sharāb** alcoholic drinks)
(b)	restaurant	*film* dekʰne
(c)	cinema	tɛrne
(d)	college	paRʰne
(e)	swimming pool	kʰānā kʰāne

(f) bar   davāī lene
(g) chemist   kapRe dʰone

2 Change the present participial phrase into its corresponding past participial form in the following sentences.

(a) vo bɛTʰte hue bolā.
(b) John sote hue hās rahā tʰā.
(c) ye shɛhɛr sotā sā lagtā hɛ.
(d) laRkī pītī huī gʰar āyī.
(e) ek aurat ne bistar par leTte hue kahā.

3 Which participial forms modify/match the noun?

likʰā   bāt
sunī   xat
hāstā   laRkā
caltī   gāRī
bʰāgtī   billī

4 Change the following sentences into their corresponding passive forms.

(a) John ne ek kahānī paRʰī.
(b) ham log kʰānā kʰā rahe hɛ̃.
(c) tum kyā karoge?
(d) mɛ̃ ne murGī kā sālan banāyā.
(e) Bill hindustān mɛ̃ paRʰegā.
(f) kyā āp ne gānā gāyā?

5 Circle the appropriate form of the subject, verb, etc. given in brackets in the following sentences.

(a) (ham ko/ham/ham ne) vahā̃ jāne kā mauqā (milā/mile).
(b) (john ne/john ko/john) hindustān (jānā/jāne) kā mauqā aksar
     miltā hɛ.
(c) ye sunhɛra mauqā (tʰā/tʰī).
(d) (āp ko/āp) kitāb likʰne kā mauqā kab (milegī/milegā)?
(e) is kāGaz par kyā (likʰā/likʰī) hɛ?
(f) billī ko mauqā (milā/milī) aur vo dūdʰ pī gayī.
(g) ye bahut (accʰā mauqā/accʰe mauqe) kī bāt hɛ.

10 باب دَس: تہوار
Festivals

By the end of this unit you should be able to:

- learn various types of relative clauses
- use complex sentences
- learn more about Urdu passives
- learn about Muslim festivals
- get cultural information about the Indian subcontinent
- learn about Perso-Arabic components in Urdu
- distinguish between formal and non-formal style

In this unit we will describe some festivals and other customs and traditions which underlie the colourful mosaic of South Asian culture. You will notice a slight shift in the style of the Urdu, which is more Persianized now. This style is preferred in formal, literary, scholarly and cultural endeavours.

Text 1

īd-ul-fitar

1 īd musalmānõ kā muqaddas tehvār hɛ.
2 ramzān ke tīs rozõ ke bād īd ātī hɛ.
3 jis rāt īd kā cãd dekʰā jātā hɛ, us ke dūsre din īd manāī jātī hɛ.
4 ramzān ke mahīne mẽ musalmānõ ke liye roze rakʰnā farz hɛ. is kā matlab ye hɛ, jo musalmān roze rakʰte hẽ vo āftāb caRʰne aur āftāb Dūbne ke darmiyān na kucʰ pī sakte hẽ aur na kucʰ kʰā sakte hẽ.
5 jɛse *Christmas* duniyā ke bahut sāre log josh se manāte hẽ, vɛse īd bʰī bahut sāre mulkõ mẽ aqīdat se manāī jātī hɛ.
6 īd ke din log savere uTʰ kar nahāte aur naye kapRe pɛhɛnte hẽ. pʰir sab log namāz paRʰne ke liye īd-gah yā baRī masjid mẽ jāte hẽ.
7 namāz ke bād sab ek dūsre se gale milte hẽ, aur bād mẽ apne apne qarībī rishtedārõ aur dostõ ke gʰar īd milne jāte hẽ, aur xɛrāt karte hẽ.
8 vāldɛn apne baccõ ko īd kī xushī mẽ īdī dete hẽ. bacce in pɛsõ se tarah tarah ke kʰilone aur miTʰāiyã xarīdte hẽ.
9 sab logõ ke gʰarõ mẽ acchī dāvatẽ hotī hɛ. is din sivaiyã pakāī jātī hẽ.
10 hindustān mẽ is mubārak din par hindū, sikʰ aur īsāī apne musalmān dostõ ke gʰarõ mẽ īd mubārak dene ke liye jāte hẽ aur unkī is xushī mẽ sharīk ho jāte hẽ.
11 kucʰ log ek dūsre ko īd mubārak ke pɛGām aur nazrāne bʰejte hẽ.
12 āj ke din aksar dushmanõ ko bʰī dost banāyā jātā hɛ.

1 *Id is an Islamic sacred festival* (lit. a sacred festival for the Muslims).
2 *Id comes after the thirty-day period of fasting during the month of Ramzan.*

3 *Id is celebrated the day after the (new) moon is seen.*

4 *It is the duty of Muslims to fast during the month of Ramzan. It means that Muslims who fast neither drink nor eat anything between sunrise and sunset.*

5 *Just as many people in the world celebrate Christmas with enthusiasm, similarly Id is celebrated with devotion in many countries.*

6 *On the day of Id, people get up early in the morning, take a bath and put on new clothes. Then everybody goes to an **Id-gah** or to a big mosque to offer prayers.*

7 *After prayers people embrace each other and later they visit the homes of close relatives and friends to offer Id greetings and they (also) give alms (to the poor).*

8 *Parents give money to their children on the occasion (lit. in the happiness) of Id. Children buy different toys and sweets with this money.*

9 *There is feasting in every home. On this day sivayan* (a sweet dessert) *is cooked.*

10 *On this auspicious day in India, Hindus, Sikhs and Christians visit the homes of their Muslim neighbours* (lit. brothers) *to exchange greetings and they participate together in this joyous occasion.*

11 *Some people send Happy Id messages and gifts to each other.*

12 *On this day even enemies often become* (lit. are often made) *friends.*

Vocabulary

īd (f.)	a Muslim festival	**tīs**	thirty
musalmān (m.)	Muslim	**rozah** (m.)	(a) fast
muqaddas	sacred	**rakʰnā** (+ne)	to keep, to put
tehvār (m.)	festival	**rozah rakʰnā**	to keep a fast
ramzān (m.)	Ramzan	**farz** (m.)	duty
	(Ramadan), the	**matlab**	meaning
	ninth month of	**āftāb** (m.)	sun
	the Muslim	**āftāb caRʰnā**	sunrise
	calendar during	**āftāb Dūbnā**	sunset
	which Muslims	**na ... kucʰ**	nothing (**na** is a
	fast in daylight		negative
	hours		particle)

ke bād (past ppl.)	after	**bād mẽ**	afterwards, later
cā̃d (f.)	moon	**apne apne**	one's own
dekʰnā (+ne)	to see	**qarīb**	close, near
jānā (-ne)	to go	**rishtedār** (m.)	relative
dekʰā jātā hɛ	is seen	**dost** (m., f.)	friend
jɛse	just like	**īd milnā**	to embrace each
duniyā (f.)	world		other cordially
josh (m.)	excitement, joy		on the occasion
vɛse	like that, similarly		of Id
aqīdat (f.)	faith, devotion	**xɛrāt** (f.)	alms
sārā	whole	**xɛrāt karnā**	to give alms
bahut sārā	many, a lot	(+ne)	
manānā (+ne)	to celebrate	**vāldɛn** (m.)	parents
manāyā jānā	to be celebrated	**xushī** (f.)	happiness, enjoy-
log (m.)	people		ment, wish
saverā (m.)	early morning	**(kī) xushī mẽ**	in the
uTʰnā (-ne)	to get up		happiness (of)
uTʰ kar	having got up	**īdī** (f.)	money given at
	(**kar**		Id to children
	construction)	**pɛsā** (m.)	money
nahānā (+ne)	to have a bath	**tarah tarah**	different
nayā	new	**kʰilonā** (m.)	toy
kapRe (m.)	clothes	**miTʰāī** (f.)	sweets
pɛhɛnnā (+ne)	to wear	**xarīdnā** (+ne)	to buy
pʰir	then, again	**dāvat** (f.)	feast, invitation,
sab	all		party
sab log	everybody	**sivaiyā̃** (f.)	name of a dessert
namāz (f.)	Muslim prayers	**īsāī** (m.)	Christians
namāz paRʰnā	to offer Muslim	**mubārak** (adj.)	blessed,
	prayers		auspicious,
īd-gah (f.)	an open space		happy
	where **īd**	**īd mubārak**	Happy Id!
	prayers are	**sharīk** (m.)	partner
	offered	**sharīk ho**	to take part in
masjid (f.)	mosque	**jānā**	(compound
ek dūsre se	with one another		verb)
galā (m.)	throat, neck	**pɛGām** (m.)	message
gale milnā	to embrace	**nazrānah** (m.)	gift
		dushman (m.)	enemy

Text 2

īd-ul-azhā *'The Muslim festival of sacrifices'*

1 musalmānõ kā ek tehvār aur bʰī hɛ jis ko baqra īd kɛhte hɛ̃. ye
   īd haj ke mahīne mẽ tīn roz manāī jātī hɛ.
2 duniyā ke musalmān haj karne ke liye makke jāte hɛ̃. Haj se fāriG
   ho kar pɛGambar ke roze ki ziyārat ke liye madīne bʰī jāte hɛ̃.
3 pākistān aur hindustān se bʰī bahut se musalmān haj karne ke
   liye makke jāte hɛ̃. jo log haj kar ke āte hɛ̃, vo hājī kɛhlāte hɛ̃,
   aur unkī bahut izzat kī jātī hɛ. jab ye hājī apne apne gʰar pahũcte
   hɛ̃, tab josh-o-xarosh ke sāth unkā istaqbāl kiyā jātā hɛ.
4 is din musalmān bakre yā bʰeR kī qurbānī karte hɛ̃, aur ye gosht
   Garībõ, dostõ, hamsāyõ aur rishtedārõ mẽ bā̃Tā jātā hɛ.
5 kahā jātā hɛ ke qurbānī kā āGāz hazrat ibrāhīm alehsata ke vaqt
   se huā hɛ, aur is din kā maqsad unkī qurbānī kī yād ko tāzah
   karnā hɛ.
6 sab musalmān īd-gah jā kar shukrāne kī namāz adā karte hɛ̃.
7 ye nihāyat azīm-ul-shān islāmī tehvār hɛ.

1 *There is another Muslim festival, which is called baqra Id. This*
   is celebrated for three days in the month of Haj (the pilgrimage
   to Mecca).
2 *Muslims from all over the world go to Mecca to perform Haj.*
   After performing Haj, people go on a holy pilgrimage to Madina.
3 *Many Muslims from India and Pakistan also go to Mecca to*
   perform Haj. Those (the people) *who perform Haj are called*
   Hajis and they are highly respected. When Hajis return to their
   homes, they are greeted with great joy and enthusiasm.
4 *On this day Muslims sacrifice a sheep or lamb and the meat is*
   distributed amongst the poor, friends, neighbours and relatives.
5 *(It) is said that such sacrifices began in the Prophet Ibrahim's*
   (Abraham) time (peace be upon him) *and the purpose of this Id*
   is to refresh the memory of his (the Prophet's) *sacrifice.*
6 *All Muslims go to an Id-gah to offer prayers of thanksgiving.*
7 *This is a very* (important) *and splendid Islamic festival.*

Vocabulary

bakrā (m.)	male goat
baqra īd (f.)	the Muslim Festival of Sacrifice in commemoration of the Prophet Ibrahim's (Abraham) offering
roz	a day, daily
haj (m.)	pilgrimage to Mecca
manāyā jānā (-**ne**)	to be celebrated
makkā (m.)	Mecca, the holy city of Muslims
duniyā (m.)	world
fāriG (adj.)	free, at leisure
fāriG honā (-**ne**)	to be free, to have done with
pɛGambar (m.)	Prophet (lit. messenger)
ziyārat (f.)	(religious) visit
madīnā (m.)	the city of Medina in Saudi Arabia
hājī (m.)	a pilgrim to Mecca
kɛhlānā (-**ne**)	to be called or named
izzat (f.)	respect
pahũcnā (+**ne**)	to reach
josh-o-xarosh	excitement
istaqbāl	welcome
istaqbāl karnā (+**ne**)	to welcome
bʰeR (f.)	a sheep
qurbānī (f.)	sacrifice
qurbānī karnā (+**ne**)	to sacrifice
gosht (m.)	meat
Garībõ (m. pl.)	the poor
dost	friend
hamsāyā	a neighbour
rishtedār	relative
bā̃Tnā (+**ne**)	to divide
āGāz (m.)	beginning, origin
āGāz honā (-**ne**)	to be started
hazrat (m.)	a title given to a Prophet, e.g. **hazrat īsā** Jesus Christ
ibrāhīm (m.)	The Prophet Ibrahim (Abraham)
vaqt (m.)	time
maqsad (m.)	purpose

yād (f.)	remembrance, memory
tāzah (adj.)	fresh
tāzah karnā (+ne)	to refresh
sab	all
īd-gah	an open space were Id prayers are offered
shukrānā	thanksgiving
namāz	Muslim prayers
adā (f.)	fulfilment, performance
adā karnā (+ne)	to perform
nihāyat (f.)	the extreme
azīm-ul-shān	magnificent
islāmī	Islamic
tehvār (m.)	festival

Perso-Arabic style

Style differences in Urdu primarily involve vocabulary. High or formal literary style is often equated with borrowing from Arabic and Persian:

informal	*formal*	
mã-bāp	**vāldɛn**	parents
nām	**ism-e-sharīf**	name
būRʰā	**buzurg**	old

Agentless passives

The Urdu equivalent of English 'this festival is celebrated' is:

ye	**tehvār**	**manāyā**	**jātā**	**hɛ.**
this	festival (m.)	celebrate (past)	(passive) go (pres.)	is

'this festival is celebrated'

Urdu tends to omit the agent. The opening clause of line 5 (text 2) of this unit further exemplifies this point. Notice the omission of the agent ('by x') in the following sentence:

kahā	**jātā**	**hɛ.**
say (past)	(passive) go (pres.)	is

'(It) is said.'

An implied agent such as 'by people' is understood in these sentences.

Relative clauses

The relative clause joins two clauses. It contains a relative pronoun, which begins with the sound **j-** in Urdu, while in English a relative pronoun begins with a **wh-**. For example, the English sentence 'The Muslims who live in this world celebrate Id' is paraphrased as 'which/who Muslims live in this world, those Muslims celebrate Id'. So, the Urdu sentence would be

jo	**musalmān**	**is**	**dunyā**	**mẽ**	**rɛhte**		**hɛ̃**	**vo**
who	Muslims	this	world	in	live (pres.)		are	those
(musalmān)	**īd**	**manāte**			**hɛ̃.**			
Muslims	Id	celebrate (pres.)			are			

'The Muslims who live in this world celebrate Id.'

The **jo**-clause is called the relative clause and is linked to the main or correlative clause. The second repeated noun (**log** 'people') can be dropped, and the final result is as follows:

jo musalmān is dunyā mẽ rɛhte hɛ̃ vo īd manāte hɛ̃.

A list of relative and correlative pronouns is given below:

	simple		*oblique*		
	singular	*plural*	*singular*	*plural*	
relative	**jo**	**jo**	**jis**	**jin**	who/which
correlative	**vo**	**vo**	**us**	**un**	this/those

The correlative pronouns are the same as the third person pronouns. Observe one more example of Urdu relative clauses:

jis	**tehvār**	**kā**	**nām**	**īd**	**hɛ,**	**vo**	**mashhūr**	**hɛ.**
which (obl.)	festival	of	name	Id	is	that	famous	is

'The festival called Id is famous.'

Other types of relative clauses found in Urdu and their markers are as follows:

	relative		*correlative*	
place	**jahã**	where, in which place	**vahã**	there, in that place
time	**jab**	when	**tab**	then
manner	**jɛse**	as, in which manner	**vɛse**	in that manner
directional	**jidʰar**	in which direction	**udʰar**	in that direction
kind	**jɛsā**	as/which kind	**vɛsā**	that kind
quantity	**jitnā**	as much/many as	**utnā**	that much/many

Relative clauses of kind and quantity behave like **ā-** adjectives
which agree with their following noun in number and gender.

An example of a time relative clause can be found in line 3 of
text 2:

jab ...	**hājī**	**apne apne**	**gʰar**	**pahū̃cte**	**hɛ̃,**	**tab**
when	Haji	own	home	reach	are	then

josh-o-xarosh	**ke sātʰ**	**unkā**	**istaqbāl**	**kiyā**
excitement	with	their	welcome	do

jātā hɛ.
(passive) go (pres.)

'When Hajis return to their homes, they are greeted with
   great joy and enthusiasm.'

Line 5 of text 1 exemplifies a relative clause of manner:

jɛse	*Christmas*	**duniyā**	**ke**	**bahut sāre**	**log**	**josh**	**se**
as	Christmas	world	of	many	people	joy	with

manāte hɛ̃,	**vɛse**			**īd**	**bʰī**	**bahut sāre**
celebrate (pres.)	in that manner			Id	also	many

mulkõ	**mẽ aqīdat**	**ke sātʰ**	**manāī**		**jātī hɛ.**
countries	in faith	with	celebrate (past)		(passive) go
					(pres.)

'As many people in the world celebrate Christmas with
   enthusiasm, similarly Id is celebrated with devotion in many
   countries.'

Text 3

muharram *'The first Muslim month'*

1 muharram musalmān taqvīm kā pɛhlā mahīnā hɛ.

2 ye xushī manāne kā tehvār nahĩ hɛ, balke shiyā musalmānõ ke liye mātam ke din hɛ̃.

3 kyõke muharram hī ke mahīne mẽ damishq ke hākim yazīd kī fauj ne Hazrat Muhammad (sa'la'lāho-alay-he-wassa'lam) ke 'azīz navāse Hussen aur unke rishtedārõ ko shahīd kiyā tʰā.

4 ye vāqi'āt yād kar, in dinõ musalmānõ mẽ bahut rañj-o-Gam pɛdā ho jātā hɛ.

5 log shahīdõ kī rūhõ ko savāb pahũcāne ke liye faqīrõ ko kʰānā kʰilāte hɛ̃.

6 isī mahīne kī nav tārīx kī rāt ko, shi'ā musalmān shahīdõ ki yād mẽ tā'ziye bāzārõ mẽ nikālte hɛ̃.

7 dūsre din ye log in tāziyõ ko le kar pānī mẽ Garq karte hɛ̃.

1 *Muharram is the first month of the Muslim calendar.*

2 *It is not an occasion for celebration; instead it is a period of mourning for Shia Muslims.*

3 *It was during the month of Muharram that Yazid, the ruler of Damascus, killed Hazrat Muhammad's* (peace be upon him) *nephew, Hussain, and his relatives* (lit. Yazid's army killed . . .).

4 *In remembrance of this incident, Muslims are in deep mourning during this period.* (lit. In these days sadness grows among the Muslims.)

5 *To offer solace to the souls of the martyrs, Muslims feed the poor.*

6 *On the ninth of this month, Shia Muslims hold processions carrying replicas of the martyrs' tombs.*

7 *The next day these replicas are immersed in water.*

Vocabulary

muharram (m.)	the first month of the Muslim calendar, held sacred on account of the death of Imam Hussain
taqvīm (f.)	calendar

pɛhlā	first
muhammad (m.)	the Prophet Muhammad
sa'la'lāho-alay-he-wassa'lam	peace be upon him
kyõke	because
bād mẽ	afterwards
xushī (f.)	happiness
manānā (+ne)	to celebrate
ke bajāe (past ppl.)	instead
mātam (m.)	mourning
ho jānā (-ne)	to become (compound verb)
damishq	Damascus
hākim (m.)	ruler
yazīd (m.)	Yazid (a name)
fauj (f.)	an army
azīz (adj.)	dear, respected
navāsā (m.)	grandson (daughter's son)
Hussɛn (m.)	Hussain, a name (the Prophet Muhammad's grandson)
rishtedār	relatives
shahīd (m.)	a martyr
shahīd karnā (+ne)	to kill (i.e. to make a martyr of)
vāqi'āt (m., pl.)	events
yād karnā (+ne)	to remember
rañj-o-Gam	sorrow
pɛdā honā (-ne)	to arise, to be born
rūh (f.)	soul, spirit
savāb (m.)	a virtuous action
pahũcānā (+ne)	to make something reach
faqīr (m., sg.)	beggar, ascetic
kʰānā (m.)	food
kʰilānā (+ne)	to feed (causative verb)
shi'ā	Shia (Muslims)
tā'ziyā	tazia (replicas of Hussain's tomb)

Grammar

The Perso-Arabic component in Urdu

The Arabic component

It is important to note that the plurals of Perso-Arabic loan words are generally formed according to the rules of Urdu grammar, e.g.

aurat	woman	**aurtẽ**	women
qalam	pen	**qalmẽ**	pens

but certain Arabic nouns in Urdu form their plurals according to the rules of Arabic grammar. So it is important for you to know these rules. Arabic plurals are classified into two groups:

1 *Sound plurals* are formed by adding -**īn** and -**āt** to the endings of singular forms, e.g.

momin	believer	**mominīn**	believers
vāqi'a	incident, events	**vāqi'āt**	incidents
axbār	newspaper	**axbārāt**	newspapers

2 *Broken plurals* are formed by altering the vowel patterns of singular nouns, e.g.

kitāb	book	**kutub**	books
shaxs	person	**ashxās**	persons
qā'idā	rule	**qavā'id**	rules

Dialogue 1 ▢▢

Marriage ceremony

Bill Hackman has received an invitation to attend the marriage ceremony of his Pakistani friend. Before he attends the ceremony, he wants to learn about the customs and traditions of Pakistani society. Javed Ahmad is from Pakistan and teaches Urdu at the University of Manchester. They live in the same area and one day Bill visits Javed's home. After greeting Bill, they begin to talk

JAVED: tashrīf rakʰiye. farmāiye mẽ āp ke liye kyā kar saktā hū̃?

BILL: mẽ pākistānī rasm aur rivāj ke bāre mẽ kucʰ jānnā cāhtā hū̃, xās tor se mẽ shādī kī rasm ke bāre mẽ āp se kucʰ savāl pūcʰnā cāhtā hū̃.

JAVED: koī bāt nahī̃, pūchiye.

BILL: kyā laRkī apnā xāvind xud intixāb kartī hɛ?

JAVED: pakistānī mu'āshre mẽ vāldɛn aksar apne beTā/beTī keliye dulhan/dūlhā kā intixāb karte hẽ. is ke baraks, shādī ke mu'āmle mẽ vāldɛn ām taur se laRkā/laRkī kī marzī hāsil karte hẽ, cū̃ke ye islāmī hukam bʰī hɛ. jab donõ xāndān ko ek dūsre kā gʰarānā pasand ātā hɛ to pʰir maŋgnī kī rasm adā hotī hɛ.

BILL: mangnī kā kyā matlab hɛ?

JAVED: mangnī kā matlab *engagement* hɛ, jiskī rasm laRkī ke gʰar mẽ adā hotī hɛ. aur laRke vāle laRkī ko aŋgūṬʰī pɛhnāte hẽ, pʰir shādī kī tārīx tɛ hotī hɛ.

BILL: shādī kī rasm kahā̃ aur kɛse adā hotī hɛ?

JAVED: ye rasm bʰī laRkī ke gʰar par hī adā hotī hɛ. us din laRke vāle bārāt le kar ā jāte hẽ jis mẽ dūlhā kā xāndān, qarībī rishtedar aur dost shāmil ho jāte hẽ. laRkī vāle un kā istaqbāl shān se karte hẽ. pʰir nikah kī rasm adā kī jātī hɛ. maulvī sāhab nikah paRʰāte hẽ.

BILL: nikah kɛse paRʰāyā jātā hɛ?

JAVED: pɛhle kucʰ log alag se laRkī ke pās jā kar us se nikah kī ijāzat lete hẽ. pʰir tamām logõ ke sāmne maulvī sāhab dūlhā se tīn bār pūcʰte hẽ ke us ko nikah qabūl hɛ ya nahī̃. jab vo iskā iqrār kartā hɛ tab sāre log dūlhā aur dulhan ko mubārak bād pesh karte hẽ. nikah ke bād sab bārātiyõ ko dāvat kʰilāyī jātī hɛ. bārātī pʰir dūlhe ke gʰar vāpas jāte hẽ.

BILL: āp kā bahut bahut shukriyā. āp ne mujʰe kāfī cīzõ se āgah kiya.

JAVED: *Please have a seat. What can I do for you?*

BILL: *I would like to know about the customs and traditions of Pakistan, I would especially like to ask you some questions about marriage customs.*

JAVED: *All right* (lit. Doesn't matter), *please ask.*

BILL: *Does a woman choose her own husband?*

JAVED: *In Pakistani culture parents quite often choose the groom/ bride for their son/daughter. Nevertheless* (lit. On the other hand), *in matters of marriage, the parents usually obtain their son's/daughter's consent, since this is in accordance with Islamic law* (lit. orders). *When both households are happy with their choice* (lit. when both families like each other's household), *then the engagement ceremony is performed.*

BILL: *What do you mean by* **maṇgnī?**

JAVED: *The meaning of* **maṇgnī** *is 'engagement', which is performed at the girl's house. The boy's side presents her with the ring* (lit. have the girl put on (her) ring (and) then). *Then the wedding dates are fixed.*

BILL: *How and where is the wedding ceremony performed?*

JAVED: *This ceremony is also performed at the girl's place. On that day the boy's side form a wedding procession accompanied by the bridegroom's family, close relatives and friends. The girl's family prepares an impressive welcome for the guests* (lit. welcome the guests with pomp). *Then the wedding ceremony is performed. The priest reads the wedding service.*

BILL: *How is the service performed?*

JAVED: *First, some people go and obtain the girl's consent in order to proceed with the service. Then, in front of all the people the groom is asked three times by the Maulvi whether or not he accepts the terms of the marriage. When he consents then people congratulate both the bride and the groom. After the wedding ceremony a meal is served to the guests, after which all the guests return to the groom's house.*

BILL: *Thank you very much. You have given me information about lots of things.*

Vocabulary

tashrīf (f.)	honouring	**farmānā** (+**ne**)	to say, to speak
rakʰnā (+**ne**)	to keep	**rasm** (f.)	custom, order
tashrīf rakʰnā (+**ne**)	to sit down	**rivāj** (m.)	custom, usage, fashion

ke bāre mē	about (post-position)	**bārāt** (f.)	a wedding procession
jānnā (+**ne**)	to know	**shāmil** (adj.)	included
xās tor se (adj.)	especially, above all	**shāmil ho jānā** (-**ne**)	to be included, participate
shādī (f.)	wedding	**istaqbāl** (m.)	reception,
kucʰ	some		welcome
savāl (m.)	question	**istaqbāl karnā**	to welcome
pūcʰ**nā** (+**ne**)	to ask	(+**ne**)	(a guest)
xāvind (m.)	husband	**shān** (f.)	pomp, splendour
xud (adj.)	self	**bārātī** (m.)	guests at a
intixāb karnā	to choose, to		wedding
(+**ne**)	pick, to elect	**matlab** (m.)	meaning
hamārā	our	**maulvī** (m.)	Muslim preacher
mu'āshrā	culture, society	**ke sāmne**	in front of (post-
aksar	often		position)
vāldɛn (m.)	parents	**paR**ʰ**ānā** (+**ne**)	to teach
dulhā (m.)	bridegroom	**nikāh paR**ʰ**ānā**	to read the
dulhan (f.)	bride	(+**ne**)	wedding
is ke baraks	opposite, on the		service
(adv.)	other hand	**ijāzat**	permission
m'āmlā (m.)	matter	**tamām** (adj.)	entire, whole
ām taur se	usually	**qabūl** (m.)	assent, acknow-
marzī (f.)	consent		ledgement
hāsil karnā (+**ne**)	to obtain	**qabūl honā**	to be accepted
cūke (adv.)	because	(+**ko**)	
hukam (m.)	order, precept	**iqrār**	agreement
gʰ**arānā** (m.)	household	**iqrār karnā**	to accept
maŋgnī (f.)	engagement	(+**ne**)	
maŋgnī honā	to be engaged	**dāvat** (f.)	meal, invitation,
(-**ne**)			party
nikāh (m.)	matrimony	**alag**	separate
adā (f.)	performance	**mubārak**	auspicious,
adā honā (-**ne**)	to be performed		blessed
		mubārakbād	congratulations
donõ	both	**pesh karna** (+**ne**)	to present
aŋgūlʰ**ī** (f.)	ring	**vāpas jānā** (-**ne**)	to return
pɛhnānā (+**ne**)	to make (some-one) wear	**āgah karānā** (+**ne**)	to cause to inform someone

Pronunciation

The Urdu word for 'society' is written as **m'āshrā**, but is pronounced in two ways: **mu'āshrā** and **māshrā**.

Exercises

1 Match the passive statements given in the right column with the two festivals given in the left column.

īd-ul-fitr   haj ke mahīne mē tīn roz manāī jātī hɛ.
īd-ul-azhā   is din sivaiyã pakāī jātī hɛ̃. gosht dostõ aur rishtedārõ
              mē bā̃Tā jātā hɛ.
              dushmanõ ko bʰī dost banāyā jātā hɛ.

2 Translate into English the sentences given in the right-hand column in the above question.

3 Read the following relative clause statements and then identify the festival associated with each statement.

(a) vo tehvār jo ramazān ke mahīne mē ātā hɛ.
(b) vo tehvār jo tīn roz kā hɛ.
(c) vo tehvār jis mē shiyā musalmān mātam karte hɛ̃.
(d) vo tehvār jis din log bakra yā bʰeR kī qurbānī karte hɛ̃.
(e) vo tehvār jis din log shahīdõ ke t'āziye nikālte hɛ̃.

Script unit 1

As mentioned before (see Urdu writing system and pronunciation unit), the vowel signs

zabar (´) **zer** (ˏ) **pesh** (´)

are used to indicate the short vowels a, i and u, respectively. However, we should mention here that these signs are not always written or printed and the vowel is determined by the context. The use of these signs is limited to children's books. However, we will make use of these signs in our script lessons and also in the text to make the learning of the Urdu (Perso-Arabic) script and the Urdu language faster and more convenient for beginners. It should be noted that the Urdu script uses a modified version of the Arabic alaphabet.

In the script units, an attempt has been made to use Urdu words as much as possible. However, some archaic Perso-Arabic words, together with nonsense words, are also employed whenever deemed necessary to introduce the finer points of the writing system. Also, some common Muslim, Hindu, Sikh and Christian names are introduced for the purpose of practising Urdu writing and pronunciation.

This unit has two sections: the first section deals with non-connector vowels and the second with non-connector consonants.

Non-connector vowels
The first letter of the alphabet, alif (ا)

Alif is a non-connector and its initial, medial and final shapes are the same as its detached (independent) shape. If a word begins with **alif**, this indicates that the word begins with a vowel. The vowel signs **zabar**, **zer** and **pesh** are employed to indicate **a**, **i** and **u**, respectively only when **alif** appears in its initial form. Look at the chart below:

letter	name	sound	shapes			
			detached (independent)	*final*	*medial*	*initial*
ا	**alif**	**a**	ا	ا	ا	ا

handwriting mode

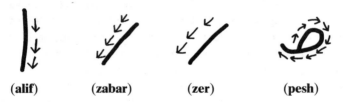

| (alif) | (zabar) | (zer) | (pesh) |

Look at the following combinations of vowel signs with the letter **alif**:

اَ	=	**a**
اِ	=	**i**
اُ	=	**u**

The superscript, **madd** (ٓ) is used above **alif** only in initial position to indicate the long vowel **ā**.

| آ | = | **ā** |

After a consonant, **alif** represents the **ā** sound.

Look at the following combinations of consonants with the vowels **a**, **i**, **u** and **ā** and try to read them aloud. You may need to refer to the consonant chart on page 20.

Remember that Urdu is written and read from right to left.

pronunciation	word	letters
a + **b** = **ab**	اَب =	اَ + ب
i + **s** = **is**	اِس =	اِ + س
u + **n** = **un**	اُن =	اُ + ن
ā + **b** = **āb**	آب =	آ + ب

The letter vāo (و)

vāo is a non-connector and has no separate positional shapes. In its initial form and after a vowel **ā** it represents only a **v/w** sound. It may represent three vowels, **o**, **ū** and **au**. But to distinguish vowels **ū** from **au**, it may occur with the signs **ulTā pesh** (ٗ) **zabar** (٘) respectively. See the chart below:

letter	name	sound	shapes			
			detached (independent)	final	medial	initial
و	vāo	v/w	و	و	و	و
		o	و	و	او	او
		ū	وٗ	وٗ	اوٗ	اوٗ
		au	وَ	اوَ	اوَ	اوَ

handwriting mode

(vāo) (madd) (ulTāpesh)

The combinations of **vāo** with other non-connector letters are given in the next section.

Non-connector consonants

First let's learn another diacritical superscript, which is shown below:

($\hat{\ }$), called **jazm**

It is written above and between two consonants to indicate a consonant cluster. For example, see the words **zard** and **dard** written below.

The following letters do not have separate initial and medial variants. Their final shape is different from the independent shape when they are connected to a preceding consonant. We will call the first four letters **re**- group letters and the last three **dāl**- group letters. Refer to the chart below:

letter	name	sound	shapes			
			detached (independent)	final	medial	initial
ر	**re**	**r**	ر	رـ ر	ر	ر
ژ	**Re**	**R**	ژ	ژـ ژ	ژ	ژ
ز	**ze**	**z**	ز	زـ ز	ز	ز
ژ	**že**	**ž**	ژ	ژـ ژ	ژ	ژ
د	**dāl**	**d**	د	دـ د	د	د
ڈ	**Dāl**	**D**	ڈ	ڈـ ڈ	ڈـ ڈ	ڈ
ذ	**zāl**	**z (ẓ)***	ذ	ذـ ذ	ذـ ذ	ذ

handwriting mode

(**re**-group)   (**dāl**-group)   (**jazm**)

Pronunciation and transcription note
As you can see from the transcription, letters

   ze (ز) zāl (ذ)

are both pronounced as **z**. **ze** occurs in most Urdu words representing the sound **z**, whereas **zāl** occurs only in a few Arabic loan words. In our English transcription, **z̤** will represent the letter **zāl**.

Following are the combinations of these consonants with the letters **vāo** and **alif**.

English	transcription	word		Urdu Letters
a + z =	az	اَز	=	ز + اَ
ā + R =	āR	آڑ	=	ڑ + آ
r + ū =	rū	رُو	=	و + رُ
d + o =	do	دو	=	و + د
D + a + r =	Dar	ڈَر	=	ر + ڈَ
au + r =	aur	اور	=	ر + او

Combinations of three or more letters

a + d + ā =	adā	اَدا	=	ا + د + اَ
r + ā + z =	rāz	راز	=	ز + ا + ر
d + a + v + ā =	davā	دَوا	=	ا + و + دَ
z̤ + a + r + ā =	zarā	ذَرا	=	ا + ر + ذَ
w + ā + r + D =	wārD	وارڈ	=	ڈ + ر + ا + و
z + a + r + d =	zard	زَرد	=	د + ر + زَ
d + a + r + d =	dard	دَرد	=	د + ر + دَ
ā + z + ā + d =	āzād	آزاد	=	د + ا + ز + آ

Exercises

1 ▪▪ Read aloud the following Urdu words. Feel free to consult the consonant chart on page 20. However, resist the temptation of transcribing and writing every letter before you pronounce the word. Treat this as an exercise in simple alphabetic addition. The difference is that you have words rather than numbers.

If you have the recording, you can compare your pronunciation with it.

(a) آداب	(b) آواز	(c) راب	(d) اور
(e) اُردو	(f) زور	(g) آرزو	(h) دور
(i) اَژدر	(j) دال	(k) دو	(l) زَر
(m) دَراز	(n) دِل	(o) زور	(p) اَب

2 Write the following words in Urdu script.

(a) ẓār	(b) azār	(c) dādā
(d) urdū	(e) darāz	(f) arvaRā
(g) doRo	(h) žāž	(i) āvārā
(j) ārzū	(k) uRā	(l) adā

Script unit 2

In script unit 1, we learned about non-connector letters. In this unit we introduce two sets of consonants which are connectors and learn to combine these letters with non-connectors. Connectors are linked to other letters by 'ligatures' (i.e. the tails which connect them to subsequent letters).

jīm **group letters**

All the letters in this section are connectors which look alike. They differ in the number and position of accompanying diacritic marks. We will call them **jīm**-group letters. These letters have similar initial and medial variants. Let us look at the chart given below:

letter	name	sound	shapes			
			detached (independent)	final	medial	initial
ج	**jīm**	**j**	ج	ج	ج	ج
چ	**ce**	**c**	چ	چ	چ	چ
ح	**he**	**h (H)***	ح	ح	ح	ح
خ	**xe**	**x**	خ	خ	خ	خ

handwriting mode

> *Script and transcription note*
>
> As mentioned in the section on Urdu Writing and Pronunciation, the letters **he** ح (**he** is also called **baRī he**) and **xe** خ are in origin Perso-Arabic sounds. There are two letters for the **h** sound:
>
> **he (ح) choTī he (ہ)**
>
> The use of **he** is limited to some Perso-Arabic loan words and will be transcribed in our script units as **H**.

Let us learn to combine these letters with the letters from Script Unit 1. Some of the words given below are nonsense words, and are used for the purpose of practising writing and pronunciation.

Initial variants

one-syllable words:

xā	خا = ا + خ	**cā**	چا = ا + چ	**jā**	جا = ا + ج
jo	جو = و + ج	**cau**	چو = و + چ	**Hū**	حو = و + ح
cār	چار = ر + ا + چ	**xar**	خر = ر + خ	**jū**	جو = و + ج

Medial variants

two-syllable words:

xacar	خچر = ر + چ + خ	**ujaH**	اجح = ح + ج + ا
jaxar	جخر = ر + خ + ج	**cacā**	چچا = ا + چ + چ

Final variants

jaj	جج = ج + ج	**Haj**	حج = ج + ح
xarc	خرچ = چ + ر + خ	**rūH**	روح = ح + و + ر
āj	آج = ج + آ	**rux**	رخ = خ + ر

Notes

When **dāl**-group letters (د ذ ز) are connected to a preceding letter, their form changes and they look similar to **re**-group letters. Needless to say, they are distinguished by the diacritic marks. Examples:

Had	حَد = د + حَ	**jaD**	جَد = د + جَ
vāHid	واحِد = د + حِ + ا + و	**xudā**	خُدا = ا + د + خُ
jaDā	جَدا = ا + د + جَ	**Haẓ**	حَذ = ذ + حَ

When **re**-type letters (ر ز ژ) are connected to a preceding letter their form also changes to (ر). Examples:

jaR	جَر = ر + جَ	**xar**	خَر = ر + خَ
āxir	آخِر = ر + خِ + آ	**carxā**	چَرخا = ا + خ + ر + چَ
Hirā	حِرا = ا + ر + حِ	**caz**	چَز = ز + چَ

Pronunciation note

Note that in some Persian loan words when **vāo** follows **xe**, it is not pronounced. Examples:

xud (xvud)	خُود = د + و + خُ
xāb (xvāb)	خواب = ب + ا + و + خ
xush (xvush)	خُوش = ش + و + خُ

sīn-**group letters**

The following letters are connectors. We will call them **sīn**-group
letters.

letter	name	sound	shapes			
			detached *(independent)*	*final*	*medial*	*initial*
س	**sīn**	s	س	ـس	ـسـ	سـ
ش	**shīn**	sh	ش	ـش	ـشـ	شـ
ص	**svād**	s (S)*	ص	ـص	ـصـ	صـ
ض	**zvād**	z (Z)*	ض	ـض	ـضـ	ضـ

handwriting mode

Pronunciation and transcription note
Note that both **sīn** and **svād** have s sounds. **sīn** is more frequent in
Urdu, whereas **svād** along with another Perso-Arabic letter **se** (ث)
(given in Script Unit 3) which also represents another sibilant
sound, s, are restricted in their use in Urdu. **svād** and **se** occur only
in some Perso-Arabic loan words. In our transcription, **s** will
represent the letter **sīn**, **S** will be used for **svād** and **s** will be used to
transcribe **se**. **Z** will represent the letter **zvād**.

Have you noticed that the first two letters **sīn** and **shīn** have two
variants each in initial and medial position? The first variant has three
hooks, called **shoshah**, and is more frequent in Urdu. The second
variant is rather restricted in use and may be used when the preceding
letter is one of the following:

  c^hoṬī ye (ی)   **baRī ye** (ے)

Let us learn to combine the four sīn-group letters with the non-connector letters discussed in Script Unit 1.

Initial variants

one-syllable words:

sā	سا = ١ + س	**shā**	شا = ١ + ش
Zā	ضا = ١ + ض	**sū**	سُؤ = ؤ + س
sho	شو = و + ش	**so**	سو = و + س
sāz	ساز = ز + ١ + س	**shād**	شاد = د + ١ + ش
shor	شور = ر + و + ش		

Medial variants

two-syllable words:

Hasad	حَسَد = د + س + ح
HuZūr	حُضُور = ر + و + ض + ح
aHsās	أحَساس = س + ١ + س + ح + أ
jashn	جَشن = ن + ش + ج

Final variants:

The following are some examples of these letters used in their final form:

ras	رَس = س + ر
sās	ساس = س + ١ + س
jāsūs	جاسُوس = س + ؤ + س + ١ + ج
sūraj	سُورج = ج + ر + ؤ + س
dozax	دوزَخ = خ + ز + و + د

Exercises

1 🔲 Read the following Urdu words aloud.
If you have the recording, you can check your pronunciation with the words recorded.

(a) چادَر   (b) جَ   (c) آشو   (d) دَرج   (e) ساسو

(f) پُوڑا   (g) خوَب   (h) سَود   (i) چور   (j) شوخ

(k) واحِد   (l) سَرا   (m) جارج   (n) جوش   (o) باجا

(p) جادُو   (q) سَو   (r) سارا   (s) صَدا   (t) اِس

(u) سَجاد   (v) ورزِش   (w) دوزَخ   (x) سُر   (y) سردار

2 Write the following words in Urdu script.

(a) **joRo**   (b) **judā**   (c) **xārij**   (d) **joRā**

(e) **rivāj**   (f) **carxā**   (g) **jis**   (h) **shād**

(i) **carc**   (j) **Zarūr**   (k) **shāx**   (l) **us**

(m) **sāzish**   (n) **Harj**   (o) **xāS**   (p) **sard**

(q) **HāZir**   (r) **dās**   (s) **rūs**

3 Form the words of the letters given below.

(a) ر + و + س =   (b) ص + خ + ش =

(c) ر + ا + ص + ج =   (d) خ + ا + ر + و + س =

(e) ا + و + ص =   (f) ا + ر + ج + ص =

Script unit 3

In this unit we introduce two more sets of consonants. All the letters in this unit are connectors.

be **group letters**

The following letters look alike; they differ mainly in the number and position of dots. We will call these **be**-group letters. They have three initial and two medial variants. Look at the chart given below:

letter	name	sound	shapes			
			detached (independent)	final	medial	initial
ب	**be**	**b**	ب	ب	ـ ـ	ـ با
پ	**pe**	**p**	پ	پ	ـ ـ	ـ پا
ت	**te**	**t**	ت	ت	ـ ـ	ـ تا
ٹ	**Te**	**T**	ٹ	ٹ	ـ ـ	ـ ٹا
ث	**se**	**s (ṣ)***	ث	ث	ـ ـ	ـ ثا
ن	**nūn**	**n**	ن	ـَن	ـ ـ	ـ نا

handwriting mode

Let us learn to combine these letters with **alif** and **vāo**.
Above consonants + **alif**

Tā	ٹا = ا + ٹ	**pā**	پا = ا + پ	**bā**	با = ا + ب
nā	نا = ا + ن	**tā**	تا = ا + ت	**ṣā**	ثا = ا + ث

consonants + **vāo**

Tau	ٹو = و + ٹ	**pū**	پُو = و + پ	**bo**	بو = و + ب
nū	نو = و + ن	**to**	تو = و + ت	**ṣau**	ثو = و + ث

Following are the combinations of the above letters with non-connector consonants.

re/ze, Re/že

Tir	ٹر = ر + ٹ	**puz**	پُز = ز + پ	**bar**	بَر = ر + ب
niz	نز = ز + ن	**ṭaR**	ٹڑ = ڑ + ٹ	**ṣur**	ثُر = ر + ث
baž	بَژ = ژ + ب	**TiR**	ٹِڑ = ڑ + ٹ	**nar**	نَر = ر + ن

dāl/Dāl/zāl

Tid	ٹِد = د + ٹ	**puD**	پُڈ = ڈ + پ	**bad**	بَد = د + ب
nad	نَد = د + ن	**taẓ**	تَذ = ذ + ت	**ṣaD**	ثَڈ = ڈ + ث

As mentioned earlier, the letters in the preceding chart have three variants in initial position and two in middle position.

Initial and medial variants

(ں) This shape is used before all non-connector letters except **vāo**, before the **be**-group consonants given above and before the following letters:

kāf (ک) **gāf** (گ) **lām** (ل)

(see Script Unit 4 for more examples.) Examples:

Initial position

but	بُت = ت + بُ	**pār**	پار = ر + ا + پ
ṣābit	ثابِت = ت + بِ + ا + ثٰ	**tandūr**	تَندُور = ر + وُ + د + ن + تَ

Medial position

xabr	خَمر = ر + ب + خ	**baTā**	بَٹا = ا + ٹ + بَ
taṣar	تاثر = ث + ا + ت	**tanā**	تَنا = ا + ن + تَ

(ں) This initial variant is used before the letter **vāo**, **sīn**-group consonants:

toi(ط) **zoi**(ظ) **ɛn**(ع) **Gɛn**(غ) **fe**(ن) **qāf**(ق) **cʰoTī**(ی) **baRī ye**(ے)

However, in medial position this variant is not used and the first initial variant (ں) is used instead. Examples:

Initial position

savāb	ثَواب = ب + ا + و + ثَ	**Top**	ٹوپ = پ + و + ٹ
per	پِیر = ر + ی + پ	**basr**	بَسَر = ر + س + بَ
pīnā	پِینا = ا + ن + ی + پ	**basʰr**	بَشَر = ر + ش + بَ

Medial position

cinor	پِنور = ر + و + ن + چ
janvarī	جَنوری = ی + ر + و + ن + ج

(/) This shape is used before **jīm**-group letters:

mīm (م) **do cashmī he** (ھ) **cʰoTī he** (ہ)

(see Script Units 4 and 5 for more examples.) Examples:

Initial position:

buxār	بُخار = ر + ا + خ + بُ	**nam**	نَم = م + نَ
taxt	تَخت = ت + خ + تَ	**bajā**	بَجا = ا + ج + بَ

Medial position

paTax	پَٹَخ = خ + ٹ + پَ	**xatm**	خَتم = م + ت + خَ
panjāb	پَنجاب = ب + ا + ج + ن + پَ	**caTax**	چَٹَخ = خ + ٹ + چَ

Script note: nasal consonant vs. vowel nasalization

The letter **nūn** has a final-position variant (**nun** without diacritic) called **nun-i-Gunnah**. It indicates nasalization at the end of a word. To indicate nasalization initially and medially, the letter **nūn** is always written with its diacritic and the symbol (◡) called **ulTā jazm**. This symbol may or may not be written over **nūn**. However, we will show the use of this symbol in our script units and text.

Vowel clusters and long ī

Following are two new symbols you should know in order to express vowel clusters and long ī.

(ء), called **hamzā**. This is written to indicate a vowel cluster in Urdu, e.g.:

ā-oṣī

(See more on **hamzā** later in this unit.)

(í), called **kʰaRā zer**. This is written below the letter **cʰoTī ye** to indicate long ī in initial and medial positions, e.g.:

اینٹ **īT**

We should mention here that this symbol is very rarely written.

Connector vowels

In this section we introduce two letters, **cʰoTī ye** and **baRī ye**, which represent three vowels, ī, e, ɛ, and a semivowel, **y**. Both these letters are connectors and, like the consonants given in the previous section, they have the same initial and medial variants.

cʰoTī ye in word-initial and medial positions may represent **y**. When a word begins with a vowel ī, it is written with the letter alif + initial variant of **cʰoTī ye**. The sign **kʰaRā zer** (í) is used under **cʰoTī** in initial and medial positions for the long vowel ī. In final position it represents only ī.

baRī ye represents the vowels **e** or **ɛ** (in which case it may occur with the superscript diacritic **zabar**). When a word begins with a vowel, **e** and **ɛ**, they are written with **alif** + initial variants of **baRī ye**.

The folowing chart gives the variants of these two letters.

letter	name	sound	shapes			
			detached (independent)	final	medial	initial
ی	cʰotī ye	y	ی		ﯾ	ﯾ ﻳ
ی	=	ī	ی	ﯿ	ﯾ	ﯾ ﻳ
ے	baRī ye	e	ے		ﯾ	ﯾ ﻳ
ے	=	ɛ	ﯦ	ﯦ	ﯾ	ﯾ ﻳ

handwriting mode

Initial and medial variants

As mentioned before, **cʰoTī ye** and **baRī ye** have identical initial and medial variants similar to the **be**-group letters in the previous section. Examples:

cʰoTī ye (ﯘ), baRī ye (ﯘ)

yār	یار = ر + ا + ی	**ek**	اﮮ = ک + اﮮ
yād	یاد = د + ا + ی	**terā**	تیرا = ا + ر + ی + ت
tīn	تین = ن + ی + ت	**jeb**	جیب = ب + ﮮ + ج

cʰoTī ye (ﯘ), baRī ye (ﯘ)

yom	یوم = م + و + ی	**ɛsā**	ایسا = ا + س + اﮮ
jyõ	جیوں = ں + و + ی + ج	**devar**	دیور = ر + و + ﮮ + د

cʰoTī ye (ﯘ), baRī ye (ﯘ)

yax	یخ = خ + ی	**ījād**	ایجاد = د + ا + ج + ای
nīc	نیچ = چ + ی + ن	**pɛc**	پیچ = چ + ﮮ + پ

Final variants

Following are some examples of vowels ī, e and ε in final position:

ārī	آری = ی + ر + آ	**nadī**	نَدی = ی + د + نَ
de	دے = ے + د	**pī**	پی = ی + پ
roze	روزے = ے + ز + و + ر	**dādī**	دادی = ی + د + ا + د
darzī	دَرزی = ی + ز + ر + دَ	**zare**	زَرے = ے + ر + زَ
darī	دَری = ی + ر + دَ	**pε**	پَے = ے + پَ
jī	جی = ی + ج		

Use of hamzā (ء)

This symbol represents a glottal stop in Arabic. However, in Urdu
it is written to indicate a vowel cluster and does not represent any
sound of its own. With **cʰoTī ye** and **baRī ye**, **hamzā** is written over
the initial variant (ئ) of **be**-group consonants. Examples:

ā + ī	آئی = ی + آ	**piTāī**	پِٹائی = ئ + ا + ٹ + پِ
jāe	جائے = ئے + ج	**jā + o**	جاؤ = ؤ + ا + ج
gāõ	گاؤں = ں + اؤ + گ	**nā + ī**	نائی = ئ + ا + ن
pā + e	پائے = ئے + ا + پ	**ā + o**	آؤ = ؤ + آ

Exercises

1 ☐☐ Read the following Urdu words aloud. If you have the
recording you can check your pronunciation with the words recorded.

(a) اِجازت	(b) خُوب	(c) ضَرورت	(d) ناراض	(e) سَجاوٹ
(f) کُمار	(g) موتی	(h) وارث	(i) خُونی	(j) بِزار
(k) دَرَخت	(l) پانچ	(m) بیوی	(n) اَرے	(o) تِجارت
(p) چاند	(q) اوُنچا	(r) زَبانی	(s) پیش	(t) دیور
(u) دونوں	(v) شَرابی	(w) پَسَند	(x) بُرائی	(y) نُخرے

2 Write the following words in Urdu script.

(a) **tīr**	(b) **ret**	(c) **tīn**	(d) **batī**
(e) **apnā**	(f) **ūn**	(g) **bū**	(h) **adab**
(i) **buniyād**	(j) **jɛsā**	(k) **bīn**	(l) **pīnā**
(m) **tālī**	(n) **nāz**	(o) **merā**	(p) **roz**
(q) **Tab**	(r) **doR**	(s) **potā**	(t) **Topī**
(u) **yūnānī**	(v) **bāp**	(w) **nas**	

3 Form the words of the letters given below:

(a) ت + ے + ر + ی (b) أ + ن + ا + ج

(c) ن + ا + ش + ے + ر + پَ (d) ب + ا + ت + و + ن + ی

(e) ن + ا + چ + ن + ا (f) ت + ر + ض + ح

(g) ص + ب + ح (h) ح + ا + س + ب

(i) ش + ا + د + ی

Script unit 4

In this unit, we introduce three sets of consonants.

Letters lām(ل) and mīm(م)

The first set includes two letters (**lām** and **mīm**) which are also connectors. The chart below gives the variants of these two consonants:

| letter | name | sound | shapes | | |
			detached (independent)	final	medial	initial
ل	**lām**	**l**	ل	ل	ل	ل
م	**mīm**	**m**	م	م	م	م

handwriting mode

Initial variants: lām (ل), mīm (م)

Examples:

lo	لو = و + ل	**lām**	لام = م + ا + ل
lāl	لال = ا + ل	**māl**	مال = ل + ا + م
mil	مِل = ل + م	**motī**	موتی = ی + ت + و + م

Medial variants: lām (ل) mīm (م)

Examples:

zalīl	ذَلیل = ل + ی + ل + ذَ	**bulbul**	بُلبُل = ل + بُ + ل + بُ
camār	جُمار = ر + ا + م + جُ	**xalīl**	خَلیل = ل + ی + ل + خَ
namī	نَمی = ی + م + نَ	**malmal**	مَلمَل = ل + م + ل + مَ

Final variants: lām (ل) mīm (م)

Examples:

shabnam	شَبنم = م + نَ + ب + شَ	**cal**	چَل = ل + چَ
ām	آم = م + آ	**ārām**	آرام = م + ا + ر + آ
dāl	دال = ل + ا + د	**shāl**	شال = ل + ا + شَ

Letters fe (ف) and qāf (ق)

The next set of consonants (**fe** and **qāf**) are connectors. They have similar initial and medial variants but differ in their final shape. Note that **fe** takes only one dot whereas **qāf** takes two dots. Look at the chart given below:

letter	name	sound	shapes			
			detached (independent)	final	medial	initial
ف	**fe**	**f**	ف	ـف	ـفـ	ف
ق	**qāf**	**q**	ق	ـق	ـقـ	ق

Handwriting mode

Let us learn to form words using letters **fe** and **qāf** in initial, medial and final positions.

Initial variants: fe (ف) qāf (ق)

Examples:

fā	فا = ا + ف	**fidā**	فِدا = ا + د + فِ
far	فر = ر + ف	**qadar**	قَدر = ر + دَ + ق
qarār	قَرار = ر + ا + ر + ق		

Medial variants: fe (ن) qāf(ق)

Examples:

safar	سَفَر = ر + ف + س	**nafrat**	نَفرَت = ت + رَ + ف + نَ
sifar	سِفَر = ر + ف + سِ	**sāqī**	ساقی = ی + ق + ا + س
bāqar	باقر = ر + ق + ا + بَ	**naql**	نَقل = ل + ق + نَ

Final variants: fe (ن) qāf(ق)

Examples:

alif	الف = ف + ل + ا	**xāliq**	خالق = ق + ل + ا + خ
Sāf	صاف = ف + ا + ص	**Sarf**	صَرف = ف + ر + صَ
varq	وَرق = ق + ر + وَ	**firāq**	فِراق = ق + ا + ر + فِ

Script note:
The letter **qāf** is borrowed from Perso-Arabic languages and is commonly used in Urdu.

Letters kāf (ک) and gāf (گ)

The following two consonants are connectors. Both these consonants
have two initial variants. Check the chart given below:

letter	name	sound	shapes			
			detached (independent)	final	medial	initial
ک	kāf	k	ک	ـک	ـ	گ
گ	gāf	g	گ	ـگ	ـ	گ

handwriting mode

Initial and medial variants (Type 1): kāf (گ), gāf (گ)

These variants are used only before **alif** and **lām** letters.

Examples:

kā	کا = ا + ک	**klās**	کلاس = س + ا + ل + ک
kal	کل = ل + ک	**gā**	گا = ا + گ
gul	گل = ل + گ	**glās**	گلاس = س + ا + ل + گ
nikal	نکل = ل + ک + نِ	**kaṇgā**	کنگا = ا + گ + ن + ک

Initial and medial variants (Type 2): kāf (ک), gāf (گ)

These variants are used elsewhere.

Examples:

ko	کو = و + ک	**karoR**	کروڑ = ڑ + و + ر + ک
kab	کب = ب + ک	**girā**	گرا = ا + ر + گِ
gum	گم = م + ک	**gīlā**	گیلا = ا + ل + ی + گِ

fikr	فِکر = ر + ک + فِ	**magar**	مَگَر = ر + گ + مَ
jigar	جِگَر = ر + گ + جِ		

Final variants: kāf (ک), gāf (گ)

Examples:

kap	کپ = پ + کَ	**taŋg**	تَنگ = گ + ن + تَ
raŋg	رنگ = گ + ن + ر	**cāk**	چاک = ک + ا + چ
nāk	ناک = ک + ا + ن	**ruk**	رُک = ک + رُ
āg	آگ = گ + آ	**jāg**	جاگ = گ + ا + ج
rāg	راگ = گ + ا + ر		

Learn to write words with two syllables or more:

koshish	کوشِش = ش + وِ + و + کَ
gulāb	گُلاب = ب + ا + لَ + گُ
kamān	کمان = ن + ا + م + کَ
nikālnā	نِکالنا = ا + ن + ل + ا + کَ + نِ
nigalnā	نِگلنا = ا + ن + لَ + گ + نِ
gulshan	گلشَن = ن + ش + لَ + گُ
kavvā	کوّا = ا + و + و + کَ
kaccā	کچّا = ا + چ + چ + کَ

Doubled consonants

Let us now learn to write doubled consonants in Urdu.

(ّ), tashdīd

When two identical consonants occur together in a word, only one is written and the superscript **tashdīd** is placed over it to indicate its gemination. However, verb forms are written with both consonants and **tashdīd** is not used.

Examples:

dillī	دِلّی = ی + ل + ل + دِ	**lassī**	لَسّی = ی + س + س + لَ	
aDDā	اَڈّا = ا + ڈ + ڈ + اَ	**abbā**	اَبّا = ا + ب + ب + اَ	
kuttā	کُتّا = ا + ت + ت + کُ			

Verb forms:

bannā بَنّا = ا + ن + ن + بَ **sunnā** سُنّا = ا + ن + ن + سُ

When an unaspirated consonant is immediately followed by its corresponding aspirated counterpart, only the aspirated consonant is written with a **tashdīd** over it. (Note: see script unit 5 for how aspirated consonants are written.)

Examples:

macc\u02b0ar	مَچّھر = ر + ھ + چ + چ + مَ
acc\u02b0ā	اَچّھا = ا + ھ + چ + چ + اَ
acc\u02b0ī	اَچّھی = ی + ھ + چ + چ + اَ
makk\u02b0ī	مَکّھی = ا + ی + ھ + ک + ک + مَ

Exercises

1 🔲🔲 Read the following Urdu words aloud. If you have the recording, you can check the pronunciation with the words recorded.

(a)	والد	(b)	اسلام	(c)	موٹا	(d)	یَلی	(e)	سَلام
(f)	شوق	(g)	قَدَم	(h)	مَحل	(i)	آلو	(j)	کوکی
(k)	کمبل	(l)	گَرَم	(m)	گالی	(n)	بگڑوا	(o)	اَککا
(p)	موتی	(q)	سرسی	(r)	مکان	(s)	کَمبا	(t)	لیکن
(u)	گاڑی	(v)	کپڑوا	(w)	پکوان	(x)	لیٹا	(y)	کسی

2 Write the following words in the Urdu script.

(a)	**faqīr**	(b)	**jism**	(c)	**fauj**
(d)	**log**	(e)	**nām**	(f)	**sabaq**
(g)	**kamrā**	(h)	**namak**	(i)	**agar**
(j)	**patlā**	(k)	**cāqū**	(l)	**camcā**
(m)	**Tokrī**	(n)	**maTkā**	(o)	**qabz**

(p) **aŋgūr**   (q) **salām**   (r) **afsos**
(s) **fasād**   (t) **farsh**   (u) **sharīf**

3 Form words from the letters given below:

(a) م + ا + گ + ل   (b) ک + ل + ش + ن
(c) خ + ا + لِ + ی   (d) مَ + ل + ا + ل
(e) م + و + سؔ + م   (f) تَ + ش + ر + ی + ف
(g) اَ + م + ی + ر   (h) اَ + ل + م + ا + ر + ی
(i) خ + چ + چ + ر   (j) ق + ر + ب + ا + ن

Script unit 5

This unit has three sections. Two letters are given in each section. First, let us learn about a new sign used in the Urdu writing system.

(˝), tanvīn do zabar

This sign is written over the final letter **alif** for the pronunciation of the sound sequence **an** in some Arabic loan words. These words are not written as a combination of **alif + nūn**.

Examples:

fauran	فوراً	=	ا + ر + و + ف			
maṣlan	مثلاً	=	ا + ل + ث + م			
qānūnan	قانوناً	=	اً + ن + و + ن + ا + ق			
jabran	جبراً	=	ا + ر + ب + ج			
majbūran	مجبوراً	=	اً + ر + و + ب + ج + م			
nisbatan	نسبتاً	=	اً + ت + ب + س + ن			

Letters cʰoTī he (ہ) and do-cashmī he (ھ)

Both the letters **cʰoTī he** (lit. small **he**) and **do-cashmī he** (lit.two -eyed **he**) are connectors. **cʰoTī he** has different variants in initial, medial and final positions. **do-cashmī he** has similar shapes in all positions. Look at the chart given below:

letter	name	sound	shapes			
			detached (independent)	final	medial	initial
٥	cʰoTī he	**h**	٥	٥	٦	۲ ٦
ھ	do-cashmī he	aspiration	ھ	ھ	ھ	ھ

Handwriting mode

Pronunciation note:

baRī he (ح) and **cʰoTī he** (٥) are both pronounced as **h** in Urdu.
However, the use of **baRī he** is limited to some Perso-Arabic loan words.

---

choTī he (٥)

You must have noticed that **cʰoTī he** has two variants in initial position.

Initial variants (Type 1): (ہ)

This variant occurs before **dāl** and **re**-group consonants and also before **alif, kāf, gāf, lām** and final **cʰoTī ye** and **baRī ye** letters.

Examples:

hār	ہار = ر + ا + ٥	**har**	ہر = ر + ٥
hε	ہل = ل + ٥	**hal**	ہل = ل + ٥

Initial variants (Type 2): (ﮩ)

This variant occurs elsewhere. Examples:

ham	نَم = م + ﻫ	**havā**	ﮨَوا = ا + و + ﮨ
haT	ﮨَٹ = ٹ + ﻫ	**hic**	ﮨِچ = چ + ﮨ

Medial variants: (ﮭ)

Examples:

mahak	مَہک = ک + ﮦ + مَ
pahāR	پہاڑ = ڑ + ا + ﮦ + پ
bɛhen	بہن = ن + ﮦ + بَ
sahārā	سہارا = ا + ر + ا + ﮦ + س
kahā	کہا = ا + ﮦ + ک

Final variants: (ﮧ)

This variant is written when the preceding letter is a connector.

Examples:

xazānah	خزانہ = ﮧ + ن + ا + ز + خ
rishtah	رشتہ = ﮧ + ت + ش + ر
peshah	پیشہ = ﮧ + ش + ے + پ

Final variants: (ﮦ)

This final variant is written when the preceding letter is a non-connector. Most of these words are also pronounced with final **ā**.

Examples:

rozah	روزه = ﮦ + ز + و + ر
āvārah	آواره = ﮦ + ر + ا + و + آ
terah	تیره = ﮦ + ر + ے + ت

Pronunciation notes

It is important to note that when c**h**oTī he occurs after a consonant in the final position, it is usually pronounced as the long vowel ā. Most of these words are Perso-Arabic loan words.

Examples:

irādā	اِرادہ =	ہ + د + ا + ر + اِ
sādā	سادہ =	ہ + د + ا + س
baccā	بَچّ =	ہ + چ + چ + بَ
zālā	زالہ =	ہ + ل + ا + ز
bandā	بَندہ =	ہ + د + ن + بَ
parvānā	پَروانہ =	ہ + ن + ا + و + ر + پَ
āhistā	آہِستہ =	ہ + ت + س + ہ + آ
ishārā	اِشارہ =	ہ + ر + ا + ش + اِ
zindā	زِندہ =	ہ + د + ن + ز
zamānā	زَمانہ =	ہ + ن + ا + م + زَ

The following are some common exceptions. They are not pronounced with ā. Instead, the final **h** is pronounced:

vāh	واہ =	ہ + ا + و	**gavāh**	گواہ =	ہ + ا + و + گ
vajah	وَجہ =	ہ + ج + وَ	**jagah**	جَگہ =	ہ + گ + جَ
āh	آہ =	+ ہ + آ	**mah**	مَاہ =	ہ + ا + مَ

Some words give the sound of **a** as in (نَ) **na**, **e** as in (کے) **ke** and in (یے) **ye**.

Aspiration (do-cashmī he) (ھ)

do-cashmī he represents aspiration in Urdu and all aspirated consonants are written by adding it to the unaspirated consonants. Learn from the consonants given below how the preceding letters are joined to it:

kʰ	کھ	**g**ʰ	گھ	**c**ʰ	چھ	**j**ʰ	جھ	**T**ʰ	ٹھ
Dʰ	ڈھ	**p**ʰ	پھ	**b**ʰ	بھ	**R**ʰ	ڑھ	**d**ʰ	دھ

Now, let us combine these aspirated consonants with other letters to form some words:

k^haRā کھڑا = ا + ڑ + ھَ + ک		g^har گھر = ر + ھ + گ	
c^hat چھت = ت + ھ + چ		b^hāī بھائی = ئی + ا + ھ + ب	
kab^hī کبھی = ی + ھ + ب + ک		and^hā أندھا = ا + ھ + د + ن + أ	
paR^h پڑھ = ھ + ڑ + پَ		lik^h لِکھ = ھ + ک + ل	
T^hīk ٹھیک = ک + ی + ھَ + ٹ		p^hal پھل = ل + ھ + پَ	
j^hal جھل = ل + ھَ + ج		D^hak ڈھک = ک + ھَ + ڈ	

Letters to'e (ط) and zo'e (ظ)

Both the letters given below are connectors. They look alike and are differentiated by a dot. Their forms never change in any position except for a minor difference, i.e. medial/final forms have a preceding ligature (ﻂ and ﻆ).

letter	name	sound	shapes			
			detached (independent)	final	medial	initial
ط	**to'e**	t (ṫ)*	ط	ﻂ	ﻄ	ط
ظ	**zo'e**	z (ż)*	ظ	ﻆ	ﻈ	ظ

handwriting mode

> *Pronunciation and transcription note*
>
> As mentioned before, the two letters ط and ظ are borrowed from Arabic,
> where they have different sounds. But in Urdu they are pronounced as **t**
> and **z**, respectively and occur only in Arabic loan words. Thus, in Urdu
> there are two letters which represent the sound **t**:
>
> ت and ط
>
> and four letters which represent the sound **z**
>
> ز ,ظ ,ذ ,and ض
>
> The symbol **ṫ** will be used for the letter **to'e** and **ż** will be used to transcribe
> the letter **zo'e.**

Combination of these letters with other consonants:

ṫā	طا = ا + ط	**ṫaq**	طاق = ط + ا + ق = طاق
ṫoṫā	طوطا = ط + و + ط + ا + ط	**żālim**	ظالم = ظ + ا + ل + م = ظالم
żulm	ظلم = ظ + ل + م + ظ	**xiṫāb**	خطاب = خ + ط + ا + ب = خطاب
xāṫir	خاطر = خ + ا + ط + ر	**iżhar**	اظہار = ا + ظ + ہ + ا + ر = اظہار
nāżir	ناظر = ن + ا + ظ + ر	**faqṫ**	فقط = ف + ق + ط = فقط
liHāż	لحاظ = ل + ح + ا + ظ	**żāhir**	ظاہر = ظ + ا + ہ + ر = ظاہر
Hāfiż	حافظ = ح + ا + فـ + ظ		

Letters ɛn (ع) and Gɛn (غ)

The following two letters are connectors. Also, note that there is a
significant difference between the final and the detached
(independent) forms. The pronunciation of the letter **ɛn** differs in
different positions. (See Pronunciation notes for details). Look at the
chart given below:

letter	name	sound	shapes			
			detached (independent)	final	medial	initial
ع	ɛn	'*	ع	ع	ـعـ	عـ
غ	Gɛn	G	غ	غ	ـغـ	غـ

handwriting mode

(*See letter **ɛn** below for the pronunciation.)

Initial variant (Type 1):

In their initial form, both these letters have two variants.
ɛn (ع) **Gɛn** (غ). These variants are used when the following letter is
alif or **lām**. The transliteration of the script is given within brackets,
while the pronunciation is given without brackets.

Examples:

ām ('ām)   عام = م + ا + ع   **ālim ('ālim)**   عالم = م + ل + ا + ع

Gār   غار = ر + ا + غ   **Gulām**   غلام = م + ا + ل + غ

ɛn (ﻉ) **Gɛn** (ﻍ). These initial variants are used elsewhere.

Examples:

amal ('amal) عمل = ل + م + ع   **aql ('aql)**   عقل = ل + ق + ع

arz ('arz) عرض = ض + ر + ع   **Gɛr**   غیر = ر + ی + غ

Gazal غزل = ل + ز + غ   **Gor**   غور = ر + و + غ

Medial variants: ɛn (ﻌ), Gɛn (ﻐ)

Examples:

tālīm
(ta'līm)   تعلیم = م + ی + ل + ع + ت

mālūm
(ma'lūm)   معلوم = م + و + ل + ع + م

afGān   أفغان = ن + ا + غ + ف + أ

pɛGām   پیغام = م + ا + غ + ی + پ

Final variants

ɛn (ﻊ), **Gɛn** (ﻎ). These variants are used when the preceding letter is a connector.

Examples:

nafā (naf'a)	نَفع = ع + ف + نَ	**jamā)** (jam'a)	جَمع = ع + م + جَ
zilā (zil'a)	ضلع = ع + ل + ضِ	**bāliG**	بالغ = غ + ل + ا + بَ
teG	تیغ = غ + ی + ت		

When the preceding letter is a non-connector, **ɛn** (ع) and **Gɛn** (غ) are written in the independent (detached) form.

Examples:

shurū (shurū')	شروع = ع + و + ر + ش
ruju (ruju')	رجوع = ع + و + ج + رُ
dimāG	دِماغ = غ + ا + م + دِ
bāG	باغ = غ + ا + ب
dāG	داغ = غ + ا + د

Pronunciation notes: the letter ɛn (ع)

As we have mentioned in the previous unit (and see Urdu writing system and pronunciation), this consonant is a glottal fricative in Arabic. However, in Urdu it is not pronounced as such and its pronunciation differs in different positions.

In initial position it indicates long **ā**, **ī** , **ɛ**, and **au** when followed by **alif**, **cʰoTī ye**, **baRī ye** and **vāo** respectively.

Examples:

ādī	عادی = ی + د + ا+ ع	**ārzī**	عرضی = ی + ض + ر + ع
āshiq	عاشق = ق + شِ + ا + ع	**īd**	عید = د + ی + ع
īsvī	عیسوی = ی + و + س + ی + ع	**īsā**	عیسا = ا + س + ی + ع
ɛsh	عیش = ش + ی + ع	**ɛb**	عیب = ب + ی + ع
ɛnak	عینک = ک + نَ + ی + ع	**aurat**	عورت = ت + ر + و + ع
aud	عود = د + و + ع		

Again, in initial position, followed by any other letter, it indicates the short vowels **a**, **i** and **u**.

Examples:

arab ('arab) عرب = ب + ر + ع   **ilm ('ilm)** علم = م + ل + ع

ajīb ('ajīb) عجیب = ب + ی + ج + ع   **izzat('izzat)** عزّت = ت + ز + ز + ع

imārat ('imārat) عمارت = ت + ر + ا + م + ع

umar ('umar) عمر = ر + م + ع   **umdā ('umdā)** عمدہ = ہ + د + م + ع

When it occurs in medial position between vowels, it is pronounced as a glottal stop by some educated Urdu speakers who have some knowledge of Arabic. Such words are pronounced with a vowel cluster by most speakers.

Examples:

māvZā (mu'āvZāh) معاوضہ = ہ + ض + و + ع + م

māf (mu'āf) معاف = ف + ا + ع + م

jamāt (jam'at) جماعت = ت + ع + ا + م + ج

In final position, after a consonant, it gives the sound of the long vowel **ā**, but loses the pronunciation when it occurs after a long vowel.

Examples:

mauqā (mauqā') موقع = ع + ق + و + م

mana (mana') منع = ع + ن + م

shurū (shurū') شروع = ع + و + ر + ش

rujū (rujū') رجوع = ع + و + ج + ر

Exercises

1 Write the following expressions in Urdu. These are very useful expressions, so their meanings are also given.

(a)   **tʰānā vahī̃ hɛ.**
      'The police station is right there.'

(b) **āp merī madad kar sakte hɛ̃?**
      'Can you help me?'

(c) **mɛ̃ vahā̃ kɛse jāū̃?**
      'How shall I get there?'

(d) **ye merī Galtī hɛ.**
      'This is my mistake.'

(e) **yahā̃ xatrā hɛ.**
      'There is a danger here.'

(f) **bacāo!**
      'Help!'

(g) **mālūmat kā daftar**
      'Enquiry office'

(h) **mɛ̃ rāstā bʰūl gayī hū̃.**
      'I (f.) am lost.' (lit. I have lost my way.)

(i) **taŋg mat karo.**
      'Do not bother me.'

(j) **mɛ̃ cābī dʰūndʰ rahā hū̃.**
      'I am looking for my key.'

(k) **nahī̃ mil rahī.**
      '(I) can't find it (f.).'

2 Combine the following letters to form words.

(a)   م + ا + ل + غ   (b)   ن + ا + ف + د + ط

(c)   ط + ف + ل   (d)   ز + ے + ہ + ر + پ

(e)   ک + ن + ی + ج   (f)   ت + د + ی + ق + ع

Syllables, stress and intonation

You must have heard the expression 'it is not what you say that matters but how you say it.' In this unit we consider some 'how to' aspects of script and pronunciation together with some other questions, such as significant and insignificant variations.

Syllables

Vowel and consonant segments can be combined into units which are called syllables. A syllable refers to the smaller unit of a word. The syllable boundary is indicated by the symbol #, as follows:

between successive vowels

word		syllabification	
جاؤ	jāo	جا # و	jā # o
نئی	naī	نَ # ئ	na # ī
کھاۓ	kʰāe	کھا # ۓ	kʰā # e

between vowels and consonants

word		syllabification	
جاتا	jātā	جا # تا	jā # tā
سونا	sonā	سو # نا	so # nā
پکا	pakā	پ # کا	pā # kā

between consonants

word			*syllabification*		
سُرکیں	saRkẽ		سُر # کیں	saR # kẽ	
آدمی	ādmī		آد # می	ād # mī	

Stress

Stress means loudness, a change in volume to express a wide variety of meanings such as emotions, contrast, focus and change in grammatical categories. It refers to the most prominent part of a syllable or word. As in English, stress distinguishes some nouns from verbs in Urdu, as in:

noun			*verb*		
گلا	*ga*lā	neck	گلا	**galā**	cause to become tender (i.e. meat)
تلا	*ta*lā	sole	تلا	**talā**	cause to fry

(The stressed syllable is in italics.)

However, stress is usually indistinguishable in Urdu. Therefore, whether one places the stress on the first syllable or on the second, the meaning will not be affected, nor will the quality of the pronunciation of the vowel:

سنا	*su*nā	su*nā*

This tendency is different from English, where the vowel in the unstressed syllable is reduced, such as in 'Alaska', and one witnesses a difference between the pronunciation of the a in the middle position (i.e. stressed syllable) and in the word-initial and -final position (i.e. unstressed syllables). This is why stress is not as distinctive and crucial in Urdu as in English. Urdu is a language like French, where the syllables are pronounced in a steady flow, resulting in a 'machine gun' effect.

The predominant pattern in Urdu is to stress the penultimate (second to last) syllable, as in:

کرایہ	**kirāyā**	rent
جانا	**jānā**	to go
چیتا	**citā**	leopard
اندو	**indu**	a name

Since short vowels are not stressed in English, the chances are you will not hear the stress on syllables with short vowels.

However, the long vowels are always stressed and thus, take precedence over the penultimate syllable rule, e.g.:

| تاریݨی | **tāriNī** | a female name |
| سرکہ | **sirkā** | vinegar |

Also, notice that if there is more than one long syllable, the stress falls on the first syllable.

In compound words the stress is usually placed on the second word, as in:

| بات چیت | **bāt**-*cīt* | conversation |
| بول چال | **bol**-*cā-l* | chit-chat |

In interrogative questions, the question word is usually stressed:

آپ کیا کریں گے؟

| **āp** | *kyā* | **karẽge?** |
| you | what | do-will |

'What will you do?'

آپ یہ کیوں کریں گے؟

| **āp** | **ye** | *kyõ* | **karẽge?** |
| you | this | why | do-will |

'Why will you do this?'

آپ کہاں جائیں گے؟

| **āp** | *kahā̃* | **jaẽge?** |
| you | where | go-will |

'Where will you go?'

Intonation patterns

Take, for example, the word **acc^hā** 'good, OK', which can be
pronounced with different intonation in different contexts. When
acc^hā is uttered in the following five contexts: (i) in a response to an
enquiry 'what kind of person is x'?; (ii) in a statement expressing
surprise, e.g. 'is that so?'; (iii–v) as an expression of agreement,
disagreement, or detachment, it will be articulated with different
intonations. Intonation is the rise and fall of the pitch of the voice.
Urdu exhibits the following four main intonation patterns:

Rising   ➚

Falling   ➘

Rising, falling and rising   ∧➚

Neutral or level   ▬

Rising intonation

As in English, the intonation rises towards the end of the sentence in
yes - no questions:

کیا آپ وہاں جائیں گے ؟

kyā	**āp**	**vahā̃**	**jāẽge?**
what	you	there	go-will

'Will you go there?'

In exclamatory sentences the intonation rises sharply:

وہ کامیاب ہو گیا؟

vo	**kāmyāb**	**ho**	**gayā!**
he	pass	be	went

'He passed (the exam)!'

Falling intonation

Statements, expressions and interrogative questions show this intonation pattern:

لڑکا اچھا ہے

laRkā	**acchā**	**hɛ.**
boy	good	is

'He is a good boy'

تمباکو نوشی منع ہے

tambāku	**naushī**	**manā**	**hɛ.**
tobacco	smoke	prohibited	is

'Smoking tobacco is prohibited.' (No smoking.)

آپ کہاں جائیں گے؟

āp	**kahā̃**	**jāēge?**
you	where	go-will

'Where will you go?'

Rising–falling and rising

In tag questions intonation rises at the beginning of the verb and falls at the termination of the verb, and then rises slightly again while the tag marker is pronounced:

آپ آئیں گے نا؟

āp	**āyēge**	**na?**
you	come-will	tag

'You will come, won't you?'

Neutral or level

Ordinary imperative sentences are uttered with a neutral or level intonation:

تم جاؤ

tum   jāo

'You go.'

Linguistic variation

As mentioned in the section on the Urdu Writing System and Pronunciation, Urdu is spoken in a vast region of South Asia and outside South Asia. Therefore, it is natural to expect linguistic variation in the regions. Some regional pronunciation differences have already been pointed out in the treatment of the description of Urdu vowels and borrowed consonant sounds. One can easily witness some variation with regard to the pronunciation of word-final and -medial pronunciation of **a**. In the eastern and southern varieties of Urdu the vowel **a** is retained in both positions. However, the **a** is dropped in Standard Urdu, as shown below:

کرسی	**kurasī**	کرسی	**kursī**	chair
سردی	**saradī**	سردی	**sardī**	winter, cold
گرمی	**garamī**	گرمی	**garmī**	summer
نزدیک	**nazadīk**	نزدیک	**nazdīk**	near
قتل	**qatal**	قتل	**qatl**	murder

Another important source of variation is the consonant h. The preceding stressed vowel a becomes ε if h is followed by a non-vowel sound. For example:

کہہ	**kah**	but pronounced as	**kε**
رہنا	**rahnā**	but pronounced as	**rεhnā**
وہ	**vah**	but pronounced as	**vo**
یہ	**yah**	but pronounced as	**ye**

The stressed vowel is in italics. The only exceptions are the third person singular pronouns which are pronounced as **vo** and **ye**, respectively.

If the **h** is preceded by **a** and followed by **u**, the **h** is dropped and the merger of the two vowels either results in **au** (as in English 'c<u>au</u>ght') or **o**. For example, **bahut** is pronounced as either **baut** or **bot**.

Exercises 📼

1 If you have the recording, listen to the following questions and answers, and the intonation patterns involved in them. Otherwise, seek the assistance of a native speaker.

(a) Yes-no type

QUESTION: **kyaa vo kāmyāb ho gayā?** *'Did he pass (the exam.)?'*

کیا وہ کامیاب ہو گیا؟

ANSWER: **hā̃.** *'yes'*

ہاں

(b) Information question

QUESTION: **kaun sā darjā milā?** *'What grade did he get?'*

کونسا درجہ ملا؟

ANSWER: **aval darjā.** *'First class.'*

اوّل درجہ

(c) Statement

vo accʰā laRkā hɛ. *'He is a good boy.'*

وہ اچھا لڑکا ہے

(d) Surprise

STATEMENT: **vo kāmyāb ho gayā.** *'He passed the exam.'*

ANSWER: **acchā!** (with surprised intonation) implying *'Is that so? I don't believe it.'*

وہ کامیاب ہو گیا؟

اچھا

(e) Agreement

SUGGESTION:	**āo, film dek^hne calē.**	*'Come, let's go and see a film.'*
AGREEMENT:	**acc^hā.** *'OK.'*	

آؤ فلم دیکھنے چلیس

اچھا

(f) Detached

SUGGESTION:	**āo, film dek^hne calē.**	*'Come, let's go and see a film.'*
AGREEMENT:	**acc^hā.** *'OK.'*	

آؤ فلم دیکھنے چلیس

اچھا

(g) Normal commands

darvāzā band karo.   *'Close the door.'*

دروازہ بند کرو

2 Listen to the stressed syllable in the following words.

(a)	ki*rā*yā	کرایہ	rent
(b)	*jā*nā	جانا	to go
(c)	cī*tā*	چیتا	leopard
(d)	*in*du	اندو	a name
(e)	*gu*lāb	گلاب	a rose
(f)	kan*i*kā	کنیکا	a female name
(g)	*tā*riNī	تاریٹی	a female name
(h)	sir*kā*	سرکہ	vinegar

Perso-Arabic transcription of texts and dialogues

Unit 1

Dialogue 1

تحسین: السلام علیکم، رضیہ

رضیہ: وعلیکم السلام۔ سب خیریت ہے؟

تحسین: مہربانی ہے، اور آپ کے مزاج کیسے ہیں؟

رضیہ: اللہ کا شکر ہے۔

(The conversation continues for some time)

تحسین: اچھا خُدا حافظ۔

رضیہ: خُدا حافظ۔

Dialogue 2

موہن: آداب عرض جناب۔

شاہد: آداب! کیا حال ہے موہن صاحب؟

موہن: ٹھیک ہے اور آپ؟

شاہد: میں بھی ٹھیک ہوں، حکم کیجیے۔

موہن: حکم نہیں، گزارش ہے۔

(The conversation continues for some time)

موہن: اچھا خُدا حافظ۔

شاہد: خُدا حافظ۔

Unit 2

Dialogue 1

بشیر: کہیئے، آپ کا اسم شریف ڈاکٹر ذاکر خان ہے نا؟

ڈاکٹر خان: جی ہاں میرا نام ذاکر خان ہے۔

(Extending his hand to shake hands)

بشیر: میرا نام بشیر ہے۔

ڈاکٹر خان: مل کر بڑی خوشی ہوئی۔ آپ کا پورا نام کیا ہے؟

بشیر: بشیر احمد ہے۔

ڈاکٹر خان: آپ کیا کرتے ہیں؟

بشیر: میں اسٹاک بروکر ہوں۔ آپ طبّی ڈاکٹر ہیں؟

ڈاکٹر خان: جی نہیں، میں طبّی ڈاکٹر نہیں ہوں۔ ایک اور قسم کا ڈاکٹر ہوں۔

Dialogue 2

فاطمہ: آپ کہاں کی ہیں؟

سائرہ: میں دلّی کی ہوں۔ اور آپ؟

فاطمہ: میں بنارس میں رہتی ہوں۔

سائرہ: آپ کتنے بھائی بہن ہیں؟

فاطمہ: ہم چار بھائی اور دو بہنیں ہیں۔

سائرہ: میرا ایک بھائی اور ایک بہن ہے۔

Dialogue 3

سائرہ: یہ میرا پتہ ہے۔

فاطمہ: یہ پتہ بہت لمبا ہے۔

سائرہ: ہاں بڑا شہر، لمبا پتہ۔

فاطمہ: لیکن چھوٹا شہر، چھوٹا پتہ۔

(Both laugh)

سائرہ: اچھا پھر ملیں گے۔

فاطمہ: جی، اچھا ملیں گے۔

Unit 3

Dialogue 1

مانا: ذرا نئے فیشن کے شلوار قمیض دکھائے۔

جاوید: کون سا شلوار قمیض چاہیے؟ ریشمی یا سوتی؟

مانا: ریشمی۔

جاوید: یہ دیکھیے، آج کل اس کا بہت رواج ہے۔ دیکھیے ریشم کتنا اچھا ہے

(Javed shows a number of shalvar qamiz. Maha asks Susan about her choice)

مانا: سوزن، آپ کو کون سا شلوار قمیض پسند ہے۔

سوزن: یہ زرد۔

(Turning to Javed to ask the price)

مانا: اس کی قیمت کیا ہے؟

جاوید: بیس پونڈ

مانا: ٹھیک بتایئے، یہ باہر سے آئی ہیں۔

جاوید: آج کل اتنی قیمت ہے۔ اچھا اٹھارہ پونڈ۔

مانا: اچھا ٹھیک ہے۔

Dialogue 2

جان:	لاہور کا ایک ٹکٹ چاہیئے۔
ایجنٹ:	کون سے دن کے لئے؟
جان:	کل کے لئے۔
ایجنٹ:	کمپیوٹر پر دیکھتا ہوں۔ ہے یا نہیں۔
جان:	صبح کی پرواز چاہیئے۔
ایجنٹ:	میرے پاس ٹکٹ ہے۔
جان:	تو دیجیئے۔ جہاز کب چلتا ہے؟
ایجنٹ:	صبح دس بجے
جان:	میرے پاس زرِ نقد نہیں ہے۔
ایجنٹ:	تو کریڈٹ کارڈ دیجیئے۔

Dialogue 3

اقبال:	ڈاکٹر صاحب، مجھے کچھ بخار ہے۔
ڈاکٹر میر:	کب سے ہے؟
اقبال:	کل رات سے۔
ڈاکٹر میر:	سر میں درد بھی ہے؟
اقبال:	جی ہاں۔

(Putting the thermometer in Iqbal's mouth)

ڈاکٹر میر:	تھرمامیٹر لگایئے۔

(After taking the thermometer from Iqbal's mouth)

ڈاکٹر میر:	تھوڑا بخار ہے۔ یہ دوائی دن میں دو بار لیجیئے۔ جلدی ٹھیک ہو جائیں گے۔

Dialogue 4

اِنسپکٹر:	تمہارا نام؟
چور:	بینر جی

(Now turning to the other)

اِنسپکٹر:	تمہارا نام؟

چور: چُوری۔

(Inspector talking to both thieves)

انسپکٹر: چوری کرتے ہو اور نام کے ساتھ جی لگاتے ہو۔

(Turning to his assistant)

انسپکٹر: ان کا نام لکھیے۔ بینرا اور چُھٹر۔

Unit 4

Dialogue 1

یاسمین: کیا آپ ہندوستان جاتے ہیں؟

پروفیسر جونز: جی ہاں کئی بار۔

یاسمین: آپ کو ہندوستانی کھانا پسند ہے؟

پروفیسر جونز: جی ہاں، تندوری مرغی، ڈوسا۔۔۔ ویسے سموسہ بھی بہت پسند ہے۔

یاسمین: آپ کے شوق کیا ہیں؟

پروفیسر جونز: مجھ کو تیرنے کا شوق ہے، اس کے علاوہ ہندوستانی موسیقی کا بھی شوق ہے۔

یاسمین: گانے کا بھی؟

پروفیسر جونز: ضرور میرے گانے سے میرے بچّے ہیڈ فون لگاتے ہیں۔

یاسمین: واہ، واہ۔

Dialogue 2

ساجد: بدمعاش میری پسندیدہ فلم ہے۔

اکبر: وہ کیسے؟

ساجد: گانے بہت اچھے ہیں۔ کہانی اور اداکاری بھی شاندار ہے۔

اکبر: ہندوستانی فلمیں تو مجھ کو بالکل پسند نہیں۔ صرف فارمولا۔

ساجد: لیکن یہ فارمولا فلم نہیں، اس کا انداز اور ہے۔

اکبر: سب ہندوستانی فلمیں ایک سی ہوتی ہیں، لڑکا لڑکی سے ملتا ہے، دونوں میں عشق ہو تا ہے۔ پھر بدمعاش آتا ہے۔

(Sajid interrupting Akbar)

ساجد: اور دونوں کی شادی ہوتی ہے۔ جی نہیں، یہ ایسی فلم نہیں۔

اکبر: تو مغرب کی نقل ہوگی۔

ساجد: تو آپ کے خیال میں صرف مغربی فلمیں اچھی ہوتی ہیں۔

اکبر: میں یہ نہیں کہہ رہا ہوں، پرانی ہندوستانی فلمیں اچھی ہوتی ہیں۔

(Mushtaq Ahmed patiently listens to this discussion and intervenes by saying)

مشتاق: فلم کی بات پر جھگڑا کیوں؟

Text 1

I سوال: کیا ہندوستانی لوگ کہتے ہیں: 'I love you'

جواب: (a) آنکھوں سے، لیکن الفاظ سے نہیں۔

(b) صرف الفاظ سے۔

Circle the correct answer.

صحیح جواب: (a)

II سوال: کیا ہندوستانی لوگ الفاظ سے کبھی کہتے ہیں کہ 'I love you'

جواب: (a) کبھی نہیں۔

(b) کبھی کبھی۔

Circle the correct answer.

صحیح جواب: (b)

III سوال: ہندوستانی لوگ الفاظوں سے کیسے کہتے ہیں:

جواب: (a) میں تم سے عشق کرتا ہوں۔

(b) مجھ کو تم سے عشق ہے۔

Circle the correct answer.

ٹھیک جواب: (b)

Dialogue 3

ڈاکٹر: ارشاد صاحب، ناشتے میں آپ کیا کھاتے ہیں؟

ارشاد: دس سموسے۔

ڈاکٹر: اور کیا پیتے ہیں؟

ارشاد: مجھے چائے بہت اچھی لگتی ہے۔ صبح چائے بہت پیتا ہوں۔

ڈاکٹر: آپ کو جسم کی بیماری نہیں، دماغ کی بیماری ہے۔ اس لئے آپ سائکیاٹرسٹ کے پاس جائیے۔

Unit 5

Dialogue 1

ایجنٹ: میں کیا خِدمت کر سکتی ہوں؟

شبیر: ہندوستان کے لئے ٹکٹ چاہئے؟

ایجنٹ: صرف اپنے لئے؟

شبیر: خاندان کے لئے۔

ایجنٹ: کتنے لوگ ہیں؟

شبیر: چار، دو بڑے اور دو بچّے۔

ایجنٹ: بچّوں کی عُمر بارہ سال سے کم ہے؟

شبیر: لڑکی کی عُمر بارہ سال ہے اور لڑکے کی چھ سال۔

ایجنٹ: کب جانا چاہتے ہیں؟

شبیر: کرسمس میں۔

ایجنٹ: اس وقت بہُت رَش ہوتا ہے۔ ٹکٹ مہنگے ہوں گے۔

شبیر: کوئی بات نہیں۔

Dialogue 2

اَل: بھئی، کِس دُنیا میں ہو؟ کیا سوچ رہے ہو؟

شبیر: ہندوستان کے بارے میں سوچ رہا تھا۔

اَل: کیوں سَب ٹھیک ہے نا؟

شبیر: ہاں، کرسمس کی چھٹیوں میں ہندوستان جا رہا ہوں۔

اَل: اَکیلے یا خاندان کے ساتھ؟

شبیر: پورے ٹرائب کے ساتھ۔

اَل: ہاں بھائی، نہیں تو بیوی طلاق دے دے گی۔ کہاں جاؤ گے؟

شبیر: دِلّی، آگرہ اور جے پور۔

اَل: آگرہ کیسے جاؤ گے؟

شبیر: ہوائی جہاز سے۔

اَل: ہوائی جہاز سے جانا بے کار ہے۔

شبیر: کیوں؟

اَل: ہوائی جہاز سے گاڑی میں وقت کم لگتا ہے۔

Dialogue 3

اَل: آگرہ کے لئے سب اچھی گاڑی تاج ایکسپریس ہے۔

شبیر: تاج ایکسپریس کہاں سے چلتی ہے؟

اَل: نئی دلّی سے، صُبح سات بجے۔

شبیر: اور واپس آنے کے لئے؟

اَل: وہی گاڑی شام کو واپس آتی ہے۔

شبیر: لیکن ہم لوگ رات کو تاج محل دیکھنا چاہتے ہیں۔

اَل: ہاں، تاج رات کو اور بھی خُوب صُورت لگتا ہے۔

شبیر: تو ایک رات آگرہ رُکیں گے۔ اگلے دن دلّی واپس آئیں گے۔

اَل: چاندنی رات، تاج محل اور بیوی ساتھ ۔۔۔ مزہ کیجئے۔

Text 1

١   ایک دن مُلک میں قحط پڑے گا۔

٢   میں آٹا بیچوں گا۔

٣   اور کچھ جانور خریدوں گا۔

٤   تو میں اَمیر بنوں گا۔

٥   ایک دن میری شادی ہو گی۔

٦   پھر میرا بچّہ ہو گا۔

٧   اب میں آرام سے کتابیں پڑھوں گا۔

٨   بچّہ میرے پاس آئے گا۔

Unit 6

Dialogue 1

حیدر:	ہیلو!
نادیہ:	ہیلو، الیاجان، میں نادیہ بول رہی ہوں۔
حیدر:	کہاں سے بول رہی ہو۔
نادیہ:	لندن سے۔
حیدر:	کیوں، ابھی ایڈنبرا نہیں پہنچی؟
نادیہ:	نہیں۔
حیدر:	کیا بات ہے۔ پریشان لگ رہی ہو۔ سب ٹھیک ٹھاک ہے نا؟
نادیہ:	میں تو ٹھیک ہوں۔ لیکن میرا سفر نامہ، میرے پیسے، اور ٹریولرس چکس کھوگئے
حیدر:	کیا!
نادیہ:	ایسا لگتا ہے کہ کسی نے میری جیب کاٹ لی۔
حیدر:	سچ!
نادیہ:	ہاں۔

Dialogue 2

نادیہ:	میرا سفر نامہ کھو گیا ہے نیا سفر نامہ چاہئے۔
آفیسر:	کب کھویا؟
نادیہ:	آج تقریباً پانچ گھنٹے پہلے۔
آفیسر:	آپ کو معلوم ہے کہ کہاں کھویا؟
نادیہ:	جی ہاں، بیٹھر و ہوائی اڈے پر۔
آفیسر:	کیسے؟
نادیہ:	جب دفتر جرت سے باہر آئی تو میرے پاس تھا۔ پھر ایڈنبرا کی پرواز کے لئے دوسرے ٹرمنل گئی، تب بھی تھا۔ جب کاؤنٹر پر پہنچی، تو دیکھا، سفر نامہ، ٹکٹ اور ٹریولرس چکس پرس میں نہیں تھے۔
آفیسر:	پولیس کو بیان دیا؟
نادیہ:	جی ہاں، یہ دیکھئے۔
آفیسر:	اچھا یہ سوالنامہ بھریئے۔ ایک دو مہینے میں نیا سفر نامہ آپ کو ملے گا۔

نادیہ: اِس سے جلدی نہیں مل سکتا؟

آفیسر: جی نہیں پہلے بیان پاکستان جائے گااور صفائی کے بعد ہی سفر نامہ مل سکتا ہے۔

نادیہ: شکریہ۔

آفیسر: کوئی بات نہیں۔

Dialogue 3

جان: میں نے حال ہی میں ایک نیا مکان خریدا ہے،اس لئے کچھ سجاوٹ کی چیزیں خریدنا چاہتا ہوں۔

نظیر: نیا مکان خریدنے پر مبارک ہو، ہمارے پاس بہت ہی خوبصورت دستکاریاں ہیں۔ اُمید ہے کہ آپ کو کوئی چیز پسند آئے گی۔

جان: میں نے کشمیر کی دستکاریوں کی خوبصورت کاریگری کے بارے میں بہت سُنا ہے۔ آپ مجھے کچھ چیزیں دکھا سکتے ہیں؟

نظیر: ہاں،ضرور۔ یہ دیکھئے صاحب کشمیری قالین۔

جان: کیا چیز ہے! یہ تو مجھے بہت ہی پسند آیا۔ کیا وہ پشمینے کی شال ہے؟

نظیر: کمال ہے! آپ نے اتنی دُور سے کیسے پہچانا؟

جان: دراصل میرے ایک عزیز دوست کے پاس ایسی ہی شال تھی۔ وہ پچھلے مہینے ایک گاڑی کے حادثے میں گزر گئے۔

نظیر: یہ بڑے اَفسوس کی بات ہے۔

Unit 7

Dialogue 1

عمران: معاف کیجئے، آپ نے کیا کہا؟

ڈرائیور: میں نے پوچھا کہ آپ کو ویسٹ اینڈ جانا ہے؟

عمران: ارے! آپ تو بہت اچھی اُردو بول سکتے ہیں۔

ڈرائیور: ہاں تھوڑی تھوڑی اُردو بول لیتا ہوں۔

عمران: اُردو آپ نے کہاں سیکھی؟

ڈرائیور: دوسری جنگ عظیم کے وقت میں برطانوی فوج میں سپاہی تھا۔ اُس وقت ہندوستان میں سیکھی۔

عمران: اَب بھی اچھی اُردو آتی ہے۔

ڈرائیور: کافی عرصے سے ایک ہندوستانی دُکان میں کام کر رہا ہوں اور اس لئے اُردو نہیں بھولی۔

عمران: یہ تو بہت اچھا ہے۔ نہیں تو یہاں ہندوستانی بھی اُردو بھول جاتے ہیں۔

ڈرائیور: یہ بات تو سچ ہے۔

Dialogue 2

عمران:	کیا آپ کو اُردو لِکھنی آتی ہے؟
ڈرائیور:	زیادہ نہیں۔ فوج میں کبھی کبھی لِکھنی پڑتی تھی، لیکن اب کوئی ضرورت نہیں۔
عمران:	اُردو میں کیوں لِکھنا پڑتا تھا؟
ڈرائیور:	سیکریٹ کوڈس اور پیغاموں کے لئے۔۔۔ خاص کر یورپ جانے والے پیغاموں کے لئے۔
	ویسٹ اینڈ میں کچھ کام ہے؟
عمران:	بجلی کا بل دینا تھا آج فرصت مِلی تو سوچا کہ خود وہاں جاؤں۔
ڈرائیور:	تو وہ دفتر آنے والا ہے۔ اصل میں اگلا اسٹاپ ہے۔
عمران:	اچھا خُدا احافِظ۔
ڈرائیور:	خُدا احافِظ۔

Dialogue 3

جان:	ہیلو، کیا ڈاکٹر نعیم ہیں؟
مسز نعیم:	جی نہیں، کوئی ضروری بات ہے؟
جان:	میری طبیعت بہت خراب ہے۔
مسز نعیم:	ایک مریض کو دیکھنے گئے ہیں۔
جان:	کتنی دیر میں واپس آئیں گے؟
مسز نعیم:	میرے خیال میں جلدی میں آ جائیں گے۔ مجھے اپنا ٹیلیفون نمبر اور پتہ دے دیجئے۔
	آتے ہی اُنھیں بھیج دوں گی۔
جان:	بہت بہت شکریہ۔

Unit 8

Dialogue 1

جان:	آداب عرض، ڈاکٹر نعیم،
ڈاکٹر نعیم:	آداب رائیڈر صاحب۔ اس بار کئی سال بعد مُلاقات ہوئی۔
جان:	جی ہاں کوئی پانچ سال بعد۔
ڈاکٹر نعیم:	تشریف رکھئے۔ میں آپ کا ہی انتظار کر رہا تھا۔ اچھا پہلے بتائیے۔ طبیعت کیسی ہے؟

جان:	طبیعت تو اچھّی نہیں، نہیں تو اتنی رات کو آپ کو تکلیف نہ دیتا؟
ڈاکٹر نعیم:	تکلیف کی بات کیا ہے؟ یہ تو میرا فرض ہے۔ خیر بخار کتنا ہے؟
جان:	جب ایک گھنٹے پہلے میں نے تھرمامیٹر لگایا تو ایک سو ڈگری تھا۔ اب شاید کچھ زیادہ ہو۔
ڈاکٹر نعیم:	اچھا ذرا پھر تھرمامیٹر لگائیے۔

(After taking John's pulse and the temperature Dr Naim
says...)

ڈاکٹر نعیم:	بخار تھوڑا بڑھ گیا ہے۔ دَست بھی ہیں؟
جان:	جی ہاں، دو گھنٹے میں سات آٹھ بار غسل خانے گیا۔
ڈاکٹر نعیم:	پچھلی بار آپ نے بہت سموسے کھائے تھے، اور اس بار؟
جان:	شام کو کچھ آم کھائے۔
ڈاکٹر نعیم:	میری صلاح مانیے ایک دو مہینے تک آپ کچھ پرہیز کیجیے۔ سموسے اور آم بند۔ میں ایک ٹیکہ لگا تا ہوں اور یہ دوائی لیجیے۔ دو گولیاں ہر دو گھنٹے بعد۔ تو کل صبح اپنی طبیعت کے بارے میں بتائیں۔ اچھا اب آرام کیجے۔ خدا حافظ۔
جان:	بہت بہت شکریہ، ڈاکٹر صاحب، خدا حافظ۔

Dialogue 2

فِلپ:	یہاں قریب کوئی تھامس ککُ کا دفتر ہے؟ میں دو دِن پہلے دہاں گیا تھا لیکن آج نہیں مِل رہا۔
اجنبی:	آپ کو پتہ معلوم ہے؟
فِلپ:	میں پتہ ہی تو بھول گیا۔
اجنبی:	(Pointing to the street) میرے خیال میں اگلی سڑک پر تھامس ککُ کا دفتر ہے۔
فِلپ:	(Seemingly puzzled) وہ سڑک تو خوبصورت ہے، لوگ اُسے اگلی سڑک کیوں کہتے ہیں؟
اجنبی:	اگلی اُردو کا لفظ ہے، انگریزی کا نہیں۔ اگلی کا مطلب انگریزی میں "نیکسٹ" ہے۔
فِلپ:	بہت خوب۔

(Philip goes to the cashier's window at the Thomas Cook
office)

فِلپ:	مجھے کچھ ٹریولرس چیک تبدیل کروانے ہیں۔
کیشیئر:	کون سے سِکّوں میں ہیں؟
فِلپ:	برطانوی پونڈ۔ زرِمُبادلہ کی شرح کیا ہے؟
کیشیئر:	ایک برطانوی پونڈ پچاس روپے کا ہے۔

(Philip signs the cheques and the cashier gives him the
equivalent amount in rupees)

کیشیئر : گل دوسوپونڈ۔ یہ رہے آپ کے دَس ہزار روپے۔ گِن لیجئے۔

فِلپ: ٹھیک ہیں شکریہ۔

Text 1

١	ایک گاؤں میں ایک چور قید خانے سے بھاگ گیا۔
٢	پولیس والا اُس کو پکڑنے کے لئے دوڑا۔
٣	اِتنے میں گاؤں والوں نے بھاگتے چور کو پکڑ لیا۔
٤	پولیس والا زور زور سے چیخ رہا تھا ''پکڑو مت جانے دو''
٥	یہ سنتے ہی گاؤں والوں نے چور کو چھوڑ دیا۔
٦	جب پولیس والا گاؤں والوں کے پاس پہنچا۔
٧	تو اُس کو بہت غُصّہ آیا۔
٨	غُصّے میں اُس نے گاؤں والوں سے پوچھا،
٩	''تم نے چور کو کیوں چھوڑ دیا''
١٠	گاؤں والوں نے جواب دیا
١١	''آپ نے ہی کہا، پکڑو مت، جانے دو''۔

Text 2

١	یہ راتیں، یہ موسم، یہ ہنسنا، ہنسانا
٢	مجھے بھول جانا، اِنہیں نہ بھلانا۔

Unit 9

Text 1

١	ایک دن دو دوست کھانا کھانے کے لئے ایک چینی طعام خانے گئے۔
٢	کھانے کے بعد بیرا فارچون لکی لایا۔
٣	دونوں نے اپنی اپنی فارچون لکی کو کھولا اور اپنی اپنی قسمت کے بارے میں کچھ پڑھا۔
٤	پھر ایک دوست نے دوسرے سے پوچھا، ''کاغذ پر کیا لکھا ہے؟''
٥	لکھا ہے۔۔۔''جلدی پیسہ آنے والا ہے۔''

٦	یہ تو بڑی خُوشی کی بات ہے۔
۷	کوئی لاٹری کا ٹکٹ خریدا؟
۸	نہیں، لیکن کل اپنی زندگی کا بیمہ کروایا ہے۔

Dialogue 1

بل:	ہندوستانی کری ابھی تک ہم نے نہیں کھائی۔
فاطمہ:	آپ کو مسالے دار کھانا پسند ہے یا کری؟
بل:	دونوں میں فرق کیا ہے؟
فاطمہ:	امریکہ میں کری ایک قسم کے کھانے کا نام ہے۔ لیکن ہندوستانی میں یہ بات نہیں ہے۔
بل:	ہمارے ہاں کری کا مطلب ''کوئی مسالے دار ہندوستانی'' کھانا ہے۔
فاطمہ:	ہندوستان میں نہ تو کری ہمیشہ مسالے دار ہوتی ہے اور نہ ہی ہندوستان میں کری پوڈر اکثر بکتا ہے۔ کری اکثر تری
والی	ہوتی ہے۔ اور یہ گوشت، سبزی، مچھلی یا پھل کی بنی ہوتی ہے۔
بل:	ارے مسالے کے بغیر کری۔۔۔ یہ تو ہم نے کبھی نہیں سنا۔
فاطمہ:	تو آپ کو کون سی کری پسند ہے؟
بل:	آم کے آم اور گٹھلیوں کے دام۔ کری کے بارے میں کچھ معلوم ہو گیا۔ اور اصلی کری چکھنے کا موقع بھی مل جائے
	گا۔ اچھا، ہم کو تیز مسالے دار گوشت کی کری بہت پسند ہے۔

(They laugh at the unexpected turn in the conversation; the
proverb has added a lighter touch to the conversation and
they continue to talk...)

Dialogue 2

بل:	واہ! واہ! شاندار خوشبو آ رہی ہے اور انتظار کرنا مشکل ہے۔
فاطمہ:	آئیے تو کھانا شروع کیا جائے۔ یہ ہے آپ کی پسند۔۔۔ تیز مرچ والی مرغی کا سالن۔

(Bill takes a lot of curry while Mrs Hassett takes only a little
bit. After taking the first substantial mouthful...)

بل:	(fanning his mouth) اوہ۔۔۔ آگ!۔۔۔ آگ!
فاطمہ:	کیوں ہوا؟
بل:	یہ تو کری نہیں ہے! یہ تو آتش فشاں ہے! اور میں اپنا آگ بُجھانے کا سامان بھی نہیں لایا۔
فاطمہ:	آگ بُجھانے کا سامان یہ ہے۔۔۔ اگر مرچیں بہت لگ رہی ہیں تو کچھ دہی لیجئے۔

(After a while Bill's mouth cools down)

بِل : سچّ،اُمریکہ میں تیز مسالے دار کھانا اتنا تیز نہیں ہوتا۔

فاطمہ : ہاں، یہ تو ہندوستان ہے۔ یہاں تیز کا مطلب بُہت تیز ہے۔ ہم لوگ بُہت تیز کھاتے ہیں۔ لیکن ہندوستان میں سبھی لوگ اتنا تیز کھانا نہیں کھا سکتے۔

بِل : غلط فہمی دور کرنے کے لئے آپ کا شکریہ۔ میں اَب سمجھ گیا کہ ''تیز'' خطرناک لفظ ہے۔

Unit 10

Text 1

١   عید مُسلمانوں کا مقدس تہوار ہے۔

٢   رمضان کے تیس روزوں کے بعد عید آتی ہے۔

٣   جس رات عید کا چاند دیکھا جاتا ہے، اُس کے دوسرے دن عید منائی جاتی ہے۔

٤   رمضان کے مہینے میں مُسلمانوں کے لئے روزے رکھنا فرض ہے۔ اِس کا مطلب یہ ہے، جو مُسلمان روزے رکھتے ہیں وہ آفتاب چڑھنے اور آفتاب ڈوبنے کے درمیان نہ کچھ پی سکتے ہیں اور نہ کچھ کھا سکتے ہیں۔

٥   جیسے کرسمس دُنیا کے بہُت سارے لوگ جوش سے مناتے ہیں، ویسے بھی عید بہُت سارے مُلکوں میں عقیدت سے منائی جاتی ہے۔

٦   عید کے دن لوگ سویرے اُٹھ کر نہاتے اور نئے کپڑے پہنتے ہیں۔ پھر سب لوگ عید نماز پڑھنے کے لئے عید گاہ یا بڑی مسجد میں جاتے ہیں۔

٧   نماز کے بعد سب ایک دوسرے سے گلے ملتے ہیں، اور بعد میں اپنے اپنے قریبی رشتے داروں اور دوستوں کے گھر عید ملنے جاتے ہیں، اور خیرات کرتے ہیں۔

٨   والدین اپنے بچّوں کو عید کی خوشی میں عیدی دیتے ہیں۔ بچّے اِن پیسوں سے طرح طرح کے کھلونے اور مٹھائیاں خریدتے ہیں۔

٩   سب لوگوں کے گھروں میں اچھی دعوتیں ہوتی ہیں۔ اُس دن سویّاں پکائی جاتی ہیں۔

١٠   ہندوستان میں اِس مُبارک دن پر ہندو، سکھ اور عیسائی اپنے مُسلمان دوستوں کے گھروں میں عید مُبارک دینے کے لئے جاتے ہیں۔ اور اُن کی اِس خوشی میں شریک ہو جاتے ہیں۔

١١   کچھ لوگ ایک دوسرے کو عید مُبارک کے پیغام اور نذرانے بھیجتے ہیں۔

١٢   آج کے دن اکثر دُشمنوں کو بھی دوست بنایا جاتا ہے۔

Text 2

١ ‏مُسلمانوں کا ایک تہوار اور بھی ہے جس کو بقر عید کہتے ہیں۔ یہ عید حج کے مہینے میں تین روز منائی جاتی ہے۔

٢ ‏دُنیا کے مُسلمان حج کرنے کے لئے مکّہ جاتے ہیں۔ حج سے فارغ ہو کر اپنے پیغمبر کے روضے کی زیارت کے لئے مدینے بھی جاتے ہیں۔

٣ ‏پاکستان اور ہندوستان سے بھی بہُت سے مُسلمان حج کرنے کے لئے مکّہ جاتے ہیں۔ جو لوگ حج کر کے آتے ہیں، وہ حاجی کہلاتے ہیں، اور اُن کی بہُت عزّت کی جاتی ہے۔ جب یہ حاجی اپنے اپنے گھر پہنچتے ہیں، تب جوش و خروش کے ساتھ اُن کا استقبال کیا جاتا ہے۔

٤ ‏اِس دِن مُسلمان بکرے یا بھیڑ کی قُربانی کرتے ہیں۔ اور یہ گوشت غریبوں، دوستوں، ہمسایوں اور رشتے داروں میں بانٹا جاتا ہے۔

٥ ‏کہا جاتا ہے کہ قُربانی کا آغاز حضرت ابراہیم علیہ السلام کے وقت سے ہُوا ہے۔ اور اِس دِن کا مقصد اُن کی قُربانی کی یاد کو تازہ کرنا ہے۔

٦ ‏تب مُسلمان عیدگاہ جا کر شُکرانے کی نماز ادا کرتے ہیں۔

٧ ‏یہ نہایت عظیم الشّان اسلامی تہوار ہے۔

Text 3

١ ‏محرّم اسلامی تقویم کا پہلا مہینہ ہے۔

٢ ‏یہ خُوشی منانے کا تہوار نہیں ہے، بلکہ شیعہ مُسلمانوں کے لئے ماتم کے دِن ہیں۔

٣ ‏کیونکہ محرّم ہی کے مہینے میں دمشق کے حاکم یزید کی فوج نے حضرت محمّد صلی اللہ علیہ وسلّم کے عزیز نواسے حُسین اور اُن کے رشتے داروں کو شہید کیا تھا۔

٤ ‏یہ واقعات یاد آ کر اِن دِنوں مُسلمانوں میں بہُت رنج و غم پیدا ہو جاتا ہے۔

٥ ‏لوگ شہیدوں کی روحوں کو ثواب پہنچانے کے لئے فقیروں کو کھانا کھلاتے ہیں۔

٦ ‏اِسی مہینے کی نو تاریخ کی رات کو شیعہ مُسلمان شہیدوں کی یاد میں تعزیے بازاروں میں نکالتے ہیں۔

٧ ‏دوسرے دِن یہ لوگ اِن تعزیوں کو لے کر پانی میں غرق کرتے ہیں۔

Dialogue 1

جاوید: ‏تشریف رکھیئے۔ فرمائیے میں آپ کے لئے کیا کر سکتا ہوں۔

بِل: ‏میں پاکستانی رسم و رواج کے بارے میں جاننا چاہتا ہوں۔ خاص کر میں شادی کی رسم کے بارے میں آپ سے کُچھ سوال پُوچھنا چاہتا ہوں۔

جاوید:	کوئی بات نہیں، پوچھئے۔
بل:	کیا لڑکی اپنے خاوند کا خود انتخاب کرتی ہے؟
جاوید:	پاکستانی معاشرے میں والدین اکثر اپنے بیٹا بیٹی کے لئے دلہن یا دلہا کا انتخاب کرتے ہیں۔ اس کے برعکس، شادی کے معاملے میں والدین عام طور سے لڑکا کر لڑکی کی مرضی حاصل کرتے ہیں۔ چونکہ یہ اسلامی حکم بھی ہے۔ جب دونوں خاندانوں کو ایک دوسرے کا گھر اناپسند آتا ہے۔ تو پھر منگنی کی رسم ادا ہوتی ہے۔
بل:	منگنی کا کیا مطلب ہے؟
جاوید:	منگنی کا مطلب "انگیجمنٹ" ہے جس کی رسم لڑکی کے گھر میں ادا ہوتی ہے۔ اور لڑکے والے لڑکی کو انگوٹھی پہناتے ہیں۔ پھر شادی کی تاریخ طے ہوتی ہے۔
بل:	شادی کی رسم کہاں اور کیسے ادا ہوتی ہے؟
جاوید:	یہ رسم بھی لڑکی کے گھر پر ہی ادا ہوتی ہے۔ اس دن لڑکے والے بارات لے کر آ جاتے ہیں، جس میں دلہا کا خاندان، قریبی رشتہ دار اور دوست شامل ہو جاتے ہیں ۔ لڑکی والے اُن کا استقبال شان سے کرتے ہیں۔ پھر نکاح کی رسم ادا کی جاتی ہے۔ مولوی صاحب نکاح پڑھاتے ہیں۔
بل:	نکاح کیسے پڑھایا جاتا ہے؟
جاوید:	پہلے کچھ لوگ الگ سے لڑکی کے پاس جا کر اُس سے نکاح کی اجازت لیتے ہیں۔ پھر تمام لوگوں کے سامنے مولوی صاحب دلہا سے تین بار پوچھتے ہیں کہ اُس کو نکاح قبول ہے یا نہیں۔ جب وہ اس کا اقرار کر تا ہے، تب سارے لوگ دلہن اور دلہا کو مبارک باد پیش کرتے ہیں۔ نکاح کے بعد سب باراتیوں کو دعوت کھلائی جاتی ہے۔ باراتی پھر دلہا کے گھر واپس جاتے ہیں۔
بل:	آپ نے مجھے کافی چیزوں سے آگاہ کیا۔

English–Urdu glossary

A set of basic vocabulary useful for everyday communication is given below. This vocabulary is classified according to the following semantic groups:

- body, health and ailments
- colours
- family and relations
- food and drink
- numbers-cardinal, ordinal, fractions and percentages
- time-hours, days, dates, months, years; asking time
- important verbs

The gender of the nouns is specified as masculine (m.) or feminine (f.). Adjectives are given in their base masculine singular form. Since the plural forms of nouns are predictable from the gender, only the singular forms are listed. Verbs taking the agentive (+/-**ne**; in perfective tenses) or experiencer subjects (+ **ko**) rather than regular nominative subjects are so indicated. Also, if the object of a verb takes a specific postposition instead of the regular **ko** postposition, it is specified in the following way:

to wait for x   **x kaa intizār karnā**

This shows that the verb **intizār karnā** 'to wait' takes the postposition **kā** 'of' instead of **ko** or the equivalent of the English 'for'. Verbs are listed in the infinitive form.

Body, health and ailments

Parts of the body

ankle	**Taxna** (m.)	ٹخنا
back	**pusht** (f.), **pīTʰ** (f.)	پُشت، پیٹھ
bald	**gañjā** (m.)	گنجا
beard	**dāRʰī** (f.)	داڑھی
blood	**xūn** (m.)	خُون
body	**jism** (m.)	جِسم
chest	**cʰātī** (f.)	چھاتی
ear	**kān** (m.)	کان
elbow	**kohnī** (f.)	کہنی
eye	**ā̃kʰ** (f.)	آنکھ
face	**cehrā** (m.)	چہرہ
finger	**uŋglī** (f.)	اُنگلی
foot	**pɛr** (m.)	پیر
forehead	**mātʰā** (m.), **peshānī** (f.)	ماتھا، پیشانی
hair	**bāl** (m.)	بال
hand	**hātʰ** (m.)	ہاتھ
head	**sar** (m.)	سَر
heart	**dil** (m.)	دِل
kidney	**gurdā** (m.)	گُردہ
knee	**gʰuTnā** (m.)	گُھٹنا
leg	**tā̃g** (f.), **lāt** (f.)	ٹانگ، لات
lip	**hõT** (m.)	ہونٹ
moustache	**mū̃ch**(f.)	مونچھ
mouth	**mū̃h** (m.)	منہ
neck	**gardan** (f.)	گردن

nose	**nāk** (f.)	ناک
shoulder	**kand^hā** (m.)	کندھا
stomach	**shikam** (m.), **peT** (m.)	پیٹ، شِکم
throat	**galā** (m.)	گلا
thumb	**aŋgūT^hā** (m.)	انگوٹھا
toe	**pɛr kī uŋglī** (f.)	پیر کی اُنگلی
tongue	**zabān** (f.)	زَبان

Health and ailments

ache, pain	**dard** (m.)	دَرد
ailment	**bīmārī** (f.)	بیماری
appetite, hunger	**b^hūk** (f.)	بھوک
blind	**and^hā** (m.)	أندھا
blister	**c^hālā** (m.)	چھالا
boil	**p^hoRā** (m.)	پھوڑا
breath	**sãs** (f.)	سانس
burning sensation	**jalan** (f.)	جَلَن
cancer	**sartān** (m.)	سَرطان
cholera	**hɛzā** (m.)	ہیضہ
common cold	**zukām** (m.)	زُکام
cough	**k^hãsī** (f.)	کھانسی
deaf	**bɛhrā** (m.)	بہرا
dumb	**gũgā** (m.)	گونگا
dysentery	**pecish** (f.)	پچش
elderly	**būR^hā** (m.)	بوڑھا
to feel breathless	**sãs p^hūlnā** (+kā)	سانس پھولنا
to feel giddy	**sar cakrānā** (+kā)	سَر چکرانا

health	**sehat** (f.)	صحت
healthy	**tandrust**	تندرست
ill	**bīmār** (m.)	بيمار
illness	**bīmārī** (f.)	بيماری
indigestion	**bad-hazmī** (f.)	بدہضمی
injury	**coT** (f.)	چوٹ
itch	**kʰujlī** (f.)	کھجلی
lame	**laŋgRā** (m.)	لنگڑا
malaria	**maleriyā buxār** (m.)	ملیریا بخار
sneeze	**chĩk** (f.)	چھینک
spot, (pimple (US))	**dānā**	دانہ
sprain	**moc** (f.)	موچ
swelling	**sūjan** (f.)	سوجن
temperature	**buxār** (m.)	بُخار
thirst	**pyās** (f.)	پياس
tuberculosis	**tap-e-diq** (m.)	ئے دق
typhoid	**miyādī buxār** (m.)	معیادی بخار
ulcer	**nāsūr** (m.)	ناسور
unconscious	**behosh**	بے ہوش

Colours

black	**kālā, siyāh**	کالا، سیاہ
blue	**nīlā**	نیلا
brown	**bʰūrā**	بھورا
colour	**raŋg** (m.)	رنگ
green	**sabz**	سبز
orange	**saŋgtarī, nāraŋgī**	سنگتری، نارنگی
pink	**gulābī**	گلابی

purple (dark)	**bēgnī**	بینگنی
purple (light)	**jāmnī**	جامنی
red	**lāl, surx**	لال، سُرخ
saffron	**kesrī, zāfrānī**	کیسری، زعفرانی
sky blue	**āsmānī**	آسمانی
white	**safed**	سفید
white (skin)	**gorā**	گورا
yellow	**zard**	زرد

Family and relations

aunt		
father's sister	**pʰūpʰī**	پھوپھی
mother's sister	**xālā**	خالہ
father's brother's wife	**cacī**	چچی
mother's brother's wife	**mumānī**	مومانی
brother	**bʰāī**	بھائی
brother-in-law		
wife's brother	**sālā**	سالا
husband's older brother	**jeTʰ**	جیٹھ
husband's younger brother	**devar**	دیور
husband's sister's husband	**nandoī**	نندوئی
wife's sister's husband	**hamzulf, sāRʰū**	ہم زُلف، ساڑھو
child	**baccā** (m.), **baccī** (f.)	بچّہ، بچّی
daughter	**beTī**	بیٹی
daughter-in-law	**bahū**	بَہو
father	**vālid**	والِد
	abbā	اَبّا
father-in-law	**susar**	سَسُر

granddaughter		
daughter's daughter	**navāsī**	نواسی
son's daughter	**potī**	پوتی
grandfather		
father's father	**dādā**	دادا
mother's father	**nānā**	نانا
grandmother		
father's mother	**dādī**	دادی
mother's mother	**nānī**	نانی
grandson		
daughter's son	**navāsā**	نواسه
son's son	**potā**	پوتا
husband	**xāvind**	خاوند
mother	**vāldah**	والده
	ammī	امی
mother-in-law	**sās**	ساس
nephew		
brother's son	**bʰatījā**	بھتیجا
sister's son	**bʰā̃jā**	بھانجا
niece		
brother's daughter	**bʰatījī**	بھتیجی
sister's daughter	**bʰā̃jī**	بھانجی
relative	**rishtedār**	رشتہ دار
sister	**behɛn, hamshīrā**	بہن، ہمشیرہ، آپا
sister-in-law		
brother's wife	**bʰābʰī**	بھابھی
wife's sister	**sālī**	سالی
husband's sister	**nand**	نند

son	**beTā**	بیٹا
uncle		
father's younger brother	**cacā**	چَچا
mother's brother	**māmū̃**	ماموں
father's sister's husband	**pʰūpʰā**	پھوپھا
mother's sister's husband	**xālū**	خالو
wife	**bīvī**	بیوی
	zaujah	زوجہ

Food and drink

Foodgrains and flours

black beans	**lobʰiyā** (m.)	لوبھیا
chickpeas	**cʰole** (m. pl.)	چھولے
corn	**makaī** (f.)	مکئی
flour	**āTā** (m.)	آٹا
flour (refined, all purpose)	**mɛdā** (m.)	میدہ
gram flour	**besan** (m.)	بیسن
lentils	**dāl** (f.)	دال
mung beans/lentils	**mū̃g dāl** (f.)	مونگ
rice	**cāval** (m.)	چاول
wheat	**gehū̃** (m.)	گیہوں

Fruits and nuts

almond	**bādām** (m.)	بادام
apple	**seb** (m.)	سیب
apricot	**xubāni** (f.)	خوبانی

banana	kelā (m.)	کیلا
cashew nuts	kājū (m.)	کاجو
fruit	pʰal (m.)	پھل
grapes	aŋgūr (m.)	انگور
guava	amrūd (m.)	أمرود
lemon	nībū (m.)	نیبو
mango	ām (m.)	آم
melon	xarbūzā (m.)	خربوزه
orange	saŋgtarā (m.)	سنگترہ
peach	āRū (m.)	آڑو
peanuts	mū̃gpʰalī (f.)	مونگ پھلی
pear	nāshpātī (f.)	ناشپاتی
pistachio	pistā (m.)	پستہ
plum	ālūbuxārā (m.)	آلو بخارا
tangerine	nāraŋgī (f.)	نارنگی
walnut	axroT (m.)	أخروٹ
watermelon	tarbūz (m.)	تربوز

Vegetables

beetroot	cuqandar (m.)	چقندر
bittergourd	karelā (m.)	کریلا
cabbage	bandgobhī (f.)	بند گوبھی
courgette	toraī (f.)	توری
cucumber	kʰīrā (m.)	کھیرا
fenugreek	metʰī (f.)	میتھی
garlic	lassan (m.)	لہسن
ginger (fresh)	adrak (f.)	أدرک
mustard	sarsõ (m.)	سرسوں

okra	**bʰiNDī** (f.)	بھنڈی
onion	**pyāz** (m.)	پیاز
peas	**maTar** (m.)	مٹر
potatoes	**ālū** (m.)	آلو
pumpkin	**kaddū** (m.)	کدّو
radish	**mūlī** (f.)	مولی
spinach	**pālak** (f.)	پالک
tomato	**TamāTar** (m.)	ٹماٹر
vegetable	**tarkārī** (f.), **sabzī** (f.)	ترکاری، سبزی

Herbs and spices

aniseed	**saũf** (m.)	سونف
asafoetida	**hĩg** (f.)	ہینگ
bay leaves	**tez pattā** (m.)	تیز پتّا
black cardamom	**baRī ilāycī** (f.)	بڑی الائچی
cardamom	**ilāycī** (f.)	الائچی
chilli	**mirc** (f.)	مرچ
cinnamon	**dārcīnī** (f.)	دارچینی
cloves	**lãũg** (m.)	لونگ
coriander	**dʰniyā** (m.)	دھنیا
cumin	**zīrā** (m.)	زیرا
ginger (dry)	**sãũTʰ** (f.)	سونٹھ
mango powder	**amcūr** (m.)	امچور
mint	**paudīnā** (m.)	پودینا
mixed spices	**garam masālā** (m.)	گرم مصالہ
mustard seeds	**rāī** (f.)	رائی
nutmeg	**jāypʰal** (m.)	جائفل
pepper (black)	**kālī mirc** (f.)	کالی مرچ

saffron	**zāfrān** (m.)	زعفران
salt	**namak** (m.)	نمک
tamarind	**imlī** (f.)	اِملی
turmeric	**haldī** (f.)	ہلدی

Food items (dishes) etc.

alcoholic drinks	**sharāb** (f.)	شراب
betel leaf	**pān** (m.)	پان
betel nut	**supārī** (f.)	سُپاری
bread (Indian)	**roTī** (f.), **capātī** (f.),	روٹی، چپاتی
	pʰulkā (m.), **nān** (m.),	پھلکا، نان
	pūrī (f.), **parāTʰā** (m.)	پوری، پراٹھا
	qulcā (m.), **bʰaTaurā** (m.)	قلچہ، بھٹورا
bread (Western)	**Dabal roTī** (f.)	ڈبل روٹی
butter	**makkʰan** (m.)	مکّھن
cheese	**panīr** (m.)	پنیر
coffee	**kāfī** (f.)	کافی
curd and water	**lassī** (f.)	لسّی
curry (Indian)	**kaRʰī** (f.)	کڑھی
egg	**aNDā** (m.)	انڈا
food	**kʰānā** (m.)	کھانا
juice	**ras** (m.)	رس
lentils	**dāl** (f.)	دال
meat	**gosht** (m.)	گوشت
milk	**dūdʰ** (m.)	دودھ
oil	**tel** (m.)	تیل
purified butter	**ghī** (f.)	گھی
sugar (brown)	**shakkar** (f.)	شکّر

sugar (white)	**cīnī** (f.)	چینی
sweets	**miTʰāī** (f.)	مٹھائی
tea	**cāy** (f.)	چائے
tobacco	**tambākū** (m.)	تمباکو
vinegar	**sirkā** (m.)	سرکہ
water	**pānī** (m.), **āb** (m.)	پانی، آب
yoghurt	**dahī** (m./f.)	دہی

Cooking processes

baked (cooked in a large earthen oven called *tandur*)	**tandūrī**	تندوری
boil	**ubālnā** (+ne)	اُبالنا
cook	**pakānā** (+ne)	پکانا
cut	**kāTnā** (+ne)	کاٹنا
fry	**talnā** (+ne)	تلنا
grill	**sēknā** (+ne)	سینکنا
grind	**pīsnā** (+ne)	پیسنا
knead	**gū̃dʰnā** (+ne)	گوندھنا
mix	**milānā** (+ne)	ملانا
peel	**cʰīlnā** (+ne)	چھیلنا
peel apart	**cīrnā** (+ne)	چیرنا
roast	**bʰūnnā** (+ne)	بھوننا
roll	**belnā** (+ne)	بیلنا
sieve	**chānnā** (+ne)	چھاننا
temper	**bagʰār denā** (+ne)	بگھار دینا

Tastes

bitter	**kaRvā**	کڑوا
delicious/tasty	**mazedār**	مزے دار
savoury/salty	**namkīn**	نمکین
sour	**kʰaTTā**	کھٹا
spicy	**masāledār, mircvālā,**	مسالے دار، مرچ والا
	caTpaTā	چٹپٹا
sweet	**mīThā**	میٹھا
taste	**zāiqā**	ذائقہ
tasteless	**pʰīkā, bezāiqā**	پھیکا، بے ذائقہ

Numbers

Cardinal

1	ek	ایک	25	paccīs	پچِیس
2	do	دو	26	cʰabbīs	چھبِیس
3	tīn	تین	27	sattāīs	ستائیس
4	cār	چار	28	aTʰāīs	أٹھائیس
5	pã̄c	پانچ	29	unatīs	أنتِیس
6	cʰe	چھ	30	tīs	تِیس
7	sāt	سات	31	ikattīs	إکتِیس
8	āTʰ	آٹھ	32	battīs	بتِیس
9	nau	نو	33	tẽtīs	تینتِیس
10	das	دَس	34	caũtīs	چونتِیس
11	gyārah	گیاره	35	pẽtīs	پینتِیس
12	bārah	باره	36	cʰattīs	چھتِیس
13	terah	تیره	37	sẽtīs	سینتِیس
14	caudah	چوَده	38	aRtīs	أڑ تِیس
15	pandrah	پندره	39	untālīs	أنتالِیس
16	solah	سوله	40	cālīs	چالِیس
17	sattrāh	ستره	41	iktālīs	إکتالِیس
18	aTʰārah	أٹھاره	42	byālīs	بیالِیس
19	unnīs	أنِّیس	43	tẽtālīs	تینتالِیس
20	bīs	بِیس	44	cavālīs	چوالِیس
21	ikkīs	إکِّیس	45	pẽtālīs	پینتالِیس
22	bāīs	بائیس	46	cʰiyālīs	چھیالِیس
23	teīs	تیئیس	47	sẽtālīs	سنتالِیس
24	caubīs	چوبِیس	48	aRtālīs	أڑ تالِیس

49	**unancās**	انچاس
50	**pacās**	پچاس
51	**ikyāvan**	اِکیاون
52	**bāvan**	باون
53	**tarepan**	ترپین
54	**cavvan**	چون
55	**pacpan**	پَچَپن
56	**cʰappan**	چھپّن
57	**sattāvan**	ستّاون
58	**aTTʰāvan**	اٹھاون
59	**unsaTʰ**	اُنسٹھ
60	**sāTʰ**	ساٹھ
61	**iksaTʰ**	اِکسٹھ
62	**bāsaTʰ**	باسٹھ
63	**tirsaTʰ**	ترسٹھ
64	**cāũsaTʰ**	چونسٹھ
65	**pɛsaTʰ**	پینسٹھ
66	**chiyāsaTʰ**	چھیاسٹھ
67	**sarsaTʰ**	سڑسٹھ
68	**aRsaTʰ**	اڑسٹھ
69	**unhattar**	اُنہتّر
70	**sattar**	ستّر
71	**ikhattar**	اِکھتّر
72	**bahattar**	بہتّر
73	**tihattar**	تہتّر
74	**cauhattar**	چوہتّر
75	**pïchattar**	پچھتّر

76	**cʰihattar**	چھہتّر
77	**sathattar**	ستّہتّر
78	**aTʰhattar**	اٹھہتّر
79	**unnāsī**	اُناسی
80	**assī**	اَسّی
81	**ikyāsī**	اِکاسی
82	**bayāsī**	بیاسی
83	**tirāsī**	تراسی
84	**caurāsī**	چوراسی
85	**picyāsī**	پچاسی
86	**cʰiyāsī**	چھیاسی
87	**sattāsī**	ستّاسی
88	**aTThāsī**	اٹھاسی
89	**navāsī**	نواسی
90	**navve**	نوے،نوّ
91	**ikyānve**	اِکیانوے
92	**bānve**	بانوے
93	**tirānve**	ترانوے
94	**caurānve**	چورانوے
95	**picyānve**	پچانوے
96	**cʰiyānve**	چھیانوے
97	**sattānve**	ستّانوے
98	**aTTʰānve**	اٹھانوے
99	**ninyānve**	ننیانوے
100	**sau**	سَو

0	**sifar**	صفر
150	**ek sau pacās**	ایک سو پچاس
1,000	**hazār**	ہزار
10,000	**das hazār**	دَس ہزار
100,000 (a hundred thousand)	**ek lāk^h**	ایک لاکھ
1,000,000 (a million)	**das lāk^h**	دَس لاکھ
10,000,000 (ten million)	**ek karoR**	ایک کروڑ
100,000,000 (a hundred million)	**das karoR**	دَس کروڑ
1,000,000,000 (a thousand million) (US: a billion)	**arab**	اَرب
10,000,000,000 (ten thousand million) (US: ten billion)	**das arab**	دَس اَرب
100,000,000,000 (a billion) (US: hundred billion)	**k^{h}arab**	کھرب

Ordinal numbers

first	**pehlā**	پہلا
second	**dūsrā**	دوسرا
third	**tīsrā**	تیسرا
fourth	**caut^{h}ā**	چوتھا
fifth	**pā̃cvā̃**	پانچواں

(For higher numbers simply add the suffix -vā̃ to the cardinal numbers.)

Fractions

¼	(a quarter)	**(ek) chaut^{h}āī**	چوتھائی
½	(half)	**ād^{h}ā**	آدھا
¾	(three quarters)	**paunā**	پونا
1¼	(one and a quarter)	**savā (ek)**	سَوا
1½	(one and a half)	**DeR^h**	ڈیڑھ
1¾	(one and a three-quarters)	**paune do**	پونے دو

	(**paunā** = three quarters; **paune** = a quarter to, less a quarter)	
2¼	**savā do**	سَوادو
2½	**Dʰāī** (the numeral two is incorporated in the word)	ڈھائی
2¾	**paune tīn**	پونے تین
3¼	**savā tīn**	سواتین
3½	**sāRʰe tīn**	ساڑھے تین
3¾	**paune cār** Then follow the pattern given below to derive other fractional numbers.	پونے چار
number + ¼	**savā** + number	
number + ½	**sāRʰe** + number	
number + ¾	**paune** + the next number	

Decimal point

decimal	**āshāriyā**	اعشاریہ
Example:		
1.5	**ek āshāriyā pãc**	ایک اعشاریہ پانچ

Percentages

percentage	**fīsadī, fīsad**	فی صدی، فی صد
Example:		
50 per cent	**pacās fīsadī**	پچاس فی صد

Time

Hours

o'clock	**baje**	بجے
1:15	**savā (ek)**	سوا

1:30	**DeRʰ**	ڈیڑھ
1:45	**paune do**	پونے دو
2:15	**savā do**	سوا دو
2:30	**Dʰāī**	ڈھائی
	(the numeral two is incorporated in the word)	
2:45	**paune tīn**	پونے تین
3:15	**savā tīn**	سوا تین
3:30	**sāRʰe tīn**	ساڑھے تین
3:45	**paune cār**	پونے چار

Examples

Q:	**kitne**		**baje**	**hɛ̃**	*or* **vaqt**	**kyā**	**hɛ?**
	how many		o'clock	are	time	what	is
	'What time is it?'						
A:	**ek bajā hɛ.**	It is 1 o'clock.					
	deRʰ baje hɛ̃.	It is 1:30.					
	paune tīn baje hɛ̃.	It is 2:45.					

9:00 a.m.	**savera/subā ke nau**	صبح کے نو
9:00 p.m.	**rāt ke nau**	رات کے نو
4:20 (twenty minutes *past* four)	**cār *bajkar* bīs minaT**	چار بج کر بیس منٹ
6:50 (10 minutes *to* seven)	**sāt bajne mẽ das minaT**	سات بجنے میں دس منٹ
year	**sāl** (m.)	سال
month	**mahīnā** (m.)	مہینہ
day	**din** (m.)	دن
hour	**gʰanTā** (m.)	گھنٹہ
minute	**minaT** (m.)	منٹ
second	**sɛkinD** (m.)	سیکنڈ

Days of the week

Monday	**pīr**	پیر
Tuesday	**maŋgal**	منگل
Wednesday	**budʰ**	بدھ
Thursday	**jumerāt**	جمعرات
Friday	**jumah**	جمعه
Saturday	**haftā**	ہفتہ
Sunday	**itvār**	اتوار

Months

Although distinct Hindu and Muslim calendars are used in particular contexts, the Christian calendar is commonly used throughout South Asia. The Urdu pronunciation of the months is given below:

January	**janvarī**	جنوری
February	**farvarī**	فروری
March	**mārc**	مارچ
April	**aprel**	اپریل
May	**maī**	مئی
June	**jūn**	جون
July	**julāī**	جولائی
August	**agast**	اگست
September	**sitambar**	ستمبر
October	**aktūbar**	اکتوبر
November	**navambar**	نومبر
December	**disambar**	دسمبر

Years

When used as part of a date the word 'year' is translated as **san**, e.g.:

1985 (the year)	**san unnīs sau pacāsī**	سنہ انیس سو پچاسی
but one *cannot* say:	**ek hazār nau sau pacāsī**	ایک ہزار نو سو پچاسی

Important verbs

Urdu verbs are listed in the infinitive form.

Abbreviations

(intr.)	intransitive verb; does not take the postposition **ne** ﻧﮯ in the perfect tenses.
(tr.)	transitive verb; takes the postposition **ne** ﻧﮯ in the perfect tenses.
(+**ne**)	takes the postposition **ne** ﻧﮯ in the perfect tenses.
(-**ne**)	does not take the postposition **ne** ﻧﮯ in the perfect tenses.
(+/- **ne**)	may or may not take the postposition **ne** ﻧﮯ in the perfect tenses.
(+**ko**)	takes **ko** ﮐﻮ with its subject; indicates non-volitional action.

accept, agree	**mānnā** (+ne)	ﻣﺎﻧﻨﺎ
ache	**dard honā** (+ko)	ﺩﺭﺩﮨﻮﻧﺎ
afraid	**Dar lagnā** (+ko)	ﮈﺭ ﻟﮕﻨﺎ
(be) angry	**Gussā honā**	ﻏﺼﮧ ﮨﻮﻧﺎ
	Gussā karnā (+ne)	ﻏﺼﮧ ﮐﺮﻧﺎ
become angry	**Gussā ānā** (+ko)	ﻏﺼﮧ ﺁﻧﺎ
appear	**lagnā** (+ko), **nazar ānā** (+ko)	ﻟﮕﻨﺎ، ﻧﻈﺮ ﺁﻧﺎ
be	**honā** (-ne)	ﮨﻮﻧﺎ
be able to	**saknā** (-ne)	ﺳﮑﻨﺎ
beat	**mārnā** (+ne)	ﻣﺎﺭﻧﺎ
begin	**shuru honā** (intr.)	ﺷﺮﻭﻉ ﮨﻮﻧﺎ
	shuru karnā (tr.)	ﺷﺮﻭﻉ ﮐﺮﻧﺎ
break	**toRnā** (+ne)	ﺗﻮﮌﻧﺎ
bring	**lānā** (-ne)	ﻻﻧﺎ
burn	**jalnā** (intr.), **jalānā** (tr.)	ﺟﻠﻨﺎ، ﺟﻼﻧﺎ
buy	**xarīdnā** (+ne)	ﺧﺮﯾﺪﻧﺎ
call	**bulānā** (+ne)	ﺑﻼﻧﺎ
catch	**pakaRnā** (+ne)	ﭘﮑﮍﻧﺎ
celebrate	**manānā** (+ne)	ﻣﻨﺎﻧﺎ
change	**badalnā** (+ne)	ﺑﺪﻟﻨﺎ
choose	**intixāb karnā** (+ne)	ﺍﻧﺘﺨﺎﺏ ﮐﺮﻧﺎ

climb	caRʰnā (-ne)	چڑھنا
collide	x se Takrānā (+ne)	سے ٹکرانا
come	ānā (-ne)	آنا
compare/compete	x ka y se muqābalā karnā (+ne)	سے مقابلہ کرنا
complain	x se y kī shikāyat karnā (+ne)	کی شکایت کرنا
complete	purā karnā (+ne)	پورا کرنا
converse	x se bāt karnā (+ne)	سے بات کرنا
cost	x (amount) lagnā (-ne)	لگنا
count	ginnā (+ne)	گننا
cover	Dʰāknā (+ne)	ڈھانکنا
cry	ronā, cillānā (-ne)	رونا،چلّانا
cut	kaTnā (intr.), kāTnā (tr.)	کٹنا،کاٹنا
dance	nācnā (+ne)	ناچنا
desire	x kī xavāish honā (-ne)	کی خواہش ہونا
die	marnā (-ne)	مرنا
disappear	Gāib honā (intr.)	غائب ہونا
	Gāib karnā (tr.)	غائب کرنا
dislike	nāpasand honā (+ko)	ناپسند ہونا
	nāpasand karnā (+ne)	ناپسند کرنا
do	karnā (+ne)	کرنا
drink	pīnā (+ne)	پینا
drink (alcohol)	sharāb pīnā (+ne)	شراب پینا
drive	gāRī calānā (+ne)	گاڑی چلانا
earn	kamānā (+ne)	کمانا
eat/dine	kʰānā kʰānā (+ne)	کھانا کھانا
eat breakfast	nāshtā karnā (+ne)	ناشتہ کرنا
enjoy	mazā honā (intr.)	مزہ ہونا
	mazā karnā (tr.)	مزہ کرنا
	mazā lenā (tr.)	مزہ لینا

enquire	pūc^h gic^h karnā (+ne)	پوچھ گچھ کرنا
enter	dāxil honā (-ne)	گھسنا
fall	girnā (-ne)	گرنا
feed	k^{h}ilānā (+ne)	کھلانا
feel happy	xush honā (-ne)	خوش ہونا
feel sad	Gamgīn honā (-ne)	غمگین ہونا
feel sick	tabīyat xarāb honā (-ne)	طبیعت خراب ہونا
fight	laRnā (-ne)	لڑنا
finish	xatam honā (intr.)	ختم ہونا
	xatam karnā (tr.)	ختم کرنا
recover,	T$^+$īk honā (intr.)	ٹھیک ہونا
repair, fix	T$^+$īk karnā (tr.)	ٹھیک کرنا
fly	uRnā (intr.), uRānā (tr.)	اُڑنا،اُڑانا
forgive, pardon	māf karnā (+ne)	معاف کرنا
get down/descend	utarnā (-ne)	اُترنا
get hot	garmī paRnā (-ne)	گرمی پڑنا
give	denā (+ne)	دینا
go	jānā (-ne)	جانا
go back	vāpas jānā (-ne)	واپس جانا
grind	pīsnā (+ne)	پیسنا
hate	x se nafrat karnā (+ne)	سے نفرت کرنا
hear	sunnā (+ne)	سننا
	sunāī denā (+ko)	سنائی دینا
hire	karāye par lenā (+ne)	کرائے پر لینا
hope	x kī ummīd honā (-ne)	کی اُمید ہونا
(get) hurt	coT lagnā (+ko)	چوٹ لگنا
invite	x ke g^{h}ar ānā (-ne)	کے گھر آنا
	dāvat denā (+ne)	دعوت دینا

jump	**kūdnā (-ne)**	كودنا
kill	**mārnā (+ne)**	مارنا
knock at	**kʰaTkʰaTānā**	كھٹکھٹانا
	dastak denā (+ne)	دستک دینا
know	**jānnā (+ne)**	جاننا
	mālūm honā (+ko)	معلوم ہونا
	patā honā (+ko)	پتہ ہونا
come to know	**patā lagnā (+ko)**	پتہ لگنا
laugh	**hãsnā (-ne)**	ہنسنا
learn	**sīkʰnā (+ne)**	سیکھنا
like	**pasand honā (+ko)**	پسند ہونا
	pasand karnā (+ne)	پسند کرنا
	accʰā lagnā (+ko)	اچھا لگنا
live	**rɛhnā (-ne)**	رہنا
look	**dekʰnā (+ne)**	دیکھنا
love	x **se ishq honā (+ko)**	سے عشق ہونا
	x **se mahobbat karnā (+ne)**	سے محبت کرنا
make	**banānā (+ne)**	بنانا
meet	**milnā (-ne)**	ملنا
melt	**pigʰalnā (-ne)**	پگھلنا
mix	**milānā (+ne)**	ملانا
need, want	**cāhiye (+ko), cāhnā (+ne)**	چاہئے، چاہنا
	x **kī zarūrat honā (+ko)**	کی ضرورت ہونا
(be) nervous	**gʰabrānā (-ne)**	گھبرانا
object	x **par ɛtrāz karnā (+ne)**	پر اعتراض کرنا
open	**kʰulnā (intr.), kʰolnā (tr.)**	کھلنا، کھولنا
order (someone; but not something)	**hukam karnā (+ne)**	حکم کرنا
peel	**cʰīlnā (+ne)**	چھیلنا

permit	**ijāzat denā** (+ne)	اجازت دینا
persuade	**manānā** (+ne)	مَنانا
place	**rakʰnā** (+ne)	رکھنا
play (game, sport)	**kʰelnā** (+ne)	کھیلنا
play (instrument)	**bajānā** (+ne)	بَجانا
pour	**Dālnā** (+ne)	ڈالنا
praise	**x kī tārīf karnā** (+ne)	کی تعریف کرنا
prepare	**teyār honā** (intr.)	تیار ہونا
push	**dʰakelnā** (+ne)	دھکیلنا
put	**rakʰnā** (+ne), **Dālnā** (+ne)	رکھنا، ڈالنا
put off	**Tālnā** (+ne)	ٹالنا
quarrel	**laRnā** (-ne)	لڑنا
rain	**bārish honā** (-ne)	بارش ہونا
reach	**pahũcnā** (-ne)	پہنچنا
read	**paRʰnā** (+ne)	پڑھنا
recognize	**pɛhcānnā** (+ne)	پہچاننا
refuse, prohibit	**x se manā karnā** (+ne)	سے منع کرنا
remember	**yād honā** (intr.; +ko)	یاد ہونا
remember, memorize	**yād karnā** (+ne)	یاد کرنا
respect	**x kī izzat karnā** (+ne)	کی عزت کرنا
rest	**ārām karnā** (+ne)	آرام کرنا
return, come back	**vāpas ānā** (-ne)	واپس آنا
	lauTnā (-ne)	لوٹنا
return (something)	**vāpas karnā** (+ne)	واپس کرنا
ripe	**paknā** (-ne)	پکنا
rise	**uTʰnā** (-ne), **caRʰnā** (-ne)	اُٹھنا، چڑھنا
run	**bʰāgnā** (-ne)	بھاگنا
	dauRnā (-ne)	دوڑنا

say	**kɛhnā** (+ne)	کہنا
seem	**lagnā** (+ko)	لگنا
sell	**becnā** (+ne)	بیچنا
send	**bʰejnā** (+ne)	بھیجنا
show	**dikʰānā** (+ne)	دکھانا
to have a bath	**nahānā** (+/-ne)	نہانا
sing	**gānā** (+ne)	گانا
sit	**bɛTʰnā** (-ne)	بیٹھنا
sleep	**sonā** (-ne)	سونا
slip	**pʰisalnā** (-ne)	پھسلنا
sneeze	**cʰĩknā** (+/-ne)	چھینکنا
snow	**baraf girnā** (-ne)	برف گرنا
speak	**bolnā** (+/-ne)	بولنا
spend (money)	**xarc karnā** (+ne)	خرچ کرنا
spend (time)	**guzārnā** (+ne), **kāTnā** (+ne)	گزارنا، کاٹنا
spill	**girānā** (+ne)	گرانا
spread	**bicʰānā** (+ne)	بچھانا
stand	**kʰaRā honā** (-ne)	کھڑا ہونا
stay	**rɛhnā** (-ne), **Tʰɛhrnā** (-ne)	رہنا، ٹھہرنا
steal	**corī karnā** (+ne)	چوری کرنا
stop	**ruknā** (intr.),	رکنا
	roknā (tr.)	روکنا
study	**paRʰnā** (+/-ne)	پڑھنا
(be) surprised	**hɛrān honā** (-ne)	حیران ہونا
swim	**tɛrnā** (-ne)	تیرنا
take	**lenā** (+ne)	لینا
take care of	**dekʰ-bʰāl karnā** (+ne)	دیکھ بھال کرنا
taste	**cakʰnā** (+ne)	چکھنا

teach	**paR^hānā (+ne)**	پڑھانا
telephone	**Tɛlīfon karnā (+ne)**	ٹیلیفون کرنا
tell, mention	**batānā**	بتانا
think (of, about)	**x kā xayāl honā (-ne)**	کا خیال ہونا
	socnā (+ne)	سوچنا
throw	**p^heknā (+ne)**	پھینکنا
tired	**t^haknā (-ne)**	تھکنا
touch	**c^hūnā (+ne)**	چھونا
try	**x kī koshish karnā (+ne)**	کی کوشش کرنا
turn	**muRnā (intr.), moRnā (tr.)**	مُڑنا، موڑنا
turn over	**palaTnā (+ne)**	پلٹنا
understand	**samaj^hnā (+/-ne)**	سمجھنا
uproot	**uk^hāRnā (+ne)**	اکھاڑنا
use	**x kā istemāl karnā (+ne)**	کا استعمال کرنا
wait	**x kā intizār karnā (+ne)**	کا انتظار کرنا
wake up	**uT^hnā (-ne)**	اُٹھنا
walk	**calnā (-ne)**	چلنا
want, need	**cāhiye (+ko), cāhnā (+ne)**	چاہئے، چاہنا
wash	**d^honā (+ne)**	دھونا
waste	**gavā̃nā (+ne)**	گنوانا
wear	**pɛhɛnnā (+ne)**	پہننا
weep	**ronā (-ne)**	رونا
win	**jītnā (+/-ne)**	جیتنا
worry	**x kī fikr karnā (+ne)**	کی فکر ہونا
worship	**parastish karnā (+ne)**	پرستش کرنا
write	**lik^hnā (+ne)**	لکھنا

Urdu–English glossary

The Urdu vocabulary items used in the dialogues are presented below in Roman alphabetical order. However, it should be pointed out that the vowel symbol ɛ follows u, whereas the nasalized vowels (with ~) precede their corresponding oral vowels. Adjectives are given in the masculine singular forms and verbs are given in their infinitive forms. See Script Unit 5 for the pronunciation of the letters cʰoTī he (ه) and ɛn (ں).

ab	اَب	now (adv.)
abbā (m.)	اَبّا	father (colloq.)
abʰī	اَبھی	right now
abʰī bʰī	اَبھی بھی	even now
accʰā	اَچّھا	good, OK
accʰāī (f.)	اَچّھائی	good (n.), quality, ideal, virtue
accʰā lagnā (+**ko**)	اَچّھا لگنا	to like
adā (f.)	اَدا	fulfilment, performance
adā karnā (+**ne**)	اَدا کرنا	to perform
adākār (m.)	اداکار	actor
adākārī (f.)	اداکاری	acting
afsos (m.)	اَفسوس	sorrow
aglā	اگلا	next
ajīb	عجیب	strange (adj.)
akelā	اَکیلا	alone
aksar	اَکثر	often, usually
alag	الگ	separate

alfāz (mpl.)	الفاظ	words
allāh (m.)	اللہ	God
amal (m.)	عمل	action
amīr	امیر	rich
anāj (m.)	اناج	grain, corn
andāz (m.)	انداز	style
and^hā (m.)	اندھا	blind
and^herā (m.)	اندھیرا	darkness
aŋgrez (m.)	انگریز	an Englishman
aŋgrezī (f.)	انگریزی	the English language
aŋgūT^hī (f.)	انگوٹھی	ring
apnā	اپنا	one's own
aqīdat (f.)	عقیدت	faith, devotion
aql (f.)	عقل	wisdom
arsā	عرصہ	time, period
arz (f.)	عرض	request
asal mẽ	اصل میں	in fact, in reality
aslī	اصلی	real, genuine
as-salām'alɛkum	السلام علیکم	Hello (a common greeting among Muslims)
aur	اور	and, more, other, else
aur b^hī	اور بھی	even more
aurat (f.)	عورت	woman
azīm-ul-shān (adj.)	عظیم الشان	magnificent, spectacular
azīz (adj.)	عزیز	dear
ãk^h (f.)	آنکھ	eye
āb (m.)	آب	water
ādāb (m.)	آداب	salutation, greetings
ādī	عادی	habituated, addicted

ādmī (m.)	آدمی	man
āftāb (m.)	آفتاب	sun
āftāb caR^hnā	آفتاب چڑھنا	sunrise
āftāb Dūbnā	آفتاب ڈوبنا	sunset
āg (f.)	آگ	fire
āgah karnā (+**ne**)	آگاہ کرنا	to inform someone
āGāz (m.)	آغاز	beginning
āGāz honā (-**ne**)	آغاز ہونا	to begin
āj-kal	آج کل	nowadays
ālim (m.)	عالم	learned man, learned(adj.)
ām (m.)	آم	mango
ānā (-**ne**)	آنا	to come
āne vālā	آنے والا	to be about to come
āp	آپ	you (hon.)
āpā (f.)	آپا	affectionate term for elder sister (colloq.)
āp kā	آپ کے	your
āp ko	آپ کو	to you
ārām (m.)	آرام	comfort, rest
ārām karnā (+**ne**)	آرام کرنا	to rest
ārzī (adj.)	عارضی	temporary
ārzū (f.)	آرزو	desire, longing
āTā (m.)	آٹا	flour
ātish fishã (m.)	آتش فشاں	volcano
āvārah (m.)	آوارہ	a vagabond
āzād (adj.)	آزاد	free
bacānā (+**ne**)	بچانا	to save
baccã (m.)	بچّہ	child

bacpan (m.)	بَچپَن	childhood
badmāsh (m.)	بَدمعاش	villain
bahār (m., adj.)	بہار	spring, outside
bahut	بہُت	very
bahut xūb	بہُت خُوب	great! splendid!
baje	بَجے	o'clock
bakrā (m.)	بَکرا	goat
banānā (+ne)	بَنانا	to make
banāras	بَنارس	Banaras (one of the oldest cities of India)
band	بَند	closed
bandah (m.)	بَندہ	servant, an individual
band honā (-ne)	بَند ہونا	to be closed
band karnā (+ne)	بَند کرنا	to close
bannā (-ne)	بَننا	to be made
baqra īd (f.)	بَقر عید	the Muslim festival of sacrifices
bartāniyā	بَرطانیہ	Britain
bartānvī (f.)	بَرطانوی	British
baRā	بَڑا	big
baRʰnā (-ne)	بَڑھنا	to increase, to advance
bayān	بَیان	report
batānā (+ne)	بَتانا	to tell
bād mē	بعد میں	afterwards, later
bādshah	بادشاہ	king
bādshāhat (m.)	بادشاہت	kingdom, reign
bāG (m.)	باغ	garden, park
bār (f.)	بار	time
bārah	بارہ	twelve

bārāt (f.)	بارات	a wedding procession
bāt (f.)	بات	matter, conversation, topic
bā̃Tnā (+ne)	بانٹنا	to distribute
becnā (+ne)	بیچنا	to sell
bekār	بے کار	useless, unemployed
beTā (m.)	بیٹا	son
beTī (f.)	بیٹی	daughter
bʰaī (m., m.pl.)	بھئی	hey, well (excl.) (colloq.)
bʰarnā (+ne)	بھرنا	to fill
bʰāgnā (-ne)	بھاگنا	to run
bʰāgte (pres. ppl.)	بھاگتے	running
bʰāī (m.)	بھائی	brother/brothers
bʰej denā (+ne)	بھیج دینا	to send (compound verb)
bʰejnā (+ne)	بھیجنا	to send
bʰeR (f.)	بھیڑ	a sheep
bʰī	بھی	also, as well
bʰūlnā (+/-ne)	بھولنا	to forget
bʰūt (m.)	بھوت	ghost
bijlī (f.)	بجلی	electricity, lightning
bimārī (f.)	بیماری	illness
bīmā (m.)	بیمہ	insurance
bīvī (f.)	بیوی	wife
bolnā (+/-ne)	بولنا	to speak
bujʰānā (+ne)	بجھانا	to extinguish, to put out (light, fire, etc.)
bulbul (f.)	بلبل	nightingale
burā	برا	bad
burāī (f.)	برائی	evil
buxār (m.)	بخار	fever

bɛhɛn (f.)	بہن	sister
bɛrā (m.)	بیرا	waiter
cakʰnā (+ne)	چکھنا	to taste
calānaā (+ne)	چلانا	to drive, to manage (business), to light firecrackers
calnā (-ne)	چلنا	to walk
carxā (m.)	چَرخا	a spinning wheel
caudā	چودہ	fourteen
cā̃d (m.)	چاند	moon
cā̃dnī	چاندنی	moonlit
cāhiye (+ko)	چاہئے	desire, want
cāhnā (+ne)	چاہنا	to want
cār	چار	four
cāy (f.)	چائے	tea
cʰatrī (f.)	چھتری	umbrella
cʰoRnā (+ne)	چھوڑنا	to leave
cʰoTā	چھوٹا	small, short
cʰupākar	چھپاکر	secretly
cʰuTTī (f.)	چھٹّی	vacation
cillānā (-ne)	چلّانا	to scream
cirāG	چراغ	a lamp
cīn (m.)	چین	China
cīnī (f.; adj)	چینی	sugar, Chinese
cīxnā (-ne)	چیخنا	to scream
cor (m.)	چور	thief
corī karnā (+ne)	چوری	to steal
cũke	چونکہ	because

daftar (m.)	دفتر	office
daftar-e-hijrat (m.)	دفتر ہجرت	immigration office
dahī (m/f)	دہی	yogurt
damishq	دمشق	Damascus
darasl (adv.)	دراصل	actually
dard (m.)	درد	pain, ache
darvāzā (m.)	دروازہ	door
das	دس	ten
dast (m.)	دست	diarrhoea
dastkārī (f.)	دستکاری	handicrafts
dauRnā (-ne)	دوڑنا	to run
davāī/davā (f.)	دوائی، دوا	medicine
davā xānā	دواخانہ	pharmacy
dāG (m.)	داغ	stain, mark
DākTar (m.)	ڈاکٹر	doctor
Dālnā (+ ne)	ڈالنا	to put in, to throw, to pour
dām (m.)	دام	price
dāvat (f.)	دعوت	feast, invitation
de denā (+ne)	دے دینا	to give (for someone else's benefit)
de jānā	دے جانا	to give
dekʰnā (+ne)	دیکھنا	to see, to look at, to notice
der (f.)	دیر	delay, time (period of, slot of)
dʰūm-dʰām se	دھوم دھام سے	with gusto
dikʰānā	دکھانا	to show
dimāG (m.)	دماغ	brain
din (m.)	دن	day
do	دو	two

donõ	دونوں	both
dost (m.)	دوست	friend
dozax (m.)	دوزَخ	hell
dulhan (f.)	دُلہن	bride
duniyā (f.)	دُنیا	world
dushman (m.)	دُشمن	enemy
dushmanī	دُشمنی	enmity, hostility
dûlhā (m.)	دُلہا	bridegroom
dūr	دُور	far, distant
dūr karnā (+ne)	دُور کرنا	to dispel, to eliminate
dūsrā (m.; adj.)	دُوسرا	second, other, another
ehsās (m.)	اَحساس	feeling
ek	ایک	one
ek aur	ایک اور	another
ek-do	ایک دو	one or two
ek dūsre se	ایک دوسرے سے	with one another, each other
ek-sā	ایک سا	alike
faqt	فَقط	simply (adv.)
faqīr (m.)	فقیر	beggar, ascetic
farishtā (m.)	فَرِشتہ	angel
farmānā (+ne)	فَرمانا	to say, to speak
farq (m.)	فَرق	difference
farz (m.)	فَرض	duty
fasal (f.)	فَصَل	crop
fasād (m.)	فَساد	an altercation

fauj (f.)	فَوج	an army
fauran	فَوراً	immediately (adv.)
fāriG (adj.)	فارغ	free, leisure
fikr (f.)	فِكر	worry
firāq (m.)	فِراق	separation
fursat (f.)	فُرصَت	free time, spare time, leisure
Galat (adj.)	غَلَط	wrong
Galat-fahmī (f.)	غَلَط فہمی	misconception, misunderstanding
gale lagānā (+**ne**)	گلے لگانا	to embrace
gale milnā (-**ne**)	گلے مِلنا	to embrace
Garq karnā (+**ne**)	غَرق کرنا	to immerse
Gaur (m.)	غور	consideration, attention
gavaiyā (m.)	گویّا	singer
gaye	گئے	went
Gazal (f.)	غَزَل	a poem or song (usually romantic)
gānā (m.), (v. +**ne**)	گانا	song (n.), to sing (v.)
gāõ (m.)	گاؤں	village
gāõ vālā (m.)	گاؤں والا	villager
gāRī (f.)	گاڑی	car, vehicle
Gɛr qānūnī	غیر قانونی	illegal
gʰanTā (m.)	گھنٹہ	hour
gʰar (m.)	گھر	house
gʰoRā (m.)	گھوڑا	horse
gʰoRī (f.)	گھوڑی	mare
ginnā (+**ne**)	گننا	to count
gīlā	گیلا	wet
golī (f.)	گولی	tablet, pill, bullet

gosht (m.)	گوشت	meat
gujarāt (m.)	گجرات	the State of Gujarat
Gulām (m.)	غلام	slave
gulshan (m.)	گلشن	garden
gulūkar (m.)	گلوکار	(performer) singer
gumnā (-ne)	گمنا	to be lost
Gusal xānā (m.)	غسل خانہ	bathroom
Gussā (m.)	غصہ	anger
guTʰlī (f.)	گٹھلی	stone (of a fruit)
guzarnā (-ne)	گزرنا	to pass by
guzar jānā (-ne)	گزر جانا	to pass away, to die
guzārish (f.)	گزارش	request
Gɛr (m.)	غیر	stranger
Gɛrvatnī (m.)	غیر وطنی	foreigner
gyārah	گیارہ	eleven
haj (m.)	حج	pilgrimage to Mecca
halāl (adj.)	حلال	lawful
halāl karnā (+ne)	حلال کرنا	to slaughter
hamārā	ہمارا	our
hamāre yahā̃	ہمارے یہاں	at our place (house, country, etc.)
hameshā	ہمیشہ	always
hamlā karnā (+ne)	حملہ کرنا	to attack
hammām (m.)	حمام	hot bath
hamsāyā (m.)	ہمسایہ	neighbour
haqīqatan	حقیقتاً	in reality
harānā (+ne)	ہرانا	to defeat
hasad (f.)	حسد	envy, jealousy

havā (f.)	ہوا	air, wind
havāī aDDā (m.)	ہوائی اڈّا	airport
hazār	ہزار	thousand
hazrat (m.)	حضرت	a title applied to a great man
hā̃	ہاں	yes
hādisā	حادثہ	accident
hājī (m.)	حاجی	a person who has performed a pilgrimage to Mecca
hākim (m.)	حاکم	ruler
hāl (m.)	حال	condition
hāl mẽ	حال میں	recently
hālā̃ ke	حالانکہ	although
hāt^h (m.)	ہاتھ	hand
hindū	ہندو	a Hindu
hindustān (m.)	ہندوستان	India
hindustāni	ہندوستانی	Indian
honā (-ne)	ہونا	to be
hukam (m.)	حکم	order
hussen (m.)	حسین	a name (the Prophet Muhammad's grandson)
huzūr (m.)	حضور	presence, your majesty! (intj.)
hū̃	ہوں	am
hẽ	میں	are
hε	ہے	is
ijāzat	اجازت	permission
ilm (m.)	علم	knowledge
imārat (f.)	عمارت	building

inglistān (m.)	انگلستان	England
intixāb karnā (+ne)	انتخاب	to choose, to pick, to elect
intizār (m/f)	انتظار	wait
intizār karnā (+ne)	انتظار کرنا	to wait
iqrār karnā (+ne)	اقرار کرنا	to accept
irādah (m.)	اراده	intention
ishārah (m.)	اشاره	gesture, sign
ishq (m.)	عشق	love
ishq karnā	عشق کرنا	to love
islāmī	اسلامی	Islamic
isliye	اس لئے	therefore, so, thus, because of this
ism-e-sharīf	اسم شریف	name (lit. distinguished appellation)
istaqbāl (m.)	استقبال	reception, welcome
istaqbāl karnā (+ne)	استقبال کرنا	to welcome (a guest)
itnā (m.; adj.)	اتنا	so much/many, this much/many
itne mē	اتنے میں	in the meanwhile
izhār (m.)	اظهار	disclosure
izzat (f.)	عزّت	respect
īd (f.)	عید	a Muslim festival
īd-gāh (f.)	عید گاه	a place or a mosque where Muslims assemble for prayers on Id day
īd-ul-azhā (f.)	عیدالاضحی	the Muslim festival of sacrifices
īd-ul-fitr (f.)	عیدالفطر	the Muslim festival celebrated at the end of Ramadan
ījād (f.)	ایجاد	an invention
īsāī	عیسائی	a Christian

īsvī	عیسوی	century of Christian calender
jab (relative pronoun)	جَب	when
jab ki	جَب کہ	while
jabran	جَبراً	by force (adv.)
jahāz (m.)	جَہاز	a ship, vessel, plane
jalānā (+ne)	جَلانا	to light, to burn; to kindle
jaldī	جَلدی	quickly, hurry
jamā (f.)	جَمع	collection, total
jamāt (f.)	جَماعت	an assembly, a class
janāb	جَناب	sir
jaŋg-e-azīm	جنگِ عظیم	world war
javāb (m.)	جَواب	answer
javāb denā (+ne)	جَواب دینا	to answer, to reply
jān (f.)	جان	life
jānā (-ne)	جانا	to go
jāne do (compound verb)	جانے دو	let (someone) go.
jāne vāle	جانے والے	those who are going
jānvar (m.)	جانور	animal
jʰagRā (m.)	جَھگڑا	quarrel, dispute
jism (m.)	جِسم	body
jī	جی	honorific word (optional with greetings)
jīt (m.)	جیت	victory
josh (m.)	جوش	exitement, passion
josh-o-xarosh	جوش و خروش	excitement
jeb (f.)	جیب	pocket
jeb kāTnā (+ne)	جیب کاٹنا	to pickpocket

jɛsā	جیسا	as
jɛse (ki)	جیسے	as, as if
kab	کب	when
kabʰī	کبھی	ever
kabʰī kabʰī	کبھی کبھی	sometimes
kabʰī naʰī̃	کبھی نہیں	never
kaccā	کچا	raw
kahā̃	کہاں	where
kahānī (f.)	کہانی	story
kaī	کئی	several
kal	کل	yesterday, tomorrow
kam	کم	less
kamāl (m.)	کمال	perfection
kamrā (m.)	کمرہ	room
kaŋgā (m.)	کنگا	comb
kapRā (m.)	کپڑا	cloth
karnā (+**ne**)	کرنا	to do
karoR	کروڑ	ten million
kaTnā (-**ne**)	کٹنا	to be cut
kaun sā	کون سا	which one
kā	کا	of
kāfī	کافی	enough, sufficient
kāGaz (m.)	کاغذ	paper
kām honā (+**ko**)	کام ہونا	to have work
kārīgar (m.)	کاری گر	an artisan
kārīgarī (f.)	کاری گری	artistic work
kāTnā (+**ne**)	کاٹنا	to cut

ke alāvāh	کے علاوہ	besides, in addition to
(ke) baGɛr	کے بغیر	without
ke bajāe	کے بجائے	instead
(ke) bād	کے بعد	after, later
ke bāre mẽ	کے بارے میں	about, concerning
ke liye	کے لئے	for
ke pās	کے پاس	have, near
ke sāt^h	کے ساتھ	with, together
k^hānā (m.), (v.+**ne**)	کھانا	food (n.), to eat (v.)
k^helnā (+/-**ne**)	کھیلنا	to play
k^hilānā (+**ne**)	کھلانا	to feed (causative verb)
k^hiloenā (m.)	کھلونا	a toy
k^hiRkī (f.)	کھڑکی	window
k^ho jānā (-**ne**)	کھو جانا	to be lost
k^holnā (+**ne**)	کھولنا	to open
kis	کس	which
kisī	کسی	someone
kitāb (f.)	کتاب	book
kitnā	کتنا	how many
kījie	کیجے	please do
koī	کوئی	some, any, someone, anyone
koshish (f.)	کوشش	effort
kuc^h	کچھ	some
kul	کل	total
kuR^hi (f.)	کڑھی	curry *(*see notes)*
kursī (f.)	کرسی	chair
kuttā (m.)	کتّا	dog
kɛhlānā (-**ne**)	کہلانا	to be called/named

kɛhnā (+ne)	کہنا	to say
kɛhte hɛ̄	کہتے ہیں	it is said
kɛsā	کیسا	how
kɛse	کیسے	how
kyā	کیا	what
kyā!	کیا	What! I do not believe it!
kyõ	کیوں	why
lafz (m.)	لفظ	word
lagām (f.)	لگام	bridle
lagānā (+ **ne**)	لگانا	to attach, to stick, to fix, to apply
lagnā (+**ko**)	لگنا	to seem, to be applied, to appear
lagnā (-**ne**)	لگنا	to take, to cost
landan	لندن	London
laRāi (f.)	لڑائی	fight, battle, war
laRkā	لڑکا	boy
laRkī	لڑکی	girl
lassī (f.)	لسّی	Indian-style drinking yoghurt
lauTnā (-**ne**)	لوٹنا	to return, to come back (colloq.)
lāl	لال	red
lālac (m.)	لالچ	greed
lānā (-**ne**)	لانا	to bring
lekin	لیکن	but
lenā (+**ne**)	لینا	to take
likʰnā (+**ne**)	لکھنا	to write
log (m.)	لوگ	people

lok dāstān (f.)	لوک داستان	folk tale
macchar (m.)	مچّھر	mosquito
macchlī (f.)	مچھلی	fish
maGrib (m.)	مغرب	west, the West
maGribī	مغربی	western, Western
mahak (f.)	مہک	fragrance
mahīnā (m.)	مہینہ	month
majbūran	مجبوراً	under pressure, being forced
malmal (f.)	ململ	muslin
manā	منع	forbidden
manānā (+**ne**)	منانا	to celebrate (festival, holiday)
maŋgnī (f.)	منگنی	engagement
maŋgnī honā (-**ne**)	منگنی ہونا	to be engaged
maqsad (m.)	مقصد	aim, purpose, intention
mard (m.)	مرد	man
marīz (m.)	مریض	patient
marnā (-**ne**)	مرنا	to die
martabā (m.)	مرتبہ	time
masālā (m.)	مسالہ	spice
masāledār	مسالے دار	spicy
mashhūr	مشہور	famous
masjid (f.)	مسجد	mosque
maslan	مثلاً	for example
mat	مت	not (see notes)
matlab (m.)	مطلب	meaning
maulvī (m.)	مولوی	Muslim priest, cleric or one learned in Muslim law
mauqā (m.)	موقع	opportunity

mausam (m.)	مَوسَم	season, weather
mausīqī (f.)	مَوسیقی	music
mazā karnā (+**ne**)	مزہ کرنا	to enjoy
mā̃ (f.)	ماں	mother
mālūm honā (+**ko**)	معلوم ہونا	to know, to be known
muāf/māf	مُعاف	forgiven
mātam (m.)	ماتم	mourning
meharbānī (f.)	مہربانی	kindness
milnā (-**ne**)	ملنا	to meet
milnā	ملنا	to be available
milnā (+**ko**)	ملنا	to find, to receive
mirc (f.)	مرچ	chilli peppers
miTʰāi (f.)	مٹھائی	sweet
mizāj (m.)	مزاج	temperament, nature
muāmlā (m.)	معاملہ	matter
mu'āshrā/māshrā	معاشرہ	culture, society
muāvzah (m.)	معاوضہ	compensation
mubārak	مُبارک	auspicious, blessed
mubārk ho	مُبارک ہو	congratulations
muGal	مُغل	Mughal
muharram (m.)	مُحرّم	Muharram (the first month of the Muslim calendar)
mujʰe	مجھے	(to) me
mulāqāt (f.)	مُلاقات	meeting
mulāqāt honā (-**ne**)	مُلاقات ہونا	to meet
muqaddas	مُقدّس	sacred
murGā (m.)	مُرغا	chicken
musalmān (m.)	مُسلمان	Muslim
musannif (m.)	مُصَنِّف	writer

mushkil	مُشکِل	difficult, difficulty
mɛ̃	میں	I
mɛ̃	میں	in, during
mɛhɛ̃gā	مہنگا	expensive
mɛhɛl (m.)	مَحل	palace
nadī (f.)	ندی	river
nafā (m.)	نفع	profit
nafrat (f.)	نفرَت	disgust, hatred
nahī̃	نہیں	not
nahī̃ to	نہیں تو	otherwise
namak (m.)	نمک	salt
namaste	نمستے	Hindu greeting and reply to greetings
namāz (f.)	نماز	Muslim prayers
namāz paRʰnā (+ne)	نماز پڑھنا	to say (one's) prayers
namī (f.)	نمی	humidity, dampness
naqal (f.)	نقل	copy, fake, imitation
nayā	نیا	new
nazar (f.)	نظر	vision
nazrānah (m.)	نذرانہ	gift
nā?	نا	isn't it?
nā...nā	نا......نا	neither...nor
nām (m.)	نام	name
nāpasand (f.)	ناپسند	dislike
nāshtā (m.)	ناشتہ	breakfast
ne	نے	agent marker in perfective tenses
nihāyat (f.)	نہایت	the extreme

nikāh (m.)	نِكاح	matrimony
nikāh paRhānā (+ne)	نِكاح پَڑھانا	to perform the marriage service
nisbatan	نِسبۃً	ratio
oh	اوہ	exclamation of pain/sorrow
pahucnā (-ne)	پَہُنچنا	to reach, arrive
pakaRnā (+ne)	پَکڑنا	to catch
par	پَر	on, at
pareshān	پَریشان	troubled
parhez (m.)	پَرہیز	abstinence
parhez karnā (+ne)	پَرہیز کَرنا	to abstain from, to avoid
parvānā (m.)	پَروانہ	moth, licence
parvāz (f.)	پَرواز	flight
paRʰnā (+ne)	پَڑھنا	to study, to read
paRnā (-ne)	پَڑنا	to fall, to lie down, to occur
pasand (f.)	پَسَند	choice, liking
pasanddīdah (adj.)	پَسَندیدہ	favourite
pashmīnā (adj.)	پَشمینہ	woollen (made from a specific variety of Kashmiri wool which is very light)
patā (m.)	پَتہ	address
patā lagnā (+ko)	پَتہ لگنا	to come to know
pālnā (-ne)	پالنا	to bring up (a child)
pānā (+ne)	پانا	to find, to obtain
pānī (m.)	پانی	water
pās	پاس	near
pɛhcānnā (+ne)	پَہچاننا	to recognize

pʰal (m.)	بَهل	fruit
pʰir	پِھر	again, then
picʰlā	پِچھلا	last
pīnā (+ne)	پینا	to drink
pulis vālā (m.)	پولیس والا	policeman
purānā	پُرانا	old (inanimate)
pūcʰnā (-ne)	پوچھنا	to ask
pūrā (m., adj.)	پُورا	full
pūrā	پُورا	complete, whole, full
pūrā karnā (+ne)	پُورا کرنا	to complete
pɛGām (m.)	پَیغام	message
pɛgambar (m.)	پَیغمبر	prophet
pɛhlā	پَہلا	first
pɛhle	پَہلے	(at) first, ago, previously
pɛhɛnnā (+ ne)	پَہننا	to wear
pɛsā (m.)	پیسہ	money; one hundredth of a Rupee
pyār (m.)	پیار	love
qabūl (m.)	قبول	assent, acknowledgement
qabūl honā (+ko)	قبول ہونا	to be accepted
qabūl karnā (+ne)	قبول کرنا	to accept
qadr (f.)	قَدر	dignity, value
qafas (m.)	قَفَس	cage, network
qamīz (f.)	قمیض	shirt
qarīb	قریب	close
qarz (m.)	قَرض	debt, loan
qāhat (m)	قَحط پڑنا	famine
qālīn (f.)	قالین	a woollen carpet

qānūn	قانون	law, principles (fig.)
qānūnan	قانوناً	by law
qismat (f.)	قسمت	fate, luck
qīmat (f.)	قیمت	price
qudrat (f.)	قدرت	nature, universe
qurbān (m.)	قُربان	a sacrifice
qurbānī (f.)	قُربانی	sacrifice
qurbānī karnā (+ne)	قُربانی کرنا	to sacrifice
qɛd xānā (m.)	قید خانہ	jail, prison
ramzān (m.)	رمضان	Ramadan (the ninth month of the Muslim calender)
rañj-o-Gam	رنج و غم	sorrow
raŋg (m.)	رنگ	colour
rasm (f.)	رسم	custom, order
rāt (f.)	رات	night
rāz (m.)	راز	secret, mystery
relgāRī (f.)	ریل گاڑی	train
resham (m.)	ریشم	silk
reshmī (adj.)	ریشمی	silk
rishtedār	رشتہ دار	relatives
rivāj (m.)	رواج	custom
roshnī (f.)	روشنی	light
roz	روز	daily
rozah (m.)	روزہ	a fast
rozah rakʰnā (+ne)	روزہ رکھنا	to keep a fast
ruknā (-ne)	رُکنا	to stop
rupaye (m.)	روپے	Rupees (Indian/Pakistani currency)

rux (m.)	رُخ	direction, face
rūh (f.)	روح	soul, spirit
rɛhnā (**-ne**)	رہنا	to live
sab	سب	all
sabaq (m.)	سَبَق	lesson, moral
sabzī (f.)	سَبزی	vegetable
sac (m.)	سَچ	truth, true
sac!	سَچ	Really! It can't be true!
safar (m.)	سَفر	travel
safar nāmah (m.)	سَفرنامہ	An account of one's travel/passport
sahārā (m.)	سَہارا	support
sajāvaT (f.)	سَجاوَٹ	decoration
saknā (**-ne**)	سَکنا	can, be able to
salāh (f.)	صَلاح	advice
salāh lenā (**+ne**)	صَلاح لینا	to seek/take advice
salāh mānnā (**+ne**)	صَلاح ماننا	to accept/take advice
salām (m.)	سَلام	Muslim greeting and reply to the greeting (colloq.)
samajʰnā (**+/-ne**)	سَمجھنا	to understand
sar (m.)	سَر	head
sau	سَو	hundred
savāb (m.)	ثَواب	a virtuous action
savāl (m.)	سَوال	question
savāl nāmā	سَوال نامہ	questionnaire, form
saverā (m.)	سَوِیرا	early (in the morning)
sādā	سادہ	simple
sāf	صاف	clean, clear

sāhab (m.)	صاحب	sir
sāl (m.)	سال	year
sāmān (m.)	سامان	baggage, goods, stuff, tools
sāqī (m.)	ساقی	one who serves a drink (i.e. drinks waiter)
sārā	سارا	whole, full
sāRī (f.)	ساڑی	saree
sās (f.)	ساس	mother-in-law
sāt baje	سات بجے	seven o'clock
se	سے	from, with, by, than
shabnam (f.)	شبنم	dew
shahīd (m.)	شہید	a martyr
shahīd karnā (+ne)	شہید کرنا	to kill (i.e. to make a martyr of)
shalvār (f.)	شلوار	loose native trousers
sharah	شرح	law/rate
sharīf	شریف	noble
sharīk (m.)	شریک	partner
sharīk honā (-ne)	شریک ہونا	to participate
shauq (m.)	شوق	hobby, fondness, interest
shādī (f.)	شادی	marriage
shādī-shudā	شادی شدہ	married
shāl (f.)	شال	a shawl
shām (f.)	شام	evening
shāmil (adj.)	شامل	comprising
shāmil ho jānā (-ne)	شامل ہو جانا	to be included
shāndār	شاندار	splendid, great
shāyad	شاید	perhaps
shiā	شیعہ	Shia (Muslim)

shor (m.)	شور	noise
shukrānā	شُکرانہ	thanksgiving
shukriyā (m.)	شُکریہ	thanks
shurū karnā (+ne)	شُروع کرنا	to begin
sheher (m.)	شہر	city
sifar (m.)	صفر	zero
sifārish	سفارش	recommendation
sifārishi	سفارشی	recommendation
sikkā (m.)	سِکّہ	a coin, currency
sipāhī (m.)	سپاہی	soldier
sirf	صرف	only
sivaihyā̃ (f.)	سویّاں	name of a dessert
sīkʰnā (+ne)	سیکھنا	to learn
socnā (+ne)	سوچنا	to think
solvī̃	سولہویں	sixteenth
subā (f.)	صُبح	morning
sultān (m.)	سُلطان	Sultan, king, emperor
sunherā (m.; adj.)	سُنہرا	golden
sunte hī (sun+ te hī part.)	سُنتے ہی	as soon as (someone) heard
sūkʰā (m., adj.)	سوکھنا	dry
sūraj (m.)	سورج	sun
sūt (m.)	سوت	cotton
sūtī (adj.)	سوتی	cotton (adj.)
tabdīlī (f.)	تبدیلی	change, transformation
tabīyat (f.)	طبیعت	health, disposition
tab tak	تب تک	by then
taklīf (f.)	تکلیف	trouble, bother

taklīf denā (+**ne**)	تکلیف دینا	to bother
talāq (m.)	طلاق	divorce
tamām (adj.)	تمام	whole, entire
taqrīban	تقریباً	approximately, roughly, about
taqvīm (f.)	تقویم	calendar
tar	تر	wet
tarah tarah	طرح طرح	different
tarī (f.)	تری	liquid
tarīqā (m.)	طریقہ	manner, method
tashrīf (f.)	تشریف	(a term signifying respect)
tashrīf lānā (-**ne**)	تشریف لانا	to grace one's place, welcome, come
tashrīf rakʰnā (+**ne**)	تشریف رکھنا	to be seated
taxt (m.)	تخت	throne
tāj (m.)	تاج	crown
tāj mɛhɛl (m.)	تاج محل	the Taj Mahal
tālīm	تعلیم	education
tāzā	تازہ	fresh
tāziyā	تعزیہ	tazia (replica of Hussain's tomb)
ta'ām xānā	طعام خانہ	restaurant
tehvār	تہوار	festival
tez	تیز	fast, quick, sharp, strong
tʰā	تھا	was
Tʰīk	ٹھیک	fine, OK
Tʰīk-Tʰāk	ٹھیک ٹھاک	fine
tʰoRā	تھوڑا	little, few
Tīkā lagānā (+**ne**)	ٹیکہ لگانا	to give an injection/a shot

to (particle)	تو	then, as regards
totā (m.)	طوطا	a parrot
tɛrnā (-ne)	تیرنا	to swim
umar (f.)	عمر	age
umdā	عمده	fine, excellent
ummīd (f.)	اُمّید	hope
uTʰnā (-ne)	اُٹھنا	to get up
ɛb (m.)	عَیب	fault, disgrace
ɛnak (f.)	عینَک	spectacles
ɛsā	اَیسا	such
ɛsh (m.)	عیش	luxury, pleasure
vahī (vah+hī)	وَہی	same, that very
vaqt (m.)	وَقت	time
varaq (m.)	وَرَق	page of a book
vādā (m.)	وَعده	promise
vādā karnā (+ne)	وعده کرنا	to promise
vāh	واہ	ah! excellent! bravo!
vāh! vāh!	واہ واہ	wow! wow! bravo!
vālid (m.)	والِد	father
vāldah (f.)	والِده	mother
vāldɛn (m.)	والدَین	parents
va-'alɛkum as-salām	وعلیکم السلام	hello (reply to Muslim greeting)
vāpas	واپَس	back
vāpas ānā (-ne)	واپَس آنا	to come back
vāqiāt (m.pl.)	واقعات	events

vo	وہ	he, she, they, that
vo kɛse	وہ کیسے	how come?
vɛse	ویسے	otherwise, in addition, like that, similarly
xabar (f.)	خبر	news
xaccar (m.)	خچّر	mule
xalīl (m.)	خلیل	a true friend
xarāb	خراب	bad
xarc (m.)	خرچ	expenditure
xarīdnā (+**ne**)	خریدنا	to buy
xatam	ختم	ended, concluded
xatarnāk	خطرناک	dangerous
xatrā (m.)	خطرہ	danger
xayāl (m.)	خیال	opinion, view
xazānah (m.)	خزانہ	a treasury, treasure
xāb (xvāb) (m.)	خواب	dream
xāliq (m.)	خالق	the Creator
xāndān (m.)	خاندان	family
xānsāmā (m.)	خانسامہ	Cook
xāskar	خاص کر	especially, particularly
xās taur se	خاص طور سے	especially, particularly
xātir (f.)	خاطر	hospitality, favour
xāvind (m.)	خاوند	husband
xidmat (f.)	خدمت	service
xitāb (m.)	خطاب	title
xud	خود	oneself
xudā (m.)	خدا	God
xudā hāfiz	خدا حافظ	goodbye

xushbū (f.)	خوشبو	fragrance (lit. happy smell)
xush-hālī (f.)	خوش حالی	prosperity
xushī	خوشی	happiness
xūbsūrat	خوبصورت	beautiful, pretty, handsome
xūnī (m.)	خونی	a murderer
xɛrāt karnā (+ne)	خیرات کرنا	to give alms
xɛriyat (f.)	خیریت	safety, welfare
yahā̃	یہاں	here
yahā̃ tak ki	یہاں تک کہ	to the point, to the exent that
yaum (m.)	یوم	day
yā	یا	or
yād	یاد	memory
yād dilānā (+ne)	یاد دلانا	to remind
yānī	یعنی	that is, in other words
yār (m.)	یار	pal, friend, lover
zabān (f.)	زَبان	language, tongue
zalīl	ذَلیل	disgraced, mean
zamānā (m.)	زَمانہ	time(s), period
zarā	ذرا	little, somewhat
zard	زَرد	yellow
zar-e-mubādilā	زَرِمُبادلہ	foreign exchange
zar-e-naqd	زَرِنقد	cash
zarūr	ضرور	of course, certainly
zarūrat (f.)	ضرورت	need, necessity
zarūrī	ضروری	important, urgent, necessary

zāhir	ظاہر	apparent, evident
zālim (m.)	ظالم	a tyrant, cruel (adj.)
zindā	زندہ	alive
zindagī (f.)	زندگی	life
ziyārat (f.)	زیارت	pilgrimage
ziyzāhir	ظاہر	apparent, evident
zor se	زور سے	loudly
zor denā (+ne)	زور دینا	to emphasize
zulm (m.)	ظلم	oppression
zyādā (invariable)	زیادہ	more

Reference grammar

Nouns

Nouns are inflected for gender, number and case.

Gender

There are two genders in Urdu, masculine and feminine. The gender system is partly semantically and partly phonologically based. The rule of thumb is that inflected nouns ending in **-ā** are usually masculine, whereas nouns ending in **-ī** are feminine. The meaning (logical sex) takes precedence over the form of the word. Overall, the gender is unpredictable: **xat** 'letter' is masculine but **kitāb** 'book' is feminine; **dāRʰī** 'beard' is feminine and so is **sipāhī** 'soldier'. Although **hātʰī** 'elephant' ends in **-ī**, it is masculine, and **havā** 'air' ends with **-ā** but is feminine.

Human beings who are of the male sex receive masculine gender whereas human beings of the female sex are assigned feminine gender. Therefore, nouns such as **laRkā** 'boy' and **ādmī** 'man' are masculine, whereas **laRkī** 'girl' and **aurat** 'woman' are feminine. The same is true of some non-human animate nouns. Nouns such as **gʰoRā** 'horse', **bandar** 'monkey' and **bɛl** 'ox' are masculine and **gʰoRī** 'mare', **bandariyā** 'female monkey' and **gāy** 'cow' are feminine.

Nouns denoting professions are usually masculine, for example, **nāī** 'barber'.

Some animate nouns (species of animals, birds, insects, etc.) exhibit unigender properties in the sense that they are either masculine or feminine. For example, **maccʰar** 'mosquito', **kīRā** 'insect', **cītā** 'leopard' and **ullū** 'owl' are masculine in gender and nouns such as **ciRiyā** 'bird', **koyal** 'cuckoo', **titlī** 'butterfly', **makkʰī** 'fly' and **mac^hli** 'fish' are feminine. To specify the sex of animate nouns, words such as **nar** 'male' and **mādā** 'female' are prefixed to give compound nouns such as **mādā-macc^har** 'female-mosquito', **nar-ciRiyā** 'male-bird'.

In the case of inanimate, abstract, collective and material nouns, gender is partly determined by form and partly by meaning. On many occasions both criteria fail to predict the gender. The names of the following classes of nouns are usually masculine:

trees: **pīpal** (the name of a tree), **devdār** 'pine family tree', **cīR** 'pine', **ām** 'mango' (however, **imlī** 'tamarind' is feminine);

minerals and jewels: **yāqūt** 'ruby', **sonā** 'gold', **koyalā** 'coal', **hīrā** 'diamond' (however, **cādī** 'silver' is feminine);

liquids: **tel** 'oil', **dūd^h** 'milk', **pānī** 'water' (however, **sharāb** 'alcohol' is feminine);

crops: **d^hān** 'rice', **bājrā** 'millet', **maTar** 'pea';

mountains and oceans: **himālaya** 'Himalayas', **bahr-e-hind** 'Indian Ocean';

countries: **hindustān** 'India', **rūs** 'Russia', **amrīkā** 'America';

God, demons and heavenly bodies: **shetān** 'devil', **āftāb** 'sun';

days and months (Islamic calendar): **pīr** 'Monday', **ramzān** 'Ramzān';

body parts: **sar** 'head', **kān** 'ear', **hāt^h** 'hand' (however, **āk^h** 'eye' and **zabān** 'tongue' are feminine);

abstract nouns: **ishq** 'love', **Gussāh** 'anger', **ārām** 'comfort' (however, some abstract nouns, including a synonym of **ishq** 'love', i.e. **mahobbat**, are feminine).

Number

Like English, Urdu has two numbers, singular and plural. However, some differences can be seen in the Urdu and the English way of looking at the singularity and plurality of objects. Words such as **pajāmā** 'pyjamas' and **qēcī** 'scissors' are singular in Urdu but plural in English. Similarly, 'rice' is singular in English but it is both singular and plural in Urdu.

Masculine nouns which end in **-ā** change to **-e** in their plural form. The group of masculine nouns which do not end in **-ā** remain unchanged. Therefore, they fall into the following two patterns:

Masculine nouns

Pattern I: ending in ā → e

beTā	son	beTe	sons
laRkā	boy	laRke	boys

Exceptions: **bādshah** king

Pattern II: not ending in ā → remain unchanged

ādmī	man	ādmī	men
kāGaz	paper	kāGaz	papers

Similarly, feminine nouns also exhibit patterns. Singular feminine nouns ending in -ī (including those ending in **i** or **iyā**) change to **iyā̃** in their plural forms, while feminine nouns not ending in -ī add **ẽ** in the plural.

Feminine nouns

Pattern I: ending in ī → iyā̃

beTī	daughter	beTiyā̃	daughters
laRkī	girl	laRkiyā̃	girls
ciRiyā	bird	ciRiyā̃	birds

Pattern II: not ending in ī → add ẽ

kitāb	book	kitābẽ	books
cīz	thing	cīzẽ	things
bahū	daughter-in-law	bahuẽ	daughters-in-law

Note that feminine nouns ending in long **ū** shorten the vowel before the plural ending.

Perso-Arabic nouns

The plurals of Perso-Arabic loan words are generally formed according to the rules of Urdu grammar, e.g.

aurat	woman	**auratẽ**	women
qalam	pen	**qalmẽ**	pens

However, certain Arabic nouns in Urdu form their plurals according to the rules of Arabic grammar. Arabic plurals are classified into the following two groups.

Sound plurals

These are formed by adding **-īn** and **-āt** to the ending of the singular form. Examples:

axbār	newspaper	**axbārāt**	newspapers
savāl	question	**savālāt**	questions
momin	believer	**mominīn**	believers

Broken plurals

These are formed by altering vowel patterns of the singular noun. Examples:

hākim	ruler	**hukkām**	rulers
shaxs	person	**ashxās**	people
qāidā	rule	**qavāid**	rules
ālim	scholar	**ulamā**	scholars

Direct and oblique case

Some nouns or noun phrases change their shape before a postposition. The form of the noun which occurs before a postposition is called the *oblique* case. The non-oblique forms are called *direct* forms, as shown above.

Masculine singular nouns which follow pattern I change under the influence of postpositions. The word-final vowel **ā** changes to

e in the oblique case. However, all plural nouns change and end in **õ** before postpositions. The following examples illustrate these rules.

Masculine nouns

Pattern I: nouns ending in -ā

	direct		*oblique* (before postpositions)	
singular	**beTā**	son	**beTe ko**	to the son
			(i.e. **ā → e**)	
plural	**beTe**	sons	**beTõ se**	by the sons
			(i.e. **e → õ**)	

Pattern II: nouns not ending in ā

	direct		*oblique* (before postpositions)	
singular	**ādmī**	man	**ādmī mẽ**	in the man
			(i.e. no change)	
plural	**ādmī**	men	**ādmiyõ mẽ**	in the men
			(i.e. **õ** added; slight change in the vowel **ī** which becomes **i** and the semivowel **y** intervenes.)	

Feminine nouns

Pattern I: nouns ending in ī

	direct		*oblique* (before postpositions)	
singular	**beTī**	daughter	**beTī par**	on the daughter
			(i.e. no change)	
plural	**beTiyā̃**	daughters	**beTiyõ par**	on the daughters
			(i.e. **ā̃** changes to **õ**.)	

Pattern II: nouns not ending in ī

	direct		*oblique* (before postpositions)	
singular	**kitāb**	book	**kitāb mē**	in the book
			(i.e. no change)	
plural	**kitābē**	books	**kitābõ mē**	in the books
			(i.e. ē changes to õ)	

Articles

Urdu has no articles equivalent to English 'a', 'an' and 'the'. This gap is filled by means of indirect devices such as the use of the numeral **ek** for the indefinite article, and the use of the postposition **ko** with an object to fulfil the function of the definite article.

Pronouns

Although the case system of pronouns is essentially the same as that of nouns, pronouns have more case forms in the oblique case than nouns do, as exemplified below by the difference in pronominal form with different postpositions.

Personal: singular

direct			*oblique*		
		general oblique	*oblique* + **ko** (e.g. 'me')	*oblique* + **kā** (e.g. 'my')	*oblique* + **ne** (agentive past)
mɛ̃	I	**mujʰ**	**mujʰ ko = mujʰe**	**merā**	**mɛ̃ne**
tū	you	**tujʰ**	**tujʰ ko = tujʰe**	**terā**	**tū ne**
vo	he/she	**us**	**us ko = use**	**us kā**	**us ne**
ye	this	**is**	**is ko = ise**	**is kā**	**is ne**

Personal: plural

direct		general oblique	oblique oblique + ko	oblique + kā	oblique + ne
ham	we	ham	ham ko = hamē	hamārā	ham ne
tum	you	tum	tum ko = tumhē	tumhārā	tum ne
āp	you	āp	āp ko	āp kā	āp ne
vo	they	un	un ko = unhē	un kā	unhõne
ye	these	in	in ko = inhē	in kā	inhõne

Other pronouns: singular

direct		general oblique	oblique oblique + ko	oblique + kā	oblique + ne
kaun	who?	kis	kis ko = kise	kis kā	kis ne
jo	who	jis	jis ko = jise	jis kā	jis ne
kyā	what	kis	kis ko = kise	kis kā	–
koī	someone	kisī	kisī ko	kisī kā	kisī ne

Other pronouns: plural

direct		general oblique	oblique oblique + ko	oblique + kā	oblique + ne
kaun	who?	kin	kin ko = kinhē	kin kā	kinhõne
jo	who	jin	jin ko = jinhē	jin kā	jinhõne

Adjectives

Adjectives can be classified into two groups – the 'inflecting' and the 'non-inflecting' type. Like masculine nouns which end in ā, inflecting adjectives also end in ā. They change their form, or agree, with the following nouns in terms of number and gender. Non-inflecting adjectives which do not end in -ā remain invariable. The following endings are used with inflecting adjectives when they are inflected for number, gender and case.

Pattern I: the inflecting type

	direct singular	plural	oblique singular	plural
masculine	-ā	-e	-e	-e
feminine	-ī	-ī	-ī	-ī

Example:

Pattern I: inflecting adjective

direct		*oblique*	
acc^hā laRkā	good boy	acc^he laRke se	by a/the good boy
acc^he laRke	good boys	acc^he laRkõ se	by good boys
acc^hī laRkī	good girl	acc^hī laRkī se	by a/the good girl
acc^hī laRkiyã	good girls	acc^hī laRkiyõ se	by good girls

Pattern II: non-inflecting adjective

direct		*oblique*	
xūbsūrat laRkā	handsome boy	xūbsūrat laRke se	by a/the handsome boy
xūbsūrat laRke	handsome boys	xūbsūrat laRkõ se	by handsome boys
xūbsūrat laRkī	beautiful girl	xūbsūrat laRkī se	by a/the beautiful girl
xūbsūrat laRkiyã	beautiful girls	xūbsūrat laRkiyõ se	by beautiful girls

Possessive adjectives (listed under oblique pronouns + **kā**), the reflexive pronoun **apnā** 'self' and *participles* behave like inflecting adjectives; therefore, they are inflected in number, gender and case.

Postpositions

The Urdu equivalents of the English prepositions such as 'to', 'in', 'at', 'on', etc., are called postpositions because they follow nouns and pronouns rather than precede them as in English.

Simple postpositions

Simple postpositions consist of one word. Here is a list of some important ones:

kā of (i.e. possessive marker)
ko to; also object marker
mẽ in
par on, at
se from, by, object marker for some verbs
tak up to, as far as
ne agent marker for transitive verbs in simple past, present perfect and past perfect tenses
vālā -er (and a wide range of meanings)

The two postpositions **kā** and **vālā** also change like inflecting adjectives; all the others act like non-inflecting adjectives.

Compound postpositions

Compound postpositions consist of more than one word. They behave in exactly the same way as simple postpositions, and thus require nouns or pronouns to be in the oblique case. Examples of some very common compound postpositions are given below:

ke-*type*		kī-*type*	
ke bāre mẽ	about	**kī taraf**	towards
ke āge	in front of	**kī jagah**	instead of
ke sāmne	facing	**kī tarah**	like
ke pehle	before	**kī bajāe**	except for
ke bād	after		
ke nīce	below		
ke ūpar	above		

Notice that most of the compound postpositions begin with either **ke** or **kī** but never with **kā**.

Question words

In English, question words such as 'who', 'when' and 'why' begin with 'wh-' (except 'how'); Urdu question words begin with the sound **k**. Some of the most common question words are listed below.

Pronouns

kyā	what	see pronouns for oblique forms
kaun	who	see pronouns for oblique forms
kaun-sā	who	**kaun** remains invariable but **sā** changes like inflecting adjectives

Possessive pronouns

See oblique + **kā** forms of **kyā** and **kaun** in the section on pronouns.

Adverbs

kab	when
kahā̃	where
kyõ	why
kɛsā	how, of what kind
kitnā	how much, how many

The last two adverbs, **kɛsā** and **kitnā** are changeable and behave like inflecting adjectives.

Question words and word order

In Urdu it is not common to move question words such as 'what', 'how' and 'where' to the beginning of the sentence. The question words usually stay in their original position, i.e. somewhere in the middle of the sentence. The only exception is yes-no questions, where the Urdu question word **kyā** is placed at the beginning of the sentence.

Verbs

The concept of time is quite different in Urdu from the 'unilinear' concept of time found in English. In other words, time is not viewed as smoothly flowing from the past through the present into the future. It is possible to find instances of the present or future tense with past time. For example, the English expression 'He said that he was going' will be 'He said that he is going' in Urdu. Similarly, the concept of habituality is also different in Urdu. It is possible to say in English 'I always went there'; however, in Urdu one has to use the past habitual instead of English simple past to indicate a habitual act. Therefore, the translational equivalent of the English sentence 'I always went there' will be 'I always used to go there' in Urdu.

Infinitive, gerundive or verbal nouns

nā is suffixed to the verbal stem to form the infinitive (or gerundive or verbal noun) form of a verb. **nā** follows the stem in Urdu rather than preceding it.

Simple infinitive

stem	*stem* + **nā**	
pī	**pīnā**	to drink, drinking
kar	**karnā**	to do, doing
jā	**jānā**	to go, going

The infinitive marker **ā** becomes **e** in the oblique case.

Causative verbs

Intransitive and transitive verbs are made causative by adding suffixes. Two suffixes **ā** (called the 'first causative' suffix) and **vā** (termed the 'second causative' suffix) are attached to the stem of a verb, and are placed before the infinitive marker **-nā**. The process of forming causative verbs brings about some changes in some stems (as in **de** 'give'); Here are examples of some causative verb types.

Type 1

No changes occur in the verbal stem.

intransitive		*transitive*	
uRnā	to fly	**uRānā**	to fly X
paknā	to be cooked	**pakānā**	to cook X

causative	
uRvānā	to cause Y to fly X
pakvānā	to cause Y to cook X

Type 2

The stem-vowel of the intransitive verb undergoes changes in its corresponding transitive and causative forms.

intransitive		*transitive*	
jāgnā	to wake (i.e. ā → a)	**jagānā**	to awaken X
leTnā	to lie down (i.e. e → i)	**liTānā**	to lay down
jʰūlnā	to swing (i.e. ū → u)	**jʰulānā**	to swing X

causative	
jagvānā	to cause Y to awaken X
liTvānā	to cause Y to lay down X
jʰulvānā	to cause Y to swing X

Type 3

The stem vowel of the transitive verb undergoes changes in its corresponding intransitive and causative forms. Also, notice that the causative verb of this type can be formed either by adding **-ā** or the **vā** suffix.

Type 3a

intransitive		*transitive*	
marnā	to die (i.e. **a → ā**)	**mārnā**	to kill
pisnā	to be ground (i.e. **i → ī**)	**pīsnā**	to grind X
kʰulnā	to be/get opened (i.e. **u → o**)	**kʰolnā**	to open X

transitive (with -ā)/causative
marānā/marvāna to cause Y to kill
pisānā/pisvānā to cause Y to grind X
kʰulānā/kʰulvānā to cause Y to open X

Type 3b

Observe the English translation of the transitive verbs with or without **ā** in Set A.

Set A

transitive (without -ā)		*transitive (with -ā)*	
paRʰnā	to read	**paRʰānā**	to teach
bolnā	to speak	**bulānā**	to call

causative
paRʰvānā to cause Y to teach X
bulvānā to cause Y to call X

Set B

The causative marker **-vā** occurs in free variation with **-lā**. The verbal stem undergoes vowel changes, as in:

transitive		*transitive (with -ā)/causative*	
denā	to give	**dilvānā/dilānā**	to cause Y to give
dʰonā	to wash	**dʰulvānā/dʰulānā**	to cause Y to wash X

Type 4

Some verbs show both consonant and vowel changes in their corresponding transitive forms. The consonant alternations are as follows: the intransitive stem-final **k** becomes **c**, and intransitive stem-final **T** becomes retroflex **R**.

intransitive		*transitive*	
biknā	to be sold	**becnā**	to sell X
TūTnā	to be broken	**toRnā**	to break X

causative	
bikvānā	to cause Y to sell X
tuRānā/tuRvānā	to cause Y to break X

Auxiliary/main verbs 'to be'

Present

The present tense auxiliary/main verb agrees in number and person with its subject.

honā 'to be'

	singular		*plural*	
first person	**hū̃**	(I) am	**hɛ̃**	(we) are
second person	**hɛ**	(you) are	**ho**	(you, fam.) are
			hɛ̃	(you, hon.) are
third person	**hɛ**	(he, she, it) is	**hɛ̃**	(they) are

Past

The past tense auxiliary/copular verb agrees in number and gender with its subject.

honā *'to be'*

	singular		*plural*	
masculine	tʰā	was	tʰe	were
feminine	tʰī	was	tʰĩ	were

Another conjugation of **honā** is as follows:

	singular		*plural*	
masculine	huā	happened	hue	
feminine	huī		huĩ	

Future

The future tense verb 'to be' agrees in number, gender and person with its subject.

honā *'to be': masculine*

	singular		*plural*	
first person	hū̃gā	(I) will be	hõge	(we) will be
second person	hogā	(you) will be	hoge	(you, fam.) will be
			hõge	(you, hon.) will be
third person	hogā	(he, she, it) will be	hõge	(they) will be

honā *'to be': feminine*

For the feminine forms, replace the final vowel of the masculine forms with **ī**.

Subjunctive

For the subjunctive forms of **honā**, simply drop the final syllable (i.e. **gā**, **ge**, **gī**) from the future tense forms.

Main verbs

Simple present/imperfective/present habitual

The simple present is formed by adding the following suffixes to the main verbal stem

	singular	*pural*
masculine	**-tā**	**-te**
feminine	**-tī**	**-tī**

The main verb is followed by the present auxiliary forms.

Examples: verb stem likʰ *'write'*

Masculine

singular

mɛ̃ likʰtā hū̃ I write

tū likʰtā hɛ you write

vo likʰtā hɛ he writes

plural

ham likʰte hɛ̃ we write

tum likʰte ho you (fam.) write

āp likʰte hɛ̃ you (hon.) write

vo likʰte hɛ̃ they write

Feminine

Replace **tā** and **te** of the masculine paradigm with **tī**.

Past habitual

The past habitual is derived by substituting the past auxiliary forms for the present auxiliary forms in the simple present tense.

*Examples: **verb stem** likʰ **'write'***

Masculine

singular		*plural*	
mɛ̃ likʰtā tʰā	I used to write	**ham likʰte tʰe**	we used to write
tū likʰtā tʰā	you used to write	**tum likʰte tʰe**	you (fam.) used to write
		āp likʰte tʰe	you (hon.) used to write
vo likʰtā tʰā	he used to write	**vo likʰte tʰe**	they used to write

Feminine

Replace **tā** and **te** of the masculine paradigm with **tī**. Also, substitute the auxilaries **tʰī** and **tʰī̃** for **tʰā** and **tʰe**, respectively.

Simple past/perfective

The simple past is formed by adding the following suffixes to the verb stem. No auxiliary verb follows the main verb.

	singular	*plural*
masculine	-ā	-e
feminine	-ī	-ī̃

*Examples: **verb stem** bɛTʰ **'sit'***

Masculine

singular		*plural*	
mɛ̃ bɛTʰā	I sat	**ham bɛTʰe**	we sat
tū bɛTʰā	you sat	**tum bɛTʰe**	you (fam.) sat
		āp bɛTʰe	you (hon.) sat
vo bɛTʰā	he sat	**vo bɛTʰe**	they sat

Feminine

The verb-final **ā** and **e** are replaced by **ī** and **ī̃**, respectively.

Transitive verbs and the agentive postposition ne

Transitive verbs take the agentive postposition **ne**, with the subject and the verb agreeing with the object instead of the subject. Observe the paradigm of the simple past tense with the transitive verb **lik^h** 'write'.

Examples: verb stem lik^h **'write'**

Masculine

singular		*plural*	
mɛ̃ ne xat lik^hā	I wrote a letter	**ham ne xat lik^hā**	we wrote a letter
tū ne xat lik^hā	you wrote a letter	**tum ne xat lik^hā**	you (fam.) wrote a letter
		āp ne xat lik^hā	you (hon.) wrote a letter
us ne xat lik^hā	he wrote a letter	**unhõne ne xat lik^hā**	they wrote a letter

The verb agrees with **xat** 'letter', which is a masculine singular noun. Therefore, the verb stays the same regardless of the change in the subject.

Important transitive verbs which do not take the postposition **ne** are **milnā** 'to meet', **lānā** 'to bring' and **bolnā** 'to speak'.

The rule of thumb is that the verb does not agree with a constituent which is followed by a postposition. For example, if the object marker **ko** is used with **xat**, the verb will agree neither with the subject nor with the object. In such situations, the verb will stay in the masculine singular form.

Present perfect

The present perfect is formed by adding the present tense auxiliary forms to the simple past tense. Transitive verbs take the postposition **ne** with their subjects.

*Examples: **verb stem** bɛTʰ **'sit'***

Masculine

singular   *plural*

mɛ̃ bɛTʰā hũ̃	I have sat (down)	**ham bɛTʰe hɛ̃**	we have sat (down)
tū bɛTʰā hɛ	you have sat (down)	**tum bɛTʰe ho**	you (fam.) have sat (down)
		āp bɛTʰe hɛ̃	you (hon.) have sat (down)
vo bɛTʰā hɛ	he has sat (down)	**vo bɛTʰe hɛ̃**	they have sat (down)

Past perfect

The past perfect is formed by adding the past tense auxiliary forms to the simple past tense. Transitive verbs take the postposition **ne** with their subjects.

*Examples: **verb stem** bɛTʰ **'sit'***

Masculine

singular   *plural*

mɛ̃ bɛTʰā tʰā	I had sat (down)	**ham bɛTʰe tʰe**	we had sat (down)
tū bɛTʰā tʰā	you had sat (down)	**tum bɛTʰe tʰe**	you (fam.) had sat (down)
		āp bɛTʰe tʰe	you (hon.) had sat (down)
vo bɛTʰā tʰā	he had sat (down)	**vo bɛTʰe tʰe**	they had sat (down)

Future

The following person-number-gender suffixes with a stem, form the future tense:

pronouns	singular		plural	
	masculine	*feminine*	*masculine*	*feminine*
first person	-ū̃gā	-ū̃gī	-ẽge	-ẽgī
second person	-egā	-egī	-oge	-ogī
			-ẽge	-ẽgī
third person	-egā	-egī	-ẽge	-ẽgī

Examples: verb stem likʰ **'write'**

Masculine

singular		*plural*	
mɛ̃ likʰū̃gā	I will write	**ham likʰẽge**	we will write
tū likʰegā	you will write	**tum likʰoge**	you (fam.) will write
		āp likʰẽge	you (hon.)will write
vo likʰegā	he will write	**vo likʰẽge**	they will write

Feminine

Replace the last syllable **gā** and **ge** of the masculine paradigm with **gī**.

Subjunctive

The subjunctive is used to express suggestion, possibility, doubt, uncertainty, apprehension, wish, desire, encouragement, demand, requirement or potential. Subjunctive formation is outlined below. Subjunctive forms do not differ for gender. Drop the **gā, ge** and **gī** endings from the future form, the remainder will be the subjunctive form.

Imperative

The imperative is formed by adding the following endings to the stem:

intimate/impolite	*familiar*	*polite*	*extra polite*	*future*
no suffix	**-o**	**-iye**	**-iyegā**	**-nā** (= infinitive)

intimate/impolite	**tū jā**	Go
familiar	**tum jāo**	Go
polite	**āp jāiye**	Please go
extra polite	**āp jāiyegā**	Please go
future	**āp jānā**	Please go (some time in the future)

Negative particles and imperatives

nahī̃ is not used with imperatives.

mat is usually used with intimate, familiar and future imperatives.

na is usually used with polite, extra-polite and future imperatives.

Present progressive/continuous

The progressive aspect is expressed by means of the independent word **rah**, which sounds identical to the stem of the verb **rahnā** 'to live'. The progressive marker agrees with the number and gender of the subject; therefore, it can appear in one of the following three forms:

Progressive marker rah '-ing'

masculine		*feminine*	
singular	*plural*	*singular*	*plural*
rahā	**rahe**	**rahī**	**rahī**

Examples: verb stem likʰ write

Masculine

singular		*plural*	
mɛ̃ likʰ rahā hū̃	I am writing	**ham likʰ rahe hɛ̃**	we are writing
tū likʰ rahā hɛ	you are writing	**tum likʰ rahe ho**	you (fam.) are writing
		āp likʰ rahe hɛ̃	you (hon.) are writing
vo likʰ rahā hɛ	he is writing	**vo likʰ rahe hɛ̃**	they are writing

Feminine

Replace **rahā** and **rahe** of the masculine paradigm with **rahī** in plural.

Past progressive/continuous

The present auxiliary verb in the present progressive construction is replaced by the past auxiliary verb in the past progressive forms.

Irregular verbs

Here is a list of Urdu irregular verbs:

	jānā	**karnā**	**lenā**	**denā**	**pīnā**
	'to go'	'to go'	'to take'	'to give'	'to drink'
simple past	**gayā**	**kiyā**	**liyā**	**diyā**	**piyā**
	(m. sg.)	(m. sg.)	(m. sg.)	(m. sg.)	(m. sg.)
	gaye	**kiye**	**liye**	**diye**	**piye**
	(m. pl.)	(m. pl.)	(m. pl.)	(m. pl.)	(m. pl.)
	gayī (f. sg.)	**kī** (f. sg.)	**lī** (f. sg.)	**dī** (f. sg.)	**pī** (f. sg.)
	gayī̃ (f. pl.)	**kī̃** (f. pl.)	**lī̃** (f. pl.)	**dī̃** (f. pl.)	**pī̃**
imperative (polite)	–	**kījiye**	**lījiye**	**dījiye**	**pījiye**
imperative (familiar)	–	–	**lo**	**do**	**piyo**

future

lenā	**lū̃gā**	**loge**	**legā**	**lẽge**
to take	(I) will take	(you) will take	will take (m. sg.)	will take (m. pl.)
denā	**dū̃gā**	**doge**	**degā**	**dẽge**
to give	(I) will give	(you) will give	will give (m. sg.)	will give (m. pl.)

Participles

Present/imperfective participle

The present participial marker is -**t**-, which immediately follows the verbal stem and is, in turn, followed by number and gender markers, as shown below:

	masculine		*feminine*	
	singular	*plural*	*singular*	*plural*
	stem-*t-ā*	stem-*t-e*	stem-*t-ī*	stem-*t-ī*

The present participle may be used as either an adjective or an adverb. The optional past participial form of the verb **honā** 'to be' may immediately follow the present participial form. The forms of the optional element are as follows:

	masculine		*feminine*	
	singular	*plural*	*singular*	*plural*
	huā	**hue**	**huī**	**huī**

Examples:

caltā (huā) laRkā	walking boy
caltī (huī) laRkī	walking girl

The present participial form and the optional 'to be' form agree in number and gender with the following head noun. The retention of the optional form makes the participial phrase emphatic. The present participle indicates an ongoing action.

Past/perfective participle

The past participial form is derived by adding the following suffixes, declined for number and gender, to the verbal stem. Like the present participle, the optional past participial form of the verb **honā** 'to be' may immediately follow the past participial form.

masculine		feminine	
singular	*plural*	*singular*	*plural*
stem-**ā**	stem-**e**	stem-**ī**	stem-**ī**

The past participle may be used as either an adjective or an adverb. The past participial form and the optional 'to be' form agree in number and gender with the following head noun. The retention of the optional form makes the participial phrase emphatic. The past participle indicate a state, as in:

bɛTʰā (huā) laRkā	a seated boy
bɛTʰī (huī) laRkī	a seated girl

The irregular past participle is formed in the same way as the past tense.

Absolutive/conjunctive participle

The absolutive/conjunctive participle is formed by adding the invariable **kar** to the verbal stem, as in:

stem		*conjunctive participle*	
likʰ	write	**likʰ kar**	having written
ā	come	**ā kar**	having come
pī	drink	**pī kar**	having drunk

-te hī participle 'as soon as'

This participle is formed by adding the invariable **-te hī** 'as soon as' to the verbal stem:

stem		*'as soon as' participle*	
likʰ	write	**likʰte hī**	as soon as (he) wrote
ā	come	**āte hī**	as soon as (he) came
pī	drink	**pīte hī**	as soon as (he) drank

Agentive participle

The agentive participle is formed by adding the marker **vālā** to the oblique infinitive form of the verb. **vālā** agrees in number and gender with the following noun and, thus, has the following three forms.

masculine		feminine	
singular	*plural*	*singular*	*plural*
vālā	**vāle**	**vālī**	**vālī**

Examples:

stem	*oblique infinitive*	*agentive participle*	
likʰ write	**likʰne**		
		likʰne vālā laRkā	the boy who writes
		likʰne vāle laRke	the boys who write
		likʰne vālī laRkī	the girl who writes
		likʰne vālī laRkiā̃	the girls who write

The Perso-Arabic component

Persian prefixes

Most of these prefixes convert a noun into an adjective. Some frequent Persian prefixes used in Urdu are given below:

bad-	bad		
tamīz (f.)	manners	**badtamīz**	rude
be-	without		
kār (m.)	work	**bekār**	unemployed
bā-	with		
qa'idā (m.)	rule	**bāqa'idā**	regularly
nā-	not (negative prefix)		
vāqif (adj.)	acquainted	**nāvāqif**	unacquainted
kam-	less		
zor (m.)	strength	**kamzor**	weak
xūb-	good		
sūrat (f.)	form	**xūbsūrat**	beautiful
Gɛr-	strange		
qānūnī	legal	**Gɛr qānūnī**	illegal

Persian suffixes

The following suffixes are added to adjectives to form abstract nouns.

ī

xūb	well	**xūbī**	quality
narm	soft	**narmī**	softness

-gī

bandā	slave	**bandagī**	slavery
zindā	alive	**zindagī**	life

The following suffixes are commonly used in Urdu. Most of them are added for deriving adjectives from nouns.

-mand

aql (f.)	wisdom	**aqlmand**	intellectual
daulat (f.)	wealth	**daulatmand**	wealthy

-ānā

dost (m.)	friend	**dostānā**	friendly
shāir (m.)	poet	**shāirānā**	poetical

-dān (m.),
-dānī (f.) container

qalam (m./f.)	pen	**qalamdān**	pen holder
cāy (f.)	tea	**cāydānī**	tea pot

-dār (this suffix is also used with Indic words)

zamīn (f.)	land	**zamīndār**	landlord
sūbā (m.)	province	**sūbedar**	governor (of a province)
Tʰekā (m.)	contract	**Tʰekedār**	contractor

-ābād (this suffix is added to nouns to form place names)

murād (f.)	Murad	**murādābād**	Muradabad
Gāzī (m.)	Gazi	**Gāzīābād**	Gaziabad

-istān/ -stān home of

pak (adj.)	pure	**pākistān**	Pakistan
hindū (m.)	Hindu	**hindustān**	Hindustan
ret /reg (f.)	sand	**registān**	desert

Adjectives

In Persian, comparative and superlative degrees are formed by adding the suffixes **-tar** and **-tarīn** respectively, to the adjectives. However, these forms are only used with adjectives of Persian origin. Following are some examples:

bad-tar	worse	**bad-tarīn**	worst
beh-tar	better	**beh-tarīn**	best

Izāfat (-e-)

The following two types of izāfat phrases are commonly used in Urdu.

The **izāfat -e** (Persian **izāfā** 'increase') indicates the possessive relationship between two nouns. Examples:

Game-e-ishq	pathos of love
ibtidā-e-kitāb	beginning of the book
zabān-e-Dehlvī	language of Delhi
wazīr-e-xazānā	minister of finance

When an adjective follows a noun, **izāfat** indicates that the adjective qualifies the noun. Examples:

zulf-e-siyā	black tresses
ism-e-sharīf	distinguished appellation
zar-e-mubādilā	foreign exchange

Key to conversation unit exercises

Urdu writing system and pronunciation

Exercise 1

1 C 2 A 3 C 4 B 5 B 6 A 7 B 8 B

Exercise 2

1 A, D 2 B, D 3 A, B 4 B, C 5 B, D 6 B, D 7 A, D 8 B, D

	Exercise 3				Exercise 4	
1	Tāk	i.e. B		1	kām	i.e. A
2	Tʰak	i.e. B		2	din	i.e. A
3	Dāg	i.e. B		3	mil	i.e. A
4	dʰak	i.e. A		4	cūk	i.e. B
5	paR	i.e. B		5	mɛl	i.e. B
6	sar	i.e. A		6	ser	i.e. A
7	kaRʰī	i.e. B		7	bic	i.e. A
8	Tʰīk	i.e. B		8	bal	i.e. B

Unit 1

Note that brackets indicate optional elements.

Exercise 1

(a) ādāb; (b) Tʰīk hɛ; (c) va-'alɛkum as-salām; (d) allāh kā shukr hɛ; (e) (accʰā), xudā hāfiz; (f) sat srī akāl jī; (g) meharbānī hɛ *or* (allāh kā) shukr hɛ; (h) namaste jī; (i) (hukam nahī̃), guzārish hɛ; (j) salām.

Exercise 2

A	B
(a) ādāb.	ādāb.
(b) kyā hāl hɛ?	Tʰīk hɛ.
(c) āp ke mizāj kɛse hɛ̃?	allāh kā shukr hɛ.
(d) xudā hāfiz.	xudā hāfiz.
(e) sab xɛriyat hɛ?	meharbānī hɛ.
(f) as-salām 'alɛkum.	va-'alɛkum as-salām.

Exercise 3

Conversation 1

A: as-salām 'alɛkum.
B: va-'alɛkum as-salām.
   sab xɛriyat hɛ?
A: meharbānī hɛ, aur āp
   ke mizāj kɛse hɛ̃?
B: allāh kā shukr hɛ.

Conversation 2

A: ādāb arz.
B: ādāb arz.
   kyā hāl hɛ?
A: Tʰīk hɛ, aur āp?
B: mɛ̃ bʰī Tʰīk hū̃.
A: accʰā, xudā hāfiz.
B: xudā hāfiz.

Exercise 4

(a) QUESTION: kyā hāl hɛ?
   ANSWER: Tʰīk hɛ.
   QUESTION: aur āp?
   ANSWER: mɛ̃ bʰī Tʰīk hū̃.
(b) QUESTION: āp kɛse hɛ̃?
   ANSWER: Tʰīk hū̃.

Exercise 5

long sentences	short sentences
(a) aur āp kɛse hɛ̃?	kɛse hɛ̃?
(b) mɛ̃ bʰī Tʰīk hū̃	Tʰīk hū̃
(c) āp kī meharbānī hɛ	meharbānī hɛ
(d) āp ke mizāj kɛse hɛ̃?	mizāj kɛse hɛ̃?

Unit 2

Exercise 1

mɛ̃ dillī *kā* hū̃. mere cār bʰāī *hɛ̃*. merā cʰoT*ā* bʰāī *Chicago* mɛ̃ kām kar*tā* hɛ. mere do baRe bʰāī *inglistān* (England) mɛ̃ rɛht*e hɛ̃*. merā nām salmān *hɛ*. mɛ̃ *school* jāt*ā* hū̃. merī do bɛhɛn*ẽ* bʰī *hɛ̃*. mere vālid sāhab bʰī kām karte hɛ̃. āp *kahā̃* rɛhte hɛ̃? āp*ke* kit*ne* bʰāī-bɛhɛn hɛ̃? āp *kī* vāldah kyā *kām* kar*tī* hɛ̃?

Exercise 2

accʰā	burā
baRā	cʰoTā
bɛhɛn	bʰāī
laRkā	laRkī
ādmī	aurat
hā̃	nahī̃

Exercise 3

banāras	se
shɛher	mɛ̃
das	bɛhɛnẽ
cār	bʰāī
do	ādmī
kitne	bʰāī
zard	sāRī

Exercise 4

kahiye
xushī
baRī xushī huī
pūrā nām
dūsrā
kitne bʰāī
milẽge

Exercise 5

Unit 3

Exercise 1

(a) mujʰe jaipur ka TikaT cāhiye/mujʰe jaipur ke liye TikaT cāhiye.
(b) kyā āp ko davāī cāhiye?
(c) mujʰe do gʰar cāhiye.
(d) mujʰ ko *garage* mẽ gāRī cāhiye.
(e) āp ko ye xūbsūrat qamīz cāhiye.

Exercise 2

(a) *merī* ek bɛhɛn hɛ.
(b) *mere* do bʰāī hẽ.
(c) *mere pās* ek *computer* hɛ.
(d) *merā* hāl Tʰīk hɛ.
(e) *mere pās* ek gāRī hɛ.
(f) *mujʰ ko* kām cāhiye.

Exercise 3

mujʰ ko	buxār hɛ.
mere pās	do rupaye hẽ.
āp ke	gʰar mẽ kitne ādmī hẽ?
merā	shɛhɛr bahut xūbsūrat hɛ.
ye xat	āp ke liye hɛ.
is kī qīmat	kyā hɛ?

Unit 4

Exercise 1

mujʰ ko paRʰnā pasand hɛ.
mujʰ ko kyā pasand hɛ?
mujʰ ko kyā-kyā pasand hɛ?
mujʰ ko gāne kā shauq hɛ.
mujʰ ko tɛrne kā shauq hɛ.
mujʰ ko kʰāne kā shauq hɛ.

By substituting **āp ko** in place of **mujʰ ko**, you can generate six more sentences.

Exercise 2

(a) Answer: gāne ke alāvāh John ko nācnā pasand hɛ.
(b) Answer: Judy ko kahāniyã aur nazmẽ likʰne kā shauq hɛ.
or
Judy ko kahāniyã aur shāirī likʰne ke shauq hẽ.
(c) Answer: sanjida ko murGī ka (or *chicken*) kʰānā nāpasand hɛ.
sanjida ko sabzī kʰānā nāpasand hɛ.
sanjida ko shāirī nāpasand hɛ.
sanjidā ko maGribī mausīqī nāpasand hɛ.
(d) Answer: sanjida ko samosā kʰānā pasand hɛ.
sanjida ko kabāb kʰānā pasand hɛ.
sanjida ko kahāniyã pasand hẽ.
sanjida ko hindustānī (*Indian*) mausīqī pasand hɛ.

Exercise 3

a1: John likes to eat/eating.
a2: John likes food.

b1: John likes to sing/singing.
b2: John likes (the) song.

Exercise 4

Sample: 1 x **karne se manā karnā** (to prohibit from doing x).
2 **unkā kɛhnā: kamrā sāf karo** (they say: clean your room).

Exercise 5

1   mujʰ ko tɛrne kā shauq hɛ.
2   mujʰ ko tɛrnā pasand hɛ.
3   mujʰ ko tɛrnā accʰā lagtā hɛ.

Unit 5

Exercise 1

(If you are a female, the final vowel of verb forms given in the italics needs to be replaced by the vowel ī.)

OFFICER: Your name (please)?
YOU: merā nām x hɛ
OFFICER: How long will you stay in Pakistan?
YOU: (number) din *rahū̃gā*.
OFFICER: Where will you go (during your stay)?
YOU: karācī aur pishāvar *jāū̃gā*
OFFICER: What is your address in Pakistan?
YOU: ye karācī (x city) kā patā hɛ:
(Fill out the address.)
OFFICER: When will you go back?
YOU: (number) dinõ ke bād.
(or x (number) tārīx ko)
OFFICER: Are you carrying any illegal baggage?
YOU: jī nahī̃.

Exercise 2

mɛ̃ āp ke liye kyā *kar* saktā *hū̃*? ham āgrā *jānā* cāhte *hɛ̃*. āgrā kitnī dūr *hɛ*? bahut dūr nahī̃, lekin āp kab jā *rahe* hɛ̃? ham kal *jāẽge*. gāRī subā dillī se *caltī* hɛ. kyā āp gāRī se *jānā cāhte hɛ̃*?

Exercise 3

azīz manzūr:
tumhārā *xat milā*. paRʰ kar xushī huī. tum kab *ā rahe ho*? kal mɛ̃ *Chicago* jā rahā *hū̃*. *Chicago* bahut *baRā* shɛhɛr hɛ. mɛ̃ *Chicago* havāī jahāz (*airplane*) se *jāū̃gā*. lekin mɛ̃ havāī jahāz se nahī̃ *jānā cāhtā hū̃*. gāRī mujʰe havāī jahāz *se zyāda pasand hɛ*. bāqī sab Tʰīk hɛ.

tumhārā dost,
iqbāl

Exercise 4

Q: āp kahā̃ jā rahī hɛ̃?
Q: āp yahā̃ kitne din rahē ge?
Q: āp kis kā kām kar rahe hɛ̃?
Q: kyā āp ko cāy bahut pasand hɛ?
Q: āp ke kitne bʰāī hɛ̃?

Exercise 5

A sample:
agar mujʰ ko ek *million dollars* milēge, to mɛ̃ duniyā kā safar karū̃gā/karū̃gī. bādshā/malkah kī tarah rahū̃gā/rahū̃gī. apne liye ek nāv aur Rolls Royce xarīdū̃gā/xarīdū̃gī. apnī bīvī/apne xāvind ke liye hīre xarīdū̃gā/xarīdū̃gī. lekin kahī̃ xushī se pāgal to nahī̃ ho jāū̃gā/jāū̃gī, kucʰ dinō ke bād apnī naukrī karne zarūr jāū̃gā/jāū̃gī.

Exercise 6

ham robot hɛ̃. ham California se *hɛ̃.* ham urdū bol *sakte hɛ̃. ham* urdū samajʰ bʰī *sakte hɛ̃. ham* urdū gāne gā *sakte hɛ̃. hamārī* yādasht (*memory*) bahut tez hɛ. *ham* har savāl pūcʰ *sakte hɛ̃* aur har javāb de *sakte hɛ̃.* yānī har kām kar *sakte hɛ̃. ham* hameshah kām kar *sakte hɛ̃. ham* kabʰī nahī̃ *tʰakte hɛ̃. hamāre* pās har savāl kā javāb hɛ. lekin masāledār kʰānā nahī̃ kʰā *sakte.*

Unit 6

Exercise 1

mere dost, vo *din kitne accʰe tʰe!* mɛ̃ *ne* socā vo din hameshah *rahēge.* vo bacpan ke *din* tʰe. mɛ̃ hameshah kʰeltā tʰā aur nāctā tʰā. har *cīz* xūbsūrat tʰī. har din nayā *tʰā⁻* aur har rāt kā apnā *andāz* tʰā. ab vo *din* nahī̃ rahe.

Exercise 2

(a) *mɛ̃* vahā̃ *gayī.*
(b) *us ne* mujʰ ko *batāyā.*

(c) *ham* gʰar *āye.*
(d) *tum* gʰar der se *pahūce.*
(e) *unhõne police* ko bayān *diyā.*
(f) *āp ko* ye kitāb kab *milī.*

Exercise 3

(a) āp ke vāldɛn kī pɛdāish kahā̃ huī?
(b) āp ke vāldɛn kab pɛdā hue?
(c) kyā un kā xāndān amīr tʰā yā Garīb tʰā?
(d) un kī shādī kab huī?
(e) un kī umar kitnī tʰī jab un kī shādī huī?
(f) kyā un kī shādī vāldɛn kī pasand se huī yā xud apnī pasand se?
(g) kyā āp kī vāldah āp ke vālid se cʰoTī hɛ̃?

Exercise 4

(a) kal *kis* kī sālgirah tʰī?
(b) *kis* ke xāndān ne ek dāvat kī?
(c) vo dāvat *kab* huī?
(d) John ko *kis cīz* ke bāre mɛ̃ mālūm nahī̃ tʰā?
(e) ye *kɛsī dāvat* tʰī?
(f) John kī sālgirah *kab* tʰī?

Unit 7

Exercise 1

(a) *mujʰ ko* sitār ātā hɛ.
   I know how to play the sitar.
(b) kyā *āp* tɛr sakte hɛ̃?
   Can you swim?
(c) *us ko* kahā̃ jānā hɛ?
   Where does he want to go?
(d) *unhõne* mausīqī kab sīkʰī?
   When did he learn music?
(e) vo *salesman* hɛ. *us ko* bāhar jānā paRtā hɛ.
   He is a salesman. He has to go (work) outdoors.

(f) John ko bahut kām hɛ. isliye *us ko* koi fursat nahî̃ hɛ.
John has a lot of work (on). That's why he has no spare time.

Exercise 2

(a) Bill ko jaldī hɛ kyõke uskī rel gāRī das minute mẽ jā*ne vālī* hɛ.
(b) *Driver* jaldī karo, mere dost kā jahāz ā*ne vālā* hɛ.
(c) sardī kā mausam tʰā, jaldī barf gir*ne vālī* tʰī.
(d) dāvat ke liye mɛhmān pah*ũcne vāle* hẽ.
(e) sʰām kā vaqt tʰā, andʰerā ho*ne vālā* tʰā.
(f) āp kabʰī hindustān ga*ye* hẽ.

Exercise 3

(a) ustād	us ko paRʰānā hɛ
(b) *Doctor*	use marīz ko dekʰnā hɛ.
(c) gulūkar	us ko gānā hɛ.
(d) *Driver*	us ko gāRī calānī hɛ.
(e) dʰobī	us ko kapRe dʰone hẽ.
(f) musannif	us ko likʰnā hɛ.

Exercise 4

(a) kyā āp mere liye sifārshī xat likʰ *dẽge*?
(b) rāt āyī aur andʰerā ho *gayā* tʰā.
(c) mẽ urdū nahî̃ paRʰ saktā, āp ye xat paRʰ *dījiye*.
(d) vo tʰoRā tʰoRā tɛr *letā* hɛ.
(e) us ko bahut accʰā nācnā *ātā* hɛ.
(f) mẽ āp kī bāt bilkul bʰūl *gayā*.

Exercise 5

Sample:

1 bacpan mẽ muj ʰe dūdʰ pinā paRtā tʰā.
2 bacpan mẽ muj ʰe DākTar ke pās jānā paRtā tʰā.
3 bacpan mẽ muj ʰe davāī pīnī paRtī tʰī.
4 bacpan mẽ muj ʰe Tīkā lagvānā paRtā tʰā.
5 bacpan mẽ muj ʰe vāldɛn ke sātʰ cīzẽ xarīdne jānā paRtā tʰā.

Unit 8

Exercise 1

āiye, tashrīf rakʰiye.
taklīf kī bāt kyā hɛ?
shāyad āp ko daftar mē kām zyādā ho.
vo āp kā intizār kar rahī tʰī.
ādāb arz.

Exercise 2

(a) mu'āf kījiye, mē *cheque* bʰejnā bʰūl gayā.
(b) mē ne kʰānā kʰā liyā.
(c) āp kā buxār baRʰ gayā.
(d) āp ne kucʰ javāb nahī̃ diyā.
(e) āp merī salāh mān lījiye.

Exercise 3

(a) ustād   shāgirdō̃ ko paRʰātā hɛ.
(b) DākTar   Tīkā lagātā hɛ.
(c) *cashier*   *cheque* tabdīl kartā hɛ
(d) darzī   kapRe sītā hɛ
(e) xānsāmā   kʰānā pakātā hɛ.
(f) *driver*   gāRī calātā hɛ
(g) *civil engineer* imāratē̃ banvātā hɛ.

Exercise 4

(a) SAJID: akram ne sājid se apnī gaRī calvāī.
(b) SAJID: akram sājid se apnā xat likʰvāyegā.
(c) SAJID: akram sājid se apnā gʰar banvā rahā hɛ.
(d) SAJID: akram sājid se apnī kahānī paRʰvā rahā tʰā.
(e) SAJID: akram sājid se apnī beTī ko jagvātā hɛ.

Exercise 5

(a) hãsnā: muj^he vo *hãstī huī* laRkī bahut pasand hɛ.
(b) k^helnā: *k^helte hue* bacce bahut xūbsūrat lag rahe t^he.
(c) gānā: *gātī huī* ciRiyā uR rahī t^hī.
(d) sitār bajānā: *sitār bajātā huā* ādmī bahut acc^hā hɛ.
(e) tɛrnā: *tɛrtī huī* mac^hliyõ ko dek^ho.
(f) ronā: DākTar ne *rote hue* bacce ko Tīkā lagāyā.

Exercise 6

mɛ̃ *railway station* par apne dost *kā* intzār kar rahā t^hā. t^hoRī der bād rel gāRī āyī aur merā dost gāRī se utrā. ham bahut xush ho kar mile. is martabā pā̃c sāl ke bād hamārī mulāqāt *huī*. t^hoRī der bād mɛ̃ ne kahā, 'is martabā bahut der ke bād yahā̃ āye ho.' usne javāb *diyā*, 'acc^hī bāt t^hī ke gāRī der se āyī, agar gāRī der se na *ātī*, to mɛ̃ āj b^hī na *ātā*.

Unit 9

Ẹxercise 1

(a) log *laundromat* kapRe d^hone ke liye jāte hɛ̃.
(b) log *restaurant* k^hānā k^hāne ke liye jāte hɛ̃.
(c) log *cinema film* dek^hne *ke liye* jāte hɛ̃.
(d) log *college* paR^hne ke liye jāte hɛ̃.
(e) log *swimming pool* tɛrne ke liye jāte hɛ̃.
(f) log *bar* pīne ke liye jāte hɛ̃.
(g) log *chemist* davāī lene ke liye jāte hɛ̃.

Exercise 2

(a) vo *bɛT^he* hue bolā.
(b) John *so(y)e* hue hãs rahā t^hā.
(c) ye shɛhɛr *soyā* sā lagtā hɛ.
(d) laRkī *piyī* huī g^har āyī.
(e) ek aurat ne bistar par *leTe* hue kahā.

Exercise 3

sunī	bāt
likʰā	xat
hãstā	laRkā
caltī	gāRī
bʰāgtī	billī

Exercise 4

(a) John se ek kahānī paRʰī gayī.
(b) ham logõ se kʰānā kʰāyā jā rahā hɛ.
(c) tum se kyā kiyā jāyegā?
(d) mujʰ se murGī kā sālan banāyā gayā.
(e) Bill se hindustān mẽ paRʰā jāyegā.
(f) kyā āp se gānā gāyā jāyegā?

Exercise 5

(a) *ham ko* vahã jāne kā mauqā *milā*.
(b) John *ko* hindustān *jāne* kā mauqā aksar miltā hɛ.
(c) ye sunhɛra mauqā *tʰā*.
(d) *āp ko* kitāb likʰne kā mauqā kab *milegā*?
(e) is kāGaz par kyā *likʰā* hɛ?
(f) billī ko mauqā *milā* aur vo dudʰ pī gayī.
(g) ye bahut *accʰe mauqe* kī bāt hɛ.

Unit 10

Exercise 1

īd-ul-fitr	is din sivaiyã pakāī jātī hɛ̃.
	dushmanõ ko bʰī dost banāyā jātā hɛ.
īd-ul-azhā	haj ke mahīne mẽ tīn roz manāī jātī hɛ.
	gosht dostõ aur rishtedārõ mẽ bā̃Tā jātā hɛ.

Exercise 2

(a) On this day sivayan (a sweet desert) is cooked.
(b) Enemies are often made friends.
(c) Celebrated for three days in the month of Haj.
(d) The meat is distributed amongst friends and relatives.

Exercise 3

(a) īd-ul-fitr
(b) īd-ul-azhā
(c) muharram
(d) īd-ul-azhā
(e) muharram

Key to script unit exercises

Unit 1

Exercise 2

(a)	زار	(b)	ازار	(c)	دادا
(d)	اُرْدُو	(e)	دراز	(f)	ارواڑا
(g)	دَوڑو	(h)	ژاڑ	(i)	آوارا
(j)	آرزُو	(k)	اُڑا	(l)	ادا

Unit 2

Exercise 2

(a)	جوڑو	(b)	جُدا	(c)	خارج	(d)	جوڑا
(e)	رواج	(f)	چرْخا	(g)	جس	(h)	شاد
(i)	چرچ	(j)	ضرور	(k)	شاخ	(l)	اُس
(m)	سازش	(n)	حرج	(o)	خاص	(p)	سرد
(q)	حاضر	(r)	داس	(s)	روس		

Exercise 3

(a)	سُنئر	(b)	شخص
(c)	حصار	(d)	سوراخ
(e)	صدا	(f)	صحرا

Unit 3

Exercise 2

(a)	تیر	(b)	ریت	(c)	تِین	(d)	بَتّی
(e)	اَپنا	(f)	اُون	(g)	یُو	(h)	اَدَب
(i)	بُنیاد	(j)	جَیسا	(k)	بِین	(l)	چِنا
(m)	تالی	(n)	ناز	(o)	میرا	(p)	روز
(q)	اُب	(r)	دَوڑ	(s)	پُوتا	(t)	اُوپی
(u)	یُونانی	(v)	باپ	(w)	نِس		

Exercise 3

(a)	تیری	(b)	اناج
(c)	پَریشان	(d)	باتُونی
(e)	ناچنا	(f)	حَضرَت
(g)	صَح	(h)	حِساب
(i)	شادی		

Unit 4

Exercise 2

(a)	فقیر	(b)	جِسم	(c)	فَوج
(d)	لوگ	(e)	نام	(f)	سَبق
(g)	کَمرا	(h)	نَمک	(i)	اَگر
(j)	پَتلا	(k)	چاقُو	(l)	چَچا
(m)	اُوکری	(n)	مَٹکا	(o)	قَیض
(p)	اَنگُور	(q)	سَلام	(r)	افسوس
(s)	فَساد	(t)	فَرش	(u)	شَریف

Exercise 3

(a)	لَگام	(b)	گُلشَن
(c)	خالی	(d)	مَلال
(e)	مَوسم	(f)	تَشریف
(g)	بَمِیر	(h)	اَلماری
(i)	خَم	(j)	قُربان

Unit 5

Exercise 1

(a) تھانا وہیں ہے

(b) آپ میری مدد کر سکتے ہیں؟

(c) میں وہاں کیسے جاؤں؟

(d) یہ میری غلطی ہے

(e) یہاں خطرہ ہے

(f) بچاؤ

(g) معلومات کا دفتر

(h) میں راستہ بھول گئی ہوں

(i) تنگ مَت کرو

(j) میں چائی ڈھونڈ رہا ہوں

(k) نہیں مِل رہی

Exercise 2

(a) غُلام   (b) طوفان

(c) لفظ   (d) پَرہیز

(e) عینک   (f) عقیدت

Index

The numbers refer to the units in the book. RG = Reference Grammar